WHAT'S RIGHT WITH PREACHING TODAY?

WHAT'S RIGHT
WITH
PREACHING TODAY?

The Enduring Influence of Fred B. Craddock

Edited by
MIKE GRAVES
and
ANDRÉ RESNER

Foreword by
THOMAS G. LONG

CASCADE *Books* · Eugene, Oregon

WHAT'S RIGHT WITH PREACHING TODAY?
The Enduring Influence of Fred B. Craddock

Cascade Books
An Imprint of Wipf and Stock Publishers
199 W. 8th Ave., Suite 3
Eugene, OR 97401

www.wipfandstock.com

PAPERBACK ISBN: 978-1-4982-9501-7
HARDCOVER ISBN: 978-1-4982-9503-1
EBOOK ISBN: 978-1-4982-9502-4

Cataloguing-in-Publication data:

Names: Graves, Mike, editor. | Resner, André, editor.

Title: What's right with preaching today? : the enduring influence of Fred B. Craddock / Edited by Mike Graves and André Resner.

Description: Eugene, OR: Cascade Books, 2021 | Includes bibliographical references.

Identifiers: ISBN 978-1-4982-9501-7 (paperback) | ISBN 978-1-4982-9503-1 (hardcover) | ISBN 978-1-4982-9502-4 (ebook)

Subjects: LCSH: Craddock, Fred B., Jr., 1928–2015. | Preaching.

Classification: BV4207 .W50 2021 (paperback) | BV4207 (ebook)

03/05/21

To Fred B. Craddock,
his life, his preaching, and his written and spoken legacy—
he continues to be one of the things most right with preaching

Sometimes I listen to a sermon that has all kinds of things wrong with it, and I'm deeply moved.

—FRED CRADDOCK

CONTENTS

FOREWORD

IF A MOON, RATHER THAN CIRCLING A SINGLE PLANET, WERE TO SPIN ITS
orbit around two equal-sized planets, its track would form an ellipse. This
book, in its own way, is an ellipse, because it traces its path around two
equally significant foci: the foci of the question *what is right about preaching?* and the foci of the life and ministry of one of America's most transformational preachers, *Fred B. Craddock.*

As for *what is right about preaching?:* the phrase recalls another transformational American preacher, Harry Emerson Fosdick. Fosdick was perhaps the most celebrated preacher of the first half of the twentieth century
(it is a humbling thought to realize that Fosdick was so prominent in his
day that he was featured on the cover of *Time* magazine twice, but that most
twenty-somethings today have never heard of him, and they are perhaps
not too much aware of *Time* magazine either). Fosdick's preaching was so
popular that the general public was admitted to the cavernous Riverside
Church, where he held forth from the pulpit, on a ticket-only basis.

Fosdick was the perfect "jazz age" preacher, and he had figured out
that restless, post-World War I Americans were tired of traditional sermons
full of moral harrumphs cantilevered off stern biblical and theological or-
thodoxy. The hunger was for sermons that spoke directly to the heart and
the will of individual hearers, that helped them wrestle with the everyday
challenges of a society in flux, that solved problems rather than expounded
doctrine. In July, 1928, Fosdick published a provocative essay in *Harper's*
magazine, sensationally titled "What Is the Matter with Preaching?," which
constituted a major take-down of the customary sermonizing of the day.
"Only the preacher proceeds upon the idea that folk come to church desper-
ately anxious to discover what happened to the Jebusites," Fosdick famously
jabbed. "The result is that folks less and less come to church at all."[1]

---

1. Fosdick, "What Is the Matter with Preaching?," 135.

Seventy-five years later, Mike Graves, one of the editors of this volume, assembled a group of writers, mostly preaching professors, to return to Fosdick's question. The result was *What's the Matter with Preaching Today?*, a diagnosis by a team of specialists about what ailed the American pulpit, not in the roaring twenties but at the beginning of a new and fraught century.

This present book, *What's Right with Preaching?*, is not just the flip side of the earlier question. It is, rather, the product of a gradual recognition that, as the butane torch of secularity blisters away the varnish of civic religion, what remains ironically reveals the beauty and courage of the life of faith and of acts of obedience and devotion, including preaching. In contrast to Fosdick's day, when a member of the clergy could make the cover of *Time* just for doing an impressive job in the pulpit, much of what is right about preaching today is that men and women still have the pluck and nerve to do it, that as numbers decline and the church grows smaller and seemingly less influential, preachers with little social support still stand up to preach and to allow themselves to be fools for Christ.

Baseball statisticians have recently come up with a new measure of a player's value and effectiveness, "wins above replacement" (ominously abbreviated as WAR). The statistic purports to quantify how many more games your team would win with a certain player on the squad over just an average Joe bench sitter. Needless to say, WAR proves that your favorite team would be better off with Babe Ruth in right field, Willie Mays in center, and Ted Williams in left, than with the three guys, whoever they might be, currently patrolling the outfield. Who wouldn't trade in a flash for Ruth, Mays, and Williams? They would bring to any team an impressive "wins above replacement."

Maybe this works in baseball, but I hope no one ever tries to develop a WAR stat for preachers. If a congregation in Nebraska could somehow trade its current preacher for a pulpit star, say a Chrysostom or a Harry Emerson Fosdick or a Gardner Taylor, would there be an uptick in WAR? The question is all wrong. The fact is that some woman or man who loves this flock has, with prayer and perspiration, crafted a sermon that seeks to speak a word from God to *these people* in *this place* and on *this day* is irreplaceable. What we now see, that we could perhaps not see as clearly in a time when the church was more powerful culturally, is that good preaching is small and locally sourced—this congregation, this neighborhood or town, this preacher, these concerns—and that this is much of what is right about preaching.

And that brings us around to the other focus of this ellipse, the other reference point of this book: Fred B. Craddock. It is said that in an elliptically shaped room, the acoustics are such that if someone whispers at one end of the oval it can be heard perfectly by someone at the other end. Just so, to speak in this book of what's right about preaching at one focal point resonates fully with Fred B. Craddock at the other, and *vice versa*. In a preaching career that spanned over a half century, Craddock blazed a genuinely new trail in sermon construction and preaching style and, in so doing, impacted not only his own generation of preachers but also the future of preaching. His preaching was "good" in the sense that the gospel news he preached is also good.

There has been much discussion and debate about what exactly made Fred B. Craddock such an excellent preacher. Some have pointed to his mastery of language, others to his near miraculous skill as a storyteller, and still others to his ability to unleash the power of biblical texts. To this list of undeniable virtues, many others could be added. I wish to suggest one more: in a positive way, Craddock made an asset of the local and the small.

In part this smallness and localness was a function of place. Andy Griffith's "Mayberry" was fashioned from his memories of his hometown, Mt. Airy, North Carolina. Garrison Keillor's "Lake Wobegon" was woven out of strands of Keillor's experiences in Stearns County, Minnesota, where he lived as a young and struggling writer. Likewise, standing behind many a Craddock sermon are his humble origins in depression-era Humboldt, Tennessee. Even when the locale of West Tennessee was not visible, it was there in the background. Craddock's sermons do not happen in the abstract, they are peopled with real characters and salted with concrete events. People have conversations in barbecue joints, working-class husbands and homebound wives have arguments about money at the family table, young men sit on the hoods of cars smoking cigarettes in the supermarket parking lot. Welcome to Humboldt.

The risk, of course, is nostalgia, and Craddock's sermons sometimes do include references that seem lost in time—a child boards a school bus carrying a "lunch bucket," and his mother wears a chenille bathrobe and has her hair rolled in pink curlers. But the power in this is that Craddock crafts a landscape small enough for the listener to imagine the gospel happening in everyday terms. In his own essay for *What's the Matter with Preaching Today?* Craddock pictured "three widows, Naomi, Orpah, and Ruth, huddled under dark veils, weeping and searching for a future,"[2] and we are, of course, in the biblical book of Ruth, but we are also standing beside a grave at the cemetery in Humboldt or in every other town, wondering from whence hope may arise. "What is of vital importance [in sermons]," Craddock wrote, "is that those who come to see God at work in the lives of persons

2. Craddock, "Preaching," 73.

not too unlike themselves will be open to the presence and power of God among them."[3]

One Sunday some years ago, as I was pulling on my robe and preparing to serve as the "guest preacher" in a church somewhere, my eye was drawn to some artwork on the wall. I was in the pastor's office, and mounted over a sofa was a drawing of first-century Jerusalem. It was so realistically done and so exacting in detail, it looked more like an aerial photograph than a piece of art. Everything familiar was there—the temple, the gates, the pool of Siloam, everything. Suddenly I realized that I knew that city, had been to that city, had walked those streets, had moved down from the Mount of Olives across the Kidron Valley and upward to the temple mount. Of course, I had done no such thing. I had lived in old Jerusalem only as an act of imagination, invited there by preachers and Sunday school teachers in my youth. What Craddock described—seeing God at work in the lives of persons not too unlike myself—had happened to me through the preaching and telling of the gospel stories.

Part of the value of imaginative narrative, Paul Ricoeur taught us, is that it projects in front of it a "world" and beckons us to enter that world, to imagine ourselves walking around in it, making decisions and coming to grips with who we are and what we are summoned to do. Eventually, of course, we must leave the narrative and return to our real world, but we do so changed. We have been somewhere, and we are different for it. In addition, the strong narrative substrate in Craddock's preaching, both in the stories told and the dramatic plot structure of many of his sermons, effects a reality that has shape and purpose, where people really do have agency, actions really do have consequences, and things really do have an ending, over against a world in which identity is threatened and malleable, where both goodness and evil seem random, and events flow on seemingly without rhyme or reason.

The narrative shape of Craddock's sermons may seem to be yet another streak of nostalgia, a wistful longing for meaning in an episodic world where all efforts at stable meaning get deconstructed. But in the hands of an able preacher like Craddock, the shape that gives meaning to life comes, as only it can, as the gospel, as divine gift. A few years ago, the theologian Gilbert Meilaender wrote a review of ethicist Stanley Hauerwas's autobiography, *Hannah's Child*. He crafted it in the form of a personal letter to his old friend Hauerwas, and near its conclusion he said,

> In the end, of course, I cannot say whether you have really succeeded in finding what you were seeking in this memoir: the

---

3. Craddock, "Preaching," 73.

pattern that gives shape and unity to your life. Without in any way diminishing the pleasure I have had in reading what you have written, may I say finally that it matters not whether you've found it. The God who alone, as Augustine says, can catch the heart and hold it still knows us better than we know ourselves. He will not fail to detect the pattern and finish the story.[4]

God alone gives the finished story. A similar conviction is at work in Craddock's preaching. His sermons have beginnings, middles, and ends. We enter a small and manageable world where events happen, plots have twists and things become complicated, but then things are resolved (even if it is the listener who finally crafts the resolution). The result is that the vast claims of the gospel get presented at the scale of everyday living. The good news is heard not in the voice of a distant angel, but in the conversation at table between the passing of the mashed potatoes and the biscuits, and big concepts like "justice" and "peace" get expressed in tangible and accessible terms, such as the painful memory of watching a proud African American man, in the pre-civil rights south, be forced to eat his sandwich on the curb of the street outside of the restaurant where he had purchased it.

This is local but universal, small but encompassing. It is part of what Fred Craddock left us as a legacy and part of what he taught us about "what's right about preaching."

Thomas G. Long
Bandy Professor Emeritus of Preaching
Candler School of Theology
Emory University

BIBLIOGRAPHY

Craddock, Fred B. "Preaching: An Appeal to Memory." In *What's the Matter with Preaching Today?*, edited by Mike Graves, 59–74. Louisville: Westminster John Knox, 2004.

Fosdick, Harry Emerson, "What is the Matter with Preaching?" *Harpers Magazine*, July 1928. harpers.org/archive/1928/07/what-is-the-matter-with-preaching/.

Graves, Mike, ed. *What's the Matter with Preaching Today?* Louisville: Westminster John Knox, 2004.

Meilaender, Gilbert. "A Dedicated Life." *First Things* 203 (May 2010) 17.

4. Meilaender, "A Dedicated Life," 17.

INTRODUCTION

A Little Christian Twitch

Mike Graves

AMONG HIS MANY STORIES, FRED CRADDOCK TELLS ONE ABOUT BEING IN the Kansas City airport when he struck up a conversation with a fellow from the University of Utrecht in The Netherlands. The man was writing a book based on a study about the influence of the conversations between doctors and nurses in the presence of patients under anesthesia. He discovered that if the medical staff were negative and grumpy, the patient in recovery was often depressed and pessimistic. If the doctors and nurses were upbeat and cheerful, the patient was more likely to be euphoric, even recover more quickly. When the time came for Fred to catch his plane, the man asked, "Are you a doctor?" Fred said, "Oh, no, I'm a preacher. But if it'll work in surgery, it'll work in the sanctuary." Reflecting on that event, Craddock added, "So when I go somewhere to speak, and people are asleep, it doesn't bother me, because I know that several days later they may get a little Christian twitch. They won't know what caused it, but I'll know."[1]

Fred really didn't have to worry about people falling asleep during his sermons, not the way some preachers might. As early as 1971, in his groundbreaking book, *As One Without Authority*, he pioneered the idea that not just the preacher's stories should be interesting, but the whole sermon. He called it "inductive preaching," and it was a clarion call for preachers to take the listeners seriously. He noted among other things how in traditional

---

1. Craddock, *Craddock Stories*, 29.

forms of preaching there was "no contributing by the hearer." He added, "If the congregation is on the team, it is as javelin catcher."[2] Ouch!

Fred Craddock was only a couple months old when in July of 1928 Harry Emerson Fosdick published his famous essay, "What Is the Matter with Preaching?" The much-celebrated preacher of Riverside Church in New York City was one of the first persons to suggest that the trouble was how preachers neglected the listeners, their concerns as well as their hopes and dreams. He wrote, "One obvious trouble with the mediocre sermon, even when harmless, is that it is uninteresting."

On the seventy-fifth anniversary of that article, I edited a collection of essays, reprinting Fosdick's original article, and enlisting eleven leading voices to name what they considered to be wrong with preaching today. Fred Craddock was one of those contributors, and he began his piece by reminding readers that he was only two months old when the article first appeared. He wrote, "Warm milk and a dry diaper were enough for me, thank you. In fact, twenty-two years passed before I read the article. It was on the required reading list for a seminary class, P301. Needless to say, I was impressed."[3]

It is remarkable to consider how in many ways Craddock would hold and eventually embody the answer to Fosdick's question. If the New York City preacher had started the so-called turn toward the listener, publishing his essay in *Harpers Magazine* of all places, the native of little old Humboldt, Tennessee, would run with the idea like no one ever had. The literature in preaching has been pursuing the idea ever since.

Craddock's *As One Without Authority* is credited with launching the "New Homiletic,"[4] and although he named the first chapter "The Pulpit in the Shadows," he was not interested in focusing solely on the negative. That 1971 classic begins, "We are all aware that in countless courts of opinion the verdict on preaching has been rendered and the sentence passed. All this slim volume asks is a stay of execution until one other witness be heard."[5]

The heart of his testimony came in the next chapter, "The Pulpit in the Spotlight," which begins, "In the words of judgment against the pulpit are to be heard the first stirrings of new life for preaching . . . Those of us vitally

---

2. Craddock, *As One Without Authority*, 46.

3. Craddock, "Preaching," 59.

4. The term itself refers to the idea of sermons being events, not just static talks. The phrase was first coined by David James Randolph in his book *The Renewal of Preaching*. Craddock and so many others after him have always acknowledged Randolph's work, who in turn noted the work of those who came before him, persons such as Donald G. Miller and P. T. Forsyth.

5. Craddock, *As One Without Authority*, 3.

concerned with preaching, perhaps possessed of unjustified hope, tend to interpret the measure of the depth to which the pulpit has fallen as also the measure of the height to which it should and can rise."[6]

Perhaps more than anyone before him or since, Craddock chose to focus on what is right with preaching, resulting in what he called that "little Christian twitch." Of course the normal question posed in preaching books, or at least implied, is, How come our preaching doesn't work? In that 2004 collection of essays I called it a "timeless question." One might say that a focus on what's wrong is the very warp and woof of the homiletical fabric. Every title in the field either starts with a negative assessment, or presumes such. If something wasn't wrong with preaching, why even bother writing about the subject?

When I first approached persons who might contribute to this project, most of us were in sunny southern California—San Diego, to be precise, attending the annual meeting of the Academy of Homiletics, a gathering of nearly 200 teachers of preaching from around the world. We sat on sun-drenched balconies, drinking coffee and eating pastries during our morning breaks, catching up with each other's lives and sharing what we were working on at the time. When I mentioned this project, the intrigue was obvious on my colleagues' faces. Most of them knew the earlier work on "what's the matter." Here was its flipside, so to speak. But within seconds, the intrigue turned to bafflement. No one came out and said it in so many words, but if I'd been playing poker, it was obvious they didn't like the cards in their hand. The subject was intriguing in the abstract, but what would they possibly say is right with preaching today? One leading voice eventually said as much in an email.

It is true, professors of preaching major in what's wrong. Not just in the books we write, but even in our teaching of preaching. For example, many of us use a pattern for debriefing after a student preaches in class, what is sometimes referred to as a "critique sandwich." This should sound familiar to most preachers. We start with the good news, specifically the question, where did you hear the good news in this sermon? And we end with more good news, affirmations of what worked well. But in between is the real "meat" of the critique sandwich, what didn't work so well. In my own teaching I try to put a positive spin on this aspect, asking instead, "What would you like to hear more of next time?" Spin it all you want, seminarians recognize this is what was wrong with their sermon on that day.

If the "meat" of critique time in seminary is the bad news, this book is about the bread on either side of that meat, the good news of preaching

6. Craddock, *As One Without Authority*, 21.

that can be the very bread of life for those who gather to listen. What is there worth celebrating in the preaching life of Christ's church? Are there developments in homiletics that should be lifted up, even celebrated? If one of the purposes of preaching, maybe the main purpose, is to offer good news for those gathered on Sundays, is there a good word as well for those who prepare those sermons? If what's wrong is a "timeless question," maybe what's right is a timely one.

In this volume André Resner and I have enlisted the help of colleagues, each tasked with the assignment of offering an encouraging word about preaching. Collectively, they offer an amazing array of positive perspectives. Ronald J. Allen celebrates the many kinds of diversity now at work in preaching in the postmodern setting—diversity according to gender, race, ethnicity, culture, biblical interpretation, theological family, congregational context, personality, sermon form, and more. In my own essay I explore the connections between the parable of the Sower and gospel preaching, how it's true that some of the seed falls among thorns and such, but some of it falls among fertile soil, yielding a significant but modest crop. Barbara Lundblad, noting how Fred Craddock painted pictures with words, invites preachers to consider the power of imagery in the biblical text as well as our world. If there is anything that marked the preaching of Fred Craddock, it was his constant use of personal experience to proclaim the gospel. To that end, Alyce McKenzie looks not just at the personal experience of the preacher but experience in general, the everydayness of life itself so often lacking in sermons. Debra Mumford considers the seriousness with which seminary students approach the task, signaling its importance in ministry. Luke Powery notes the fact we still pray before and/or after we preach says something theologically important about the preaching we do, that this is a spiritual happening.

Extending the diverse range of the essays, co-editor André Resner takes us back to one of the most fundamental and foundational aspects of the preaching task, namely the contemporaneous speaking of gospel in conversation with the witness of biblical texts. Using a threefold taxonomy of gospel, he helps preachers think about what their theological presuppositions are with regard to the good news and how those serve preachers in reading the Bible for preaching. Mary Donovan Turner directs our attention to how our interpretations of biblical texts are shaped by our own contexts, calling for a level of humility on the part of us preachers and inviting us into conversation with those who read differently. Richard Ward focuses on how training in "sermon delivery" has matured, being tutored and in deeper conversation with theology, not just rhetorical theory. Dawn Ottoni-Wilhelm celebrates the turn toward listeners in recent homiletical theory and practice, and their active participation in the preaching of the good news. Paul Scott Wilson lifts up homiletics, the academic discipline that focuses on the study of preaching, and how it enables teachers of preaching to hold one another responsible for scholarly engagement of key biblical, theological, and social issues, how it encourages interdisciplinary discussion, and how it foments creative discussion.

Wilhelm's emphasis on the "turn toward listeners" should not be missed, for it lies at the heart of Fosdick's original essay and Craddock's later work. For that reason, this book is not just for preachers but for those who listen to them as well. Each of the contributors has been asked to lift up something right with preaching, and to do so in conversation with preachers and listeners alike. Those who listen can get more out of preaching when they understand the task more fully, and those who preach can benefit from listener insights. In keeping with this emphasis on listeners, we also invited personal remembrances of Fred by those who heard him preach, clergy as well as laity. You might think of them as a different kind of "Craddock story."

Therefore, we offer these essays in hopes of accomplishing at least three things: celebrating what is happening in preaching these days; initiating a conversation about preaching between listeners and preachers (seminarians and seasoned ministers alike); and offering a word of encouragement for the whole church. During a time of a global pandemic, a word of encouragement seems especially fitting. Unfortunately, the essays and remembrances in these pages were compiled prior to our current situation, although thankfully the conclusion to this volume does address the current situation.

Sundays come and Sundays go. Sermons are preached, often without much fanfare. Yet the good news of the gospel goes forth, doing its work. In the words of the King James Version, Jesus says once again to all of us, "Be of good cheer."

BIBLIOGRAPHY

Craddock, Fred B. *As One Without Authority*. Rev. ed. St. Louis, MO: Chalice, 2001.

———. *Craddock Stories*. Edited by Mike Graves and Richard F. Ward. St. Louis, MO: Chalice, 2001.

———. "Preaching: An Appeal to Memory." In *What's the Matter with Preaching Today?*, edited by Mike Graves, 59–74. Louisville: Westminster John Knox, 2004.

Fosdick, Harry Emerson. "What Is the Matter with Preaching?" Reprinted in *What's the Matter with Preaching Today?*, edited by Mike Graves, 7–21. Louisville: Westminster John Knox, 2004.

Randolph, David James. *The Renewal of Preaching*. Philadelphia: Fortress, 1969.

BLESS YOU, FRED

A Remembrance

Robin Meyers

FRED CRADDOCK WAS THE SINGLE MOST IMPORTANT INFLUENCE ON MY life as a preacher and teacher. Yesterday, I was preaching at West End United Methodist church across the street from Vanderbilt, where Fred studied New Testament, and I found out that Fred's last public lecture was also given in that church. So I must say that he seemed especially present to me in that place, and honestly I don't know how to express my gratitude to my teacher and mentor except through a *blessing*. So here goes . . .

Bless you, Fred Craddock, for being Fred Craddock. You were the smallest giant I ever met. You could barely see over the pulpit; your voice was squeaky; your head was bald (not that there is anything wrong with that); and the lilt of your voice sounded almost forlorn, as if it was seeking some other, kinder country. Someone would always find you a box, or in my case, build you one, so you could step up on it and peer over the pulpit and say, "I was six-foot five when I started teaching preaching, but the students have worn me down."

Bless you, Fred, for listening to my first sermon in class and for telling me that it was absolutely underwhelming. Thanks for writing at the bottom of my very first sermon manuscript, "Some of this is clever, but I'm waiting for Robin Meyers to wrestle with a more worthy adversary, like the text."

Bless you, Fred, for showing us that the Scripture is not a scaffolding on which to hang three points and a joke, but a dance partner we think we know, but may be meeting for the very first time—and that no matter how well we think we dance, we should let her lead.

Bless you, Fred, for telling us the truth about preaching in the sixties and seventies—that it was dead as a doornail—a cartoon in the minds of very smart, modern people—and yet when you preached no one seemed to want the sermon to end. Smart people did not even realize that their mouths were hanging open.

Bless you, Fred, for all the great stories you made up. When someone would ask you if everything that happened in your stories "really happened," you would tell them you don't know much about what "really happened," but you are very interested in what is "always happening." And besides, you said Jesus made up stories too.

Bless you, Fred, for telling us the truth about how we live and learn things—*inductively*, from the concrete particulars of life to the sacred lessons they point us to. Aristotle would not have liked you, Fred—perhaps because he woke up every morning with a fully developed thesis sentence in his head, or had a major premise for breakfast, over-easy, or blew his nose and out came Roman numeral I for God's sake—but not the rest of us. We live our lives mostly around the small end of the outline, somewhere under 2b. Remember what day it is, get coffee, and then start making great plans for the day that will end immediately when the phone rings, or there is a knock at the door, or a child calls out to us after waking from a bad dream—that's when it begins. That's when God comes to us, disguised as the utterly ordinary, the holy conspiracy of small things. Or as a poet put it, "as if Someone was building Eternity as a swallow its nest out of clumps of moments."

Bless you, Fred, for saying so many things in class that I still remember as if you said them yesterday. Things like, "Come to think of it, I think I know why so many people are obsessed with the second coming. Perhaps it's because, deep down, they are really disappointed in the first one." I asked you one day what you thought of the Trinity and you said, "I don't think about it much, I'm more of a Bible person myself."

Bless you, Fred, for preaching sermons that people weren't sure were even sermons. They sounded more like trips to the grocery store, where a woman thought you were hitting on her, or the listener met someone as "poor as Job's turkey." I liked it when you talked about people who pray for Georgia to win a football game, which you described as more obscene than anything you have ever seen on a bathroom wall. You said we should never make points in a sermon until we have gotten the point.

Bless you, Fred, for going to hear Albert Schweitzer at his only appearance in America, carrying a marked-up copy of *The Quest for the Historical Jesus*, ready to cross-examine him on his theology, which you found rather weak. But before you could question him about it, Dr. Schweitzer looked right at you and invited you to go with him to Africa to help him heal dying patients. That was his theology. Bless you Fred, for not asking any follow-up questions.

Bless you, Fred, for standing up to the board of your first church in Oak Ridge, Tennessee, which voted that only residents and land owners could be members of that little church (this to keep out the riff-raff that was moving into town to work on enriching uranium for the Manhattan Project), and you said this to the board: A church should only reject something that the church believes Jesus would have rejected. So let's make a list. Long silence, but the vote stood. They said, "We run this church, young man," and so you said, "I resign." Today that same church building is a barbeque restaurant, which you claim is an improvement.

Bless you, Fred, for being so good that a lot of us tried to imitate you and failed. You wanted us to find our own voice, tell our own stories, look down more and watch the world carefully enough to make our own report. So we will, we will try, Fred. But honestly, Fred, we wish we were still listening to you. Because we liked it, even though we've never heard anything like it.

And last but not least, bless you, Fred, for saying this: "When I was in my late teens, I wanted to be a preacher. When I was in my late twenties, I wanted to be a good preacher. Now that I am older, I want more than anything else to be a Christian. To live simply, to love generously, to speak truthfully, to serve faithfully, and to leave everything else to God."

Well done good and faithful servant, well done. Do you hear us, Fred? Or do you overhear us?

Bless you, Fred Craddock, for being Fred Craddock. Amen.

— 1 —

DIVERSITY IS DIVERSE

Ronald J. Allen

IF ASKED TO NAME ONE PREACHER WHO REPRESENTS WHAT IS RIGHT WITH preaching, I would respond with the name "Fred Craddock." Everything in his approach to preaching seems so right. He made penetrating biblical exegesis immediately accessible to the listener. He brought theological acuity to text and context. His identification with the congregation would have made Aristotle envious. His eye for human detail was so perceptive. He could open up a whole world with just a word, a phrase. He defined storytelling in preaching. His voice had an almost magical quality. His sense of how to end a sermon is legendary. I heard him preach almost every year from 1970 to his death in 2015 and never heard him "bomb."

Professor Craddock was so natural and unassuming that I realized only after digging into the literature of preaching in seminary and graduate school that he anticipated many emphases in preaching. While he did not use the word *diversity* in the first part of his career, he had an innate sense of respect for the diverse voices in the Bible and for the diversity of preaching situations and, hence, for the fact that preachers need to cultivate diverse ways of preaching. His comments on types of literature in the Bible and modes of preaching on that literature fall into that category:

> The Bible is rich in forms of expression: poetry, saga, historical narrative, proverb, hymn, diary, biography, parable, personal correspondence, drama, myth, dialogue, and gospel, whereas most sermons which seek to communicate the message of that

4

treasury of materials are all in essentially the same form. Why
should the multitude of forms and moods within biblical literature and the multitude of needs in the congregation be brought
together in one unvarying mold . . . ?

This interest in the diversity of biblical and homiletical form illustrates how
Professor Craddock anticipated many other dimensions of diversity.

Concern for diversity has now become a signal of our values, feelings,
practices, and behaviors of our postmodern era. Many Christians, Jews, and
other religious people, along with many people who are not connected with
religion, celebrate the notion of diversity and seek for communities to become more diverse. Indeed, two defining characteristics of the postmodern
ethos are: 1) respecting diversity and bringing diverse communities into
mutually supporting relationships; and 2) recognizing the relativity of all
perception. For example, in previous eras in North America—and in many
sectors of this continent still—Eurocentric, heterosexual, male, middle- and
upper-class people assumed that Eurocentric culture, values, and practices
are the norm in both the larger social world and in the church. Christians
in this culture thought (and some continue to think) of preaching as a male
domain both in terms of the bodies in the pulpits and the perspectives in-
forming sermons. The publishing houses of many historic denominations
largely published Eurocentric approaches to preaching. Seminaries taught
in the same vein. If Eurocentrics noticed other peoples and cultures at all,
we tended to see them on the margins of our social worlds and often from
the perspective of how they could serve our middle-class lifestyles.

Thinkers today often speak of a deconstructive approach to such things,
that is, taking apart that which has been assumed and analyzing it more
closely to identify the things it supports and the things it devalues. Thus,
a call to diversity is a call to break up the Eurocentric, male, heterosexual,
middle- and upper-class power structures that continues to have a disproportionate place in so much of North American life, including in the church
and in preaching. From a constructive perspective, the call to recognize,
respect, and express diversity intends to recalibrate North American and
global social systems so that all people, including those whom Eurocentrics
have previously assumed to be on the margins, may now live in contexts of
respect, dignity, freedom, mutual support, material and emotional security,
with access to the power to determine their own lives and to help shape the
wider community.

Thus, one big thing right about preaching in many circles today is an
increasing emphasis on this kind of diversity. More and more preachers
are urging congregations, denominations, wider religious movements, and

social systems to promote respect and mutual support among different communities from all races, ethnicities, cultures, and subcultures. Eurocentric scholarship in preaching, and the practice of preaching itself, is increasingly open to the scholarship and preaching of other communities. I believe that many people in other communities and cultures are committed to working together toward similar values and relationships.

In a word, we are at a moment when embracing diversity across preachers, communities, and cultures can enrich preaching in all cultures. I speak not of a preaching version of a melting pot in which different communities lose their own identities, but of communities of others in which members maintain their own identities while respectfully asking, "What can we learn from one another?" For example, what might Christians learn from Jews? From Muslims? From people who engage in indigenous religions? What might practicing Christians learn from people who claim to be spiritual but not religious, or from agnostics or atheists? Indeed, what might different kinds of Christians have to learn from one another, say, progressives from evangelicals? Such communities would compare, contrast, and critique approaches to preaching, and identify the take-aways from such encounters. Preachers can learn from one another by listening carefully and critically, by offering perspectives with humility, by being brave enough to raise hard questions of one another, and by venturing fresh possibilities.

After identifying how a good many preachers and theoreticians of preaching still gravitate toward "one size fits all" approaches to preaching, this chapter offers a brief theology of diversity and reviews of some of the most important gains in diversity. It considers some aspects of diversity related to gender, race, ethnicity, culture, and sexual orientation. This essay then turns to other spheres of diversity that are less discussed under the heading of diversity, especially purposes of preaching and modes of expression in preaching.[1] The chapter concludes with a question: "What to do when diverse perspectives are not simply different, but are different in such ways as to be in tension, and even in conflict?"

At one level, then, this piece seeks to reinforce preaching that calls for a genuinely and respectfully diverse world. At another level, it invites preachers to become more diverse in their own approaches to preaching. For the preacher, diversity itself can be diverse.

---

1. A theological caution comes with the absolute call to diversity. Preachers can so focus on particular aspects of diversity that they idolize those aspects. Diversity that is truly diverse relativizes impulses towards idolatry.

MOVING PAST THE "ONE SIZE FITS ALL" APPROACH TO PREACHING

I begin with something a little odd in contemporary preaching. While the church and wider culture are seeking to broaden their embrace of various kinds of diversity, some scholars and preachers effectively operate with singular perspectives on preaching. They may not consciously subscribe to the Enlightenment search for *the* universal approach to preaching. Indeed, they sometimes advocate the kind of diverse church and social world we described earlier while operating with a "one size fits all" approach to preaching. For example, when I was actively teaching (before retirement), every semester I encountered students who wanted only to preach sermons that made points or students who wanted to move verse by verse through a text. Even as sophisticated a teacher of preaching as David Buttrick calls for a sermon to have a plot made up of a limited number of moves that are constructed in the same way.[2]

Such preachers and scholars of preaching promote particular patterns of preaching that they bring to every sermon. This kind of monotone can obviously pertain to style, but it can also embrace how the preacher thinks theologically about preaching, how the preacher engages in exegesis and hermeneutics, how the preacher analyzes the various contexts of the sermon (e.g., congregational, national, global), and other matters.

Books about preaching sometimes argue for *a* way to preach—one way to think about the purpose of preaching, one way to organize the content of a sermon, and even one way to embody a sermon. Indeed, occasional books and classes offer the preacher *a* formula as *the* way to preach. I even hear preachers and teachers of preaching insist that unless ministers preach a certain way, congregations cannot fully receive the sermon.

However, the multiple kinds of diversity at work in the human being, in the church, and in the world today suggest that one size does not fit all. For example, cultures differ in degree and mode of expressiveness. Denominations and theological movements value different emphases in the content and style of preaching. Different schools of biblical interpretation take account of the perspectives of different social locations. Generations have their own patterns of communication. Individuals are more and less receptive to different kinds of communication. And within each of these broad categories we find distinct communities, sub-communities, and individual orientations.

2. Buttrick, *Homiletic*, 21–33.

A BRIEF THEOLOGY OF DIVERSITY

A responsible theology of diversity begins with the great poem of creation in Genesis 1. For here, the priestly theologians depict God creating a world in which diverse elements live in mutual support; each element is necessary for the world to be the community God wants it to be (Gen 1:1–2:4a). In this context, the call for justice is the call for all elements in creation—all human beings and all elements of nature—to live in relationships that make it possible for every entity in creation to be fully what God intends it to be. The different participants in creation not only enrich one another, but are necessary for one another so that all may be fully what God wants them to be as individuals and as community. That is possible only when all things live together in the model of Genesis 1:1–2:4a. Diversity, then, is part of the very structure of creation.[3]

When God made the creature that is in God's own image, God made them female and male (Gen 1:26–28). The image of God is thus not one singular icon, but manifests diversity represented by the differing (yet related) characteristics of women and men.

---

3. We should not romanticize diversity in the biblical materials. Mythologically speaking, the story of the fall in Genesis 3 explains that the ideal community among people and between humankind and nature (assumed in Genesis 1–2) is now fractured. Diversity is no longer automatically presumed to be good: some of the diverse people and diverse elements of nature work against God's covenantal purposes. Even so, prior to the building of the Tower of Babel, humankind shared common life and language (Gen 11:1–9). When the people attempted to build a tower with its top in the heavens under the banner of making a name for themselves, God gave them different languages and scattered them to different places on the earth. Scholars vary wildly on how to interpret this story. While a majority of scholars believe that God divided humankind into different groups with different languages to punish them and to prevent them from trying again (and again) to build such towers, some scholars see the story in more positive ways, even as affirmation of diversity. In my view, the former opinion has the greater exegetical likelihood as I think the Priestly theologians developed the present form of this story around the time of the Babylonian exile as part of their critique of Babylon. I see the separation into different languages and different places of living as a judgment. However, some of the end-time (apocalyptic) literature does point to the re-communion of the scattered elements of the human family (and elements of nature) as part of the realm of God. For example, the book of Acts envisions the eschatological work of the Spirit as prompting people of different languages and nations towards shared understanding of God's deeds of power, i.e., shared understanding of the present, partial manifestations of the realm of God through the ministry of Jesus and the church (Acts 2:1–13). In a dramatic image the book of Revelation points to people coming together in a great multitude "from every nation, from all tribes and peoples and languages" (e.g., Rev 5:9; 14:6). Evidently, these end-time theologians envision the realm as an arena in which distinctions of race, language, tongue, and culture do not disappear but are gathered into mutually supportive community in the service of the living God.

Trinitarians believe, further, that the very nature of God is social. God is one, but God's oneness is simultaneously as Creator, Redeemer, and Sustainer.[4] Each person of the Trinity has a certain distinction while all persons of the Trinity are one God without partition or division. God in Godself is diverse.

The importance of honoring and responding appropriately to the other is one of the most permeating themes of contemporary theology. While many preachers initially think of the other in human terms—e.g., other human beings, other communities or cultures—otherness, more broadly, includes animals and the rest of the natural world. From this perspective we can think of biblical texts, theological doctrines, and ethical precepts as others.

Two aspects of the current discovery of otherness are especially important for preaching. For the first aspect, each other has its own integrity and has the right to be what it is. Those who interact with the other are obligated to understand the other from the perspective from which the other wants to be understood. For example, when people of color take to the streets to protest injustice, Eurocentric people tend to refer to the act as a riot whereas people of color often perceive such events as uprisings. When recognizing that people of color interpret their actions in the street as an uprising against injustice, a Eurocentric person might respond to the event quite differently than thinking of it as nothing more than a riot. Those who interact with others should resist the temptation to reduce the other to their perception of the other.

For the second aspect, interaction with others (especially the Bible, theological doctrines, and other human beings individually and in communities) can cause the preacher and congregation to imagine possibilities of thinking and behavior they had not previously considered, or can cause preacher or congregation to reconsider things they have taken for granted.

This emphasis upon otherness, of course, is a call for all in the world of the sermon to relate appropriately to the diversity of others. Going a step further, each preacher is an other to congregations. As noted above, preachers have their own distinct voice and should speak out of the depths of their otherness in both theological content and approach to the sermon. The preacher who subscribes to a homiletic of sameness disrespects that

---

4. Occasionally Christians argue that the precise terms "Father, Son, and Holy Spirit" must be used, especially in formal occasions in order for the rite to be theologically valid (e.g. baptism, and the invocation at the Sacred Table). However, my sense is that most Christians believe that other designations are appropriate, e.g., Creator, Redeemer, Sustainer. So, we have diversity even in talk about the Godhead.

preacher's own otherness, and denies the congregation the full benefit that comes from interacting with the other.

Moreover, recent study of the self points out that the self is not a single, unitary entity, but is comprised of multiple elements. My colleague Helene Tallon Russell puts it this way.

> The self is a matrix of interrelated self-states that are also open to more and to other relationships. There are sub-selves, which are centers of connection, memory, and tendencies, and secondly, connectors, which are conduits of relation. This conglomeration of stuff is a network with many points of concentration as well as wires that flow back and forth in all directions.[5]

Russell uses an "old-fashioned tinker toy set" as a rough analogy. The many different pieces are different sizes and shapes. The pieces have different functions, are different colors, and they can be connected in different ways to create different things. But, when the different parts are connected to make an object, the parts maintain their individuality while working together. They can be connected in different ways to make different objects—a horse one time, a building another, an abstract piece of art another time.

In a similar way, the self is not a singular chunk of being but is made up of different parts that work together in different ways at different times. The self is always in process, changing in response to external and internal stimuli, creating and recreating. The self is itself diverse. It follows, then, that the preacher's means of expression in sermons can vary according to the dimension of the theological and homiletical self that is in play.

From this point of view, the preacher should not only advocate diversity in the social world, but should embody diversity in preaching itself.

VOICE AND VOICES IN DIVERSE PREACHING

This part of our discussion needs to be nuanced. One of the most important movements in preaching over the past twenty-five years focuses on helping preachers find their own voices, that is, encouraging preachers to speak clearly and honestly out of their own experience in ways that reflect their own identities. As Mary Donovan Turner and Mary Lin Hudson point out, this coming to voice does not end in a static state of being. "Coming to voice has been, and will continue to be, a lifelong experience."[6]

---

5. Russell, *Irigaray and Kierkegaard*, 247.

6. Turner and Hudson, *Saved from Silence*, ix.

In particular, Turner and Hudson rightly note that women have been silenced for millennia. Coming to voice after being silenced, these scholars observe, is itself an experience of salvation.[7] One purpose of preaching, from this perspective, is to help listeners come to voice. Only when all in a group have voice can the group become a truly liberated and liberating *community*. A preacher with voice can help a congregation develop its own voice.

In calling attention to the widening range of diversity in the preacher's view finder, I am not suggesting that preachers mute our own voices and impose the style and perspectives of others onto their sermonic repertoires for the sake of adding diverse elements to their homiletical repertoire. Just the opposite. I am suggesting that preachers often have more variations in their voices than we may recognize and claim. Indeed, as Turner and Hudson indicate, some aspects of preachers' voices may evolve over time, that is, a preacher's perspectives and ways of expression may change in response to changing circumstances and changing perceptions of themselves. Preachers will lose credibility if we do not maintain integrity with our own voices. This caution applies to integrity with respect to our personhood and to our theologies, ecclesial, and social commitments, and modes of expression.

The bottom line is that, in a way similar to the way the self is made up of diverse elements, so preachers can be consistent with the multiple dimensions of our own voices, while modulating our sermons in diverse ways that are true to the self while helping the congregation toward its best interpretations of God's purposes and appropriate responses. Indeed, particular dynamics in the culture, in the church, or in the self may compel preachers towards such modulation.

DIVERSITY WITH RESPECT TO GENDER, RACE, ETHNICITY, CULTURE, AND SEXUAL ORIENTATION

The first categories that come to my mind when I think of diversity in relationship to preaching (and to the church and world more generally) are gender, race, ethnicity, culture, and sexual orientation. As the mind widens, I recognize many other expressions of diversity—e.g., theological perspective, class, political commitment, theological perspective, geographical location, vocation, philosophical mind-set, pattern of mental operation, and personality type. In fact, there are probably as many kinds of diversity as there are others. For this abbreviated discussion, I use gender, race, ethnicity, culture, and sexual orientation as representing a host of other diverse qualities.

7. Turner and Hudson, *Saved from Silence,* 7–17.

I have mentioned several times that, from a theological perspective of embracing diversity, the preacher's vocation today includes helping congregations to recognize and live towards God's intention for the world to be a place of genuine community of people who are different in gender, race, ethnicity, culture, sexual orientation, and other manifestations of diversity. Nature, too, is included in this vision. From this perspective, respect for diversity is a theological norm by which to gauge the content of sermons.

Going a step further, as part of sermon preparation, preachers today have increasing opportunities to listen to scholars, preachers, and a wide range of interpreters who are other to the preacher. Eurocentric heterosexual middle- and upper-class male preachers, in particular, should attend to the interpretive perspectives of others—e.g., women, people of color, people of different classes, and people of different ethnicities and cultures. For example, when I finished graduate school in 1977, biblical interpretation had begun to diversify in methodologies. In addition to classical historical criticism, various forms of literary criticism had begun to appear. Feminist criticism was just on the horizon. But most biblical interpretation took place under an umbrella that was modern, Eurocentric, male, heterosexual, and middle class.

I do not mean to be cute when saying that today's preachers move their interpretive trays along an international salad bar of approaches to the Bible and to theological reflection. To cite some biblical criticisms easily available to the preacher: feminist, womanist, Mujerista, African American male, Asian, post-colonial, Latino, disability, post-Holocaust, psychological, Queer, and ecological. When we take theological families into account— each of which has its own axioms for the place of the Bible in theology, and the number of interpretive others multiples exponentially. Among the theological families from history (many of whose emphases extend into today): Roman Catholic, Orthodox, Lutheran, Reformed, Anglican, Wesleyan, Anabaptist, Friends, and Pentecostal. Among contemporary theological families: fundamentalism, evangelicalism, neo-orthodox, postliberal, liberal, process, liberation, racial/ethnic, and, of course, theologies of otherness.

However, while the perceptual world of many Eurocentric, heterosexual, middle- and upper-class preachers is enclosed within their own experience and perspectives, such males are not the only preachers to exist largely within the boundaries of their own experience and communities. I say this hesitantly but directly: A theology of diversity insists that women, people of color, members of the LGBTQIA community also seek to understand the perspectives of others, including Eurocentric, male heterosexuals of the middle class.

In my view, every preacher today should regularly engage at least one approach to biblical criticism that is outside the preacher's regularly traveled route. The same is true of theological family. To receive the maximum benefit from the preacher's encounter with others in these ways, preachers should engage perspectives that are quite different. As a Eurocentric process theologian trained in classical historical criticism, for instance, significant others to me might be womanists and evangelicals.

To understand the perspective of the other is not automatically to agree and support. But mutual understanding is an essential aspect of diverse community, and is often a beginning point for conversation (and other interactions) that can lead to positive change. And, indeed, this is one of the things that, from time to time, is right about preaching today: some sermons do begin or reinforce conversations that move in the direction of change. I think, for instance, of a congregation in which a series of sermons on Eurocentric privilege led to the congregation forming a group that studied the topic more deeply and began to explore what to do in relationship to privilege to work towards a world that is more egalitarian.

Going yet one more step, congregations should consider calling preachers who have a differing demographic profile than that of the congregation.[8] Of course, the preacher is always an other in relationship to the congregation. Nevertheless, some preachers are especially other to particular congregations. While many congregations today are more diverse today than in previous generations with regard to such things as race, ethnicity, class, culture, and sexual orientation, many congregations continue to be pretty homogenous with regard to such qualities.

A theology of diversity summons congregations to consider calling preachers who are other. Here are some examples. A congregation that is heavily Eurocentric should consider preachers from other races and cultures. A congregation that has never had a woman in the pulpit week to week should consider a woman. A congregation made up primarily of heterosexuals should consider a preacher who is LGBTQIA. In such situations, the preacher needs to be open to the congregation as other in the same way that the preacher hopes the congregation will be open to the preacher's otherness.

A preacher and congregation face the possibility of challenging times when they are significantly other. But when challenges take place in a

---

8. Recent studies in the make-up of congregations call our attention to the fact that every congregation contains different cultures. A congregation that is predominantly Eurocentric, for instance, typically contains people of different genders and sexual orientations, different classes, even different theological assumptions. For economy of discussion, I write as if congregations are more unitary in composition than they really are.

context of respect, challenges can be occasions for growth and constructive change. Even when a challenge does not eventuate in a positive change, the act of considering the possibility raised by the other can help preacher and congregation better understand their own perspectives and live in empathetic community with those who are other.

DIVERSITY IN PERCEPTION AND EXPRESSION

Preachers and scholars of preaching often discuss the purpose of the sermon and the form (genre, style, pattern of movement) of the sermon as separate categories. For discussion, especially with students, this separation often has heuristic value. But when thinking about diversity in preaching, we should consider purpose and form together. When we do so, we see yet another reason for preachers becoming more diverse in our approaches to the homily, and we get a clue for some of the kinds of diversity a preacher might embrace. But first, we need to consider diversity in perception and expression.

One of the last generation's essential insights from literary criticism and philosophy of art is the inseparability of form and meaning. The form or genre or style in which something is expressed is not simply a container for meaning. Rather the experience of the expressive piece in its own medium is a part and parcel of the meaning. From this perspective, perception is multi-dimensional. We know some things at a conscious, straightforward level. Much of our awareness, however, takes place at the deep level of feeling. This level of awareness is not inchoate. It has its own patterns of meaning that contribute to self and community, but such awareness cannot be fully articulated in conventional language.

Modes of expression and modes of receiving expressions correspond to these two levels of perception—at the straightforward level of consciousness and at the level of deep feeling. At the straightforward level, communicators can speak with direct statements, often with the precision of mathematical formulae. Listeners hear what the communicator says and information/perception transfers from the speaker to the listener in as much of a one-to-one correlation as is possible. (A certain amount of slippage, even reconceptualization, always occurs as material goes from the mouth of one to the ears of another). At the level of feeling, however, a communicator—such as a poet, a musical composer, a rap artist, a painter, a sculptor, a dancer, a film maker—cannot set out the meaning of the communication in propositional language in a fully satisfactory way. The experience of the expression in the medium for which it was created is itself a part of the meaning of the piece for the reader, the listener, or the viewer.

When people talk about the significance of a deep feeling level expression in conventional language, dimensions of meaning are lost because propositional language can seldom evoke the full range of significance evoked during the encounter with the expression in its own medium. For instance, a class visits an art gallery and stands in front of an impressionist painting. The teacher asks the class, "What did the artist want to accomplish with this painting?" Students can respond insightfully, but their descriptions never quite capture the fullness of what happened to them when they received the painting in its own medium.

DIVERSITY IN PURPOSES AND FORMS OF PREACHING

There are as many moments in congregational life as there are congregations and congregational dynamics. Each congregation is its own culture. And, congregations are touched in different ways by different things. Think of the distinct qualities associated with birth, baptism, graduation, encountering others in mission projects, struggling around the budget, conflict regarding whether a minister should continue to serve in the congregation, events in the larger world impinging on (or even preoccupying) congregational mental and emotional space, the effects of different kinds of deaths in the community. Sunday can differ from Sunday as much as night differs from day, sunshine from rain, or snow from sand. Each moment has its own levels of awareness—some conscious and articulate, and others at the level of feeling, beneath the surface of consciousness, but powerful.

Similarly, there can be as many modes of expression for the sermon as there are preachers and Sundays. Some preachers are by nature more deductive, that is, making the big point at the beginning and drawing out implications, while others are more inductive, that is, beginning with questions and issues and moving towards the big point—the conclusion—at the end of the sermon. Some are more propositional while others are more imagistic, that is, some sermons are made up mostly of straightforward statements while other sermons rely more on word-pictures. Some more naturally bend to reason and argument while others to storytelling. Preachers today have the chance to find and develop their optimum patterns of communication.

Yet, a preacher is more than *a* preacher. In the manner described above, a minister contains multiple selves that can express themselves in different ways. The preacher who is essentially a mechanic with words likely has something of a poet in the closet of one of the rooms of the self. Somewhere in the storyteller is at least a shadow of a logician. The essayist probably has some neurons that fire on the rap circuit.

The preacher seeks an expression that fits the self and the moment. A preacher who is naturally deductive may need to tap into that dimension of the self that handles the inductive. For example, a preacher who typically announces the big point at the beginning of the sermon might be in a situation in which to do so would immediately anger the congregation to the point that they would cease listening, whereas a more inductive approach would have a greater chance easing the congregation into the topic. A preacher who is by nature imagistic and storytelling may need to move in a direction that is more logical and argumentative. There are times, after all, when a preacher simply needs to say straightaway what she or he means to say. A preacher who likes to resolve every theological issue may need to preach a sermon that is open-ended. A preacher who is a firebrand may need to speak out of an inner sage.

Such a diverse approach to preaching releases the preacher from trying to force every sermon into one pattern. Preachers can—and should—be sensitive to possibilities for shaping the sermon that are appropriate to the congregation, the moment, and the preacher. For instance, when a congregation suffering a significant loss it may be better served by a lyrical lament than a clinical analysis of loss. When a congregation participates in injustice, the sermon may need to have a confrontive character. A congregation struggling with theological identity may call for old fashioned teaching sermons. A preacher may find an approach already available in the homiletical storehouse, or may adapt such an approach, or may release or create modes of expression that are new, at least to the preacher.

Most Sundays, a preacher is in the position of *talking* about a biblical text or a theological theme. Apropos of the idea (mentioned above) that modes of awareness and modes of expression interpenetrate, and are sometimes intuitive and trans-verbal, the preacher must sometimes find a manner of speaking that comes as close as the preacher can get to the medium of awareness. Sometimes a preacher might spend part of the sermon talking about something about which speech is not truly adequate. But, at some point in the sermon, the preacher should reach for language that evokes the deeper, more intuitive dimensions of awareness. A minister might, for instance, preach in free verse. Preachers who can take this route typically help the congregation develop a deep, innate, even visceral awareness that transcends logical rationality.

From the perspective of the inherent inter-relationship of purpose and form, preachers today have opportunities to create sermons (or parts of sermons) in media other than talking. It is easy to imagine sermons (or moments in sermons) in the mode of such things as chancel drama, in rap, as comedic monologue, as body movement or dance. I think some aspects of the use of the Big Screen in the service of worship are appropriate, though I have hesitations about the use of the Big Screen in the sermon itself. Nevertheless, Big Screens do give the preacher an opportunity to bring expressive media into the sermon that can speak to the life of feeling, e.g., photographs, paintings, film clips, comments from people far away, excerpts of music.

WHEN DIVERSE PERSPECTIVES
COME INTO CONFLICT

Many contemporary theologians, scholars of preaching, and preachers discuss the move toward a diverse world and diverse communities in almost universally positive terms. Indeed, in some circumstances, "diversity" is a code word for moving toward a community in which all people are welcomed, valued, and affirmed. A preacher might say, "The board for such-and-such in the denomination is now diverse," meaning that Eurocentric women, people of color, people of different sexual orientations, and people with still other qualities are now on the board, in sufficient number and with sufficient power to shape the agenda of the board in ways that enhance the diversity of the denomination or movement.

At the idealized level at which this chapter typically discusses diversity, I envision the diverse community as one in which all people and all elements of nature live in respect, dignity, freedom, mutual support, and abundance. People and communities with different values and practices live alongside one another in peace and mutual respect. Interaction with the other enlarges one's own sense of possibility and world. In a diverse community permeated by the spirit of respect for the other, difference does not have to mean disagreement. As I heard someone say, "We can agree to disagree agreeably."

But the fact is that occasionally people and groups hold values, and especially engage in practices, that violate fundamental convictions of other peoples and groups. Stoning women to death for adultery is part of the otherness of some peoples and cultures. But, in my view, this act of taking the life of another violates the otherness of the victim to the degree that it is simply wrong. Some communities assume patriarchy that allows repression of women. In my view, this structure of relationship violates the otherness of women and is simply wrong. In the United States, many Eurocentric people believe in the superiority of people of European origin. In my view this perception is simply wrong, whether such awareness is conscious and buttressed by arguments of white supremacy, or whether it exists as a prejudice that permeates self and community without specific articulation. As a Eurocentric student said, who came from the latter community, "Racism was just in the air we breathed." While these wrongheaded things persist, I believe that more and more preachers today are doing something right by analyzing such wrongs from the perspective of justice and urging congregations and wider communities to reenvision their ways of living around values of love, peace, justice, and abundance for all. The call to justice is something very right about much preaching today.

What does a preacher do when faced with communities that hold values and engage in practices that violate others, even resulting in death? At base, the preacher would seek to understand the perspectives of the other community from the point of view of the other community. What are the values at stake? Why does the other community hold the values the preacher finds objectionable? As noted earlier, to understand is not necessarily to accept and approve. But it is fundamental for the integrity of interaction among others.

The preacher could critically reflect on values and behaviors associated with the other community and could articulate points of comparison and contrast between the perception and behavior of the other community and the perception and behavior of the preacher's own community. At what points does the preacher perceive the attitudes and actions of the community in view to be disrespectful, to violate an other? The preacher would share these perceptions through the sermon.

A preacher can understand why a racist would say, "Racism was just in the air we breathed." But a Christian preacher should offer a substantial rationale for inviting such people to turn away from racism and to turn towards diverse, mutually supportive community. The preacher needs to do better than simply say, "Diversity is just in the air this diverse community breathes." One hopes that diversity is the air of the diverse community, but the members of the community need to be able to answer the question, "*Why* is the air in the diverse community cleaner (so to speak) than the air in the racist community?"

Seeking to offer all parties the opportunity to be affected in optimum ways by interaction with the other, the preacher may invite the other community to reconsider its own understandings of how to relate to others. How might individuals and groups within the other community benefit from more respectful attitudes of otherness?

In full respect for the possibilities of interacting with others in truly diverse community, the preacher should think with the congregation about how the other prompts the congregation to think about its own values and practices, and its own treatment of others. Coming to clarity with regard for the reasons for its criticism of the practice of stoning women accused of adultery, a congregation in the United States might come to apply similar logic to capital punishment.

With respect to the next step of this discussion, I share the ambiguity of a good many preachers. Some communities sanction what I consider the violation of others that can only (seemingly) be stopped by force. Is it less damaging for the preacher to tolerate the continued violation in the name of respecting the differences on the part of the other community, or to tolerate intervention by force in the hope of changing the violating behaviors in the situation?

This discussion is not quite the same as the centuries-old debate as to whether war can be just. From the standpoint of the most mature biblical and theological perspectives on justice, a war can never be truly just, but it might lead to saving some lives that would otherwise be lost even as it licenses killing. The preacher must decide not whether a forceful intervention can be just, but whether such intervention has a good chance of leading to lesser violations of the other than standing by while full-scale violations of the other continue.

Such an intervention would take place not with the kind of flag waving that launches wars, but by displaying the kinds of flags that mark cars in a funeral procession. A dramatic move with force would be accompanied not by bands playing patriotic marches, but by bands playing dirges. Preachers would not rally the congregation for battle, but would lead in confession of sin. The mood in the pulpit would not be cheering but regret that the choice before the community is the lesser of two evil behaviors.

THE PREACHER'S UNPARALLELED OPPORTUNITY

What is right about preaching? As this chapter seeks to show, one big thing right about preaching is this: the continually emerging emphasis on diversity at all levels of homiletical consciousness and practice. A theology of diversity presents preachers with almost unparalleled opportunities to help congregations explore (and claim) interpretations of God's presence and purposes and how to respond appropriately. Preachers today are limited only by the interaction of what they can imagine for preaching by the degree to which the congregation is ready to participate in a sermon in traditional or inventive modes.

I was born in 1949, and have been involved in a spectrum of traditional congregations my whole life. My experience as a Bible study leader and preacher in congregations is anecdotal, but it is still my experience: I find that many people in congregations are more willing to be adventurous than many preachers anticipate. Indeed, lay people sometimes reveal in a Bible study session or a remark after the sermon that they are actually more willing than their resident ministers to try out fresh ways of interpreting the Bible, of thinking theologically, of being Christian community, and of living and engaging in mission in the world. There are exceptions, of course. Some listeners effectively inhabit bunkers of thought that are enclosed by limited thinking that is as mentally thick as six or eight feet of concrete wall. But, my limited experience is that such folk tend to be fewer in number than many preachers imagine.

However, some preachers are hesitant to swim too far from the familiar homiletical dock. Secure in their current practices of preaching, they wonder, "Why run the risk of creating waves where there are none?" Other preachers think it is too much work to try something new and untested. Nearly every minister has been confronted by congregants playing their power cards face-up because the congregants are distressed by something the preacher has said or done. Such confrontations can leave painful scars on sensitive souls. Many preachers are empathetic when listening to congregants who are fearful of change. Preachers are often economically vulnerable, especially if they lose a job suddenly. Many ministers in my generation thought of ministry as a career track parallel to a career track in industry. Fewer people do that today, but preachers can still be anxious about news of a disruption in the congregation reaching the ecclesial figures who play a central role in congregations calling ministers, or showing up on letters of recommendation. I could be wrong, but my impression is that such threats are not as potent as I once assumed. Indeed, as just noted, my experience is that many people are receptive to creative and promising change.

If this chapter were a sermon in a Disciples congregation, I would follow the sermon with an invitation to discipleship, that is, an appeal for listeners to accept the grace of God and to commit themselves to living for God. Some would come forward to make an initial confession of faith to be followed by immersion. Others would transfer membership, and still others would rededicate their lives to faithful discipleship. This essay may not be a sermon, but that model still comes to mind. Indeed, I hear a congregation singing an invitational hymn softly in the background. In the typical Sunday morning congregation, the minister issues the invitation to discipleship to the laity. Here, however, the situation is the other way around. Hence, I close with an invitation to preachers. "With every eye open and every head up, this is a time for you to step into the unparalleled diversity of opportunities afforded for helping congregations interpret God's life-giving purposes for our time."[9]

BIBLIOGRAPHY

Buttrick, David G. *Homiletic: Moves and Structures*. Philadelphia: Fortress, 1987.

Craddock, Fred B. *As One Without Authority*. Revised and with New Sermons. St. Louis, MO: Chalice, 1991.

Russell, Helene Tallon. *Irigaray and Kierkegaard: On the Construction of the Self*. Macon, GA: Mercer University Press, 2010.

Turner, Mary Donovan, and Mary Linn Hudson. *Saved from Silence: Women's Voice in Preaching*. St. Louis, MO: Chalice, 1999.

9. The reference to "every eye open and every head up" is a play on the expression "With every eye closed and with every head bowed." Until fairly recently, many preachers in churches that regularly practice the invitation to discipleship in worship settings used the latter expression as part of the invitation. The expression is intended to create a nonthreatening environment for those who consider accepting the invitation. With the congregation singing, and with most of the congregation's eyes closed and heads bowed, a person can slip out of the pew and come down the aisle to meet the minister to make a confession of faith. I hope ministers will accept the invitation to diversity with eyes open and heads up, i.e., consciously and in full critical awareness.

MY DAY WITH FRED CRADDOCK

A Remembrance

Amy Violette

"Black, a little cream, no sugar."

I met Fred Craddock on Tuesday, September 17, 2013. I was twenty-seven years old. He was eighty-four. We sat together in his office in Cherry Log, Georgia, and watched it rain. It was quarter to 10 AM when I made him his coffee, poured it in a six-ounce white Styrofoam cup, and walked it over to him.

I was in Atlanta doing an internship at First Baptist Church Decatur. I had read his book *Preaching* in seminary and listened to several of his sermons. Unlike some of my colleagues who claimed Fred to be "completely irrelevant," I disagreed. Growing up in East Tennessee where front porch sitting and storytelling is as common as waiting for the mailman, I immediately recognized the skill and mastery in Fred's sermons. His word choices. His pace. The artistry. How he talked about the weather or the sky or something his neighbor had told him earlier that morning. It all led somewhere and often never made sense until the end.

For me, listening to Fred was like listening to B. B. King play *Lucille* or Will Campbell talk about standing on the balcony of the Lorraine Motel hours after Dr. Martin Luther King, Jr. was shot. I was mesmerized.

I handed Fred his coffee and sat down in the chair adjacent to his desk. A simple cherry desk with books, papers, three-ring binders, compact disks stacked high. A phone. A black desk lamp pushed up against the wall. A framed eight-by-ten Thomas Merton poem, "My Lord God, I have no idea where I am going . . ."

"Thank you for meeting with me today!" I said.
You drove from Decatur?
"Yes sir."
How was the drive?
"Good, rainy."
Would you like an apple?
"Yes, thank you . . . I wanted to meet you."
He smiled.
I'm glad you did.

For the next two hours we talked. No agenda. We swapped stories. I told him about seminary. Why I loved preaching. Why I wanted to meet him. I asked him about the future of preaching. He wanted to know what I was reading. He was very disappointed I wasn't reading more fiction! He gave me a reading list. We talked about his life, the Baylor Oral History Project, his friends Tom Long and Barbara Brown Taylor.

We talked about the Pink Pig BBQ and a server and her son who worked there. He told me about the importance of journaling, of reading books, how ordinary people are important, and gave me a list of preachers to watch.

From my time with Fred I have eight takeaways:

1. *Read more.* Read everything you can get your hands on. Cookbooks. Fiction. Gardening tutorials. Crime novels. "Read just because." "Read about things unrelated to anything."

2. *Respect words.* Don't pick cheap words. Have a reverence for words. Words matter. Pick the right one at the right time. "Let words dance." Words have power to convey information (e.g., a cookbook) or create experience (i.e., power).

3. *Keep a journal.* Write down "not the things you've done but things that happened. Jot it down. Don't let it get away." Fred said, "I keep an index card with me at all times to jot down what happened. At night I set down and write about it on one page in an accountant's notebook. No more than one page. Then at the end of a year you have 365 illustrations."

4. *Be around ordinary people.* Find your own Pink Pig BBQ. Find people who do not care who you are or what you have done.

5. *Prize Oral Tradition.*

6. *Don't get above your raising.*

7. *Read your Bible.*

8. *Keep your promises.*

The rain stopped. I knew my time with Fred was coming to an end. I also knew this would be the last time I would ever see him. I thanked him for his time. I gathered my things to leave. He leaned in and said:

> I imagined what you'd be like.
> I smiled. "What did you come up with?"
> I thought you would be short, energetic, and full of questions. I was two for three.
> I smiled.
> He smiled.
> Until next time, he said.
> "Until next time," I said.

Fred gave me a book of his sermons as I departed. The inscription reads: "To Amy—with gratitude for a great conversation—Fred Craddock, 2013."

"LISTEN TO HOW EVERYDAY FOLKS PUT THINGS INTO WORDS"

Remembering Fred

Richard F. Ward

IT WAS TO BE THE LAST TIME I SAT DOWN WITH FRED, FACE TO FACE, FOR A conversation about preaching. We were on his back porch at his house in Cherry Log, sipping iced tea and listening to the creek that ran under his house. The ruin of an old mill just at the edge of his back yard caught my eye and I couldn't help but wonder if Fred ever considered the evocative possibilities of this image: a brick ruin being slowly reclaimed by nature, overseeing the stream that changed its course, but never stopped running.

I was there because I had just been named to the chair in preaching and worship that Phillips Theological Seminary had established in his honor. I had flown from Denver to Atlanta, rented a car, and drove through one of those classic "*southun THUNDastoms*," rehearsing what I wanted to ask him while I had his ear. By the time I arrived, the rain had moved on, the spring sunlight had returned, and Fred was standing on a stoop at the front door, waving, making sure I would turn in to the right driveway.

Stepping over fresh puddles, hugs, greetings, jokes, and regal Nettie in the living room, ever the gracious hostess, offering the tea or coffee, Fred leading the way to the rocking chairs on the back porch. We shared impressions about Oklahoma, its rustic charm, agreeing that autumn was the best season, the complicated story of how Phillips had moved from Enid to Tulsa, and how difficult it was to find representation for one's concerns in Oklahoma's political climate. As you might expect, the conversation featured stories where his compassion for the small rural churches shone through. "Don't spend all your time going to the big steeples with the handsome honorarium. If those little churches ever invite you to speak there," he said, "go, let them know that the seminary respects and honors them. Don't let them feel forgotten." I think about that exchange whenever the conversation in the seminary moves to consider the "gap" between classroom and pew.

"If you were teaching preaching today," I asked, "what would you do first?" Without hesitating, he said, "I would tell the students to listen to how everyday folk put things into words." He gave some examples, like how people used the word "looking." "Up here someone isn't 'pretty,' they are "good-lookin.' Or if they're mean, they are 'mean-lookin.'" We went on like that for a while and then the conversation turned to what words we'd like to retire or at least put on the shelf for a while. Words like "awesome" or even the word "like" got way too much air time when folks talked to one another. Why not spend a bit more time cultivating more picturesque speech? I'm not sure I could ever use a Craddockian expletive like "Great honk!" or a descriptive like "mad as a boiled owl" like he did and get away with it, but I could certainly work to create better word pictures with my speech and encourage my students to do the same.

I had something else on my mind. It seemed to me that homiletics was officially losing its fascination with narrative in its turn towards doctrine, even as more and more of my students were anxious to take classes in storytelling. Some of the assumptions that guided my own development as a preacher, that listeners "thought in story" in order to make sense of their experiences for example, just weren't holding up in this tech-savvy generation. How much of an emphasis should we continue to place on the narrative arts? Again Fred was quick to respond. "What's the first thing a movie producer asks the agent who is pitching the work of a screenwriter? What's the *story?* They still want to know what the story is." Maybe that was still true of congregations, even the tech-savvy ones, I wondered. Do they still want to know what the *Story* is?

The conversation on the back porch had to end soon after that. Fred needed an afternoon rest and I needed to catch my flight home. As this book of essays and remembrances attests, however, conversations with Fred continue in our lives and in our imaginations. Fred once said that every preacher "has a critic sitting in the balcony" that challenges, objects, sometimes even inhibits our preaching. That may be so, but let us thank God that Fred now sits with the "cloud of witnesses," not as a critic, but as a coach encouraging us to "run with perseverance that race set before us" (Heb 12:1).

THE STRAIGHT-EDGED POINTER FINGER

A Remembrance of Fred

Ryan Motter

IT WAS MY THIRD YEAR OF PREACHING EVERY SUNDAY, AND I WAS FEELING exhausted. The relentless impending Sunday morning, combined with a prayer life that ranked very low on my list of priorities, combined with an over-abundance of administrative details, made the weekly sermon feel like a chore.

It happened that, in the midst of those years, I gathered with a group of young pastors, all somewhere within the first five years of ministry with a congregation, at a retreat center just outside of Atlanta. Fred was in the phase of his speaking life where he no longer traveled, unless it was within an easy drive from Cherry Log. We asked for an hour of his time. Fred gave us an entire morning. As Fred took the podium, it was clear that he was there to have a conversation with people he saw as his equals. His presence exuded hospitality, simple, true, and welcoming. Putting his elbows on the lectern, he said, "So, what do y'all want to talk about it? We've got this time, might as well use it." I half-listened to the questions of my colleagues as I brewed my own question, somewhat nervous to ask *the* Fred Craddock a question.

Finally, I raised my hand and asked, "What advice do you have for the pastor who is feeling beat down by the every-Sunday-to-every-Sunday constant grind of preaching?" Fred didn't like the question. It was obvious that he didn't. He barely let me finish asking it. Taking his elbows off the lectern, he gripped it with one hand and with the other hand brought out his pointer finger. Quickly, he had me in his cross hairs. "You know, I hear all these stories about pastors around the coffee pot and at lunch after Sunday service, who say, 'It's just so exhausting to preach every Sunday,' and 'I feel like I'm saying the same thing over and over again,' and 'These people just don't understand how good these sermons are.' Every person who preaches has the privilege of sharing the word of God with people. That is a privilege, a sacred right of your calling, and it's something not to be taken lightly. Consider, too, that people willingly choose to wake up, get dressed, and get themselves smelling decent, just to come hear you preach each week. When else in our culture and society do people do that? They don't! It must mean that they are hungry for something that only you, by the goodness of God, are able to give to them. They trust you to shepherd their spirit, in a world that offers to them a thousand opportunities to find meaning in the meaningless, to the deep well." The important words were reinforced by that pointer finger which, with every joust, made me feel like the only person in the whole entire world, let alone the room.

"So, tired? I've never been tired of the privilege of sharing the word of God with the people of God. In need of a deeper prayer life, I've been that. In need of more time in the word of God, I've been that. In need of spending more time loving the church folk I serve, maybe been that too. But . . . I've never been tired of the privilege of sharing the word of God with the people of God."

There was a tense silence in the room. I think we all felt the call to accountability. Fred put his pointer finger away, took a deep breath, and leaned back onto his elbows on the podium. Sighing, he cracked his wry smile. That smile was grace in that moment. He said, "That was a good question. It gave me a chance to use my pointer finger." His eyes met mine, gentle and warm. "Hope the answer didn't hurt too much, though."

The straight-edged pointer finger and the wry smile appear most weeks when I'm sitting with the Bible open, the pen to paper. It's a privilege when they appear, like old friends who help you remember who you are.

— 2 —

GOD'S LITTLE FARM

Preaching as the Planting of Gospel Seeds

Mike Graves

"GOD LIVES ON A LITTLE FARM." THAT'S A LINE FROM JAMES MICHENER'S epic tale *The Source*, a historical novel set in the Holy Land. The particular scene during which the line is uttered occurs decades after the ministry of Jesus, just prior to the fall of Jerusalem in the year 70 CE, when the people of Jerusalem and smaller villages revolted against the Romans. Of course, not every Jewish person favored revolt, even if every one of them despised the Empire's lording it over them.

Michener describes a debate between two characters, Yigal, a grower of olives who refuses to bow his knee to the gods of the emperors, and a rabbi, Rab Naaman, faithful to Israel's God but also wanting to play it safe. The rabbi says, "You're right. We are faced with the loss of our religion, but not if we stay here. But if the Romans move us from this land . . . There'll be no synagogue in the land of our slavery." The debate continues, and then the rabbi declares, "We're in terrible peril, Yigal, and you want to fight over a little farm." That's when Yigal replies, "God lives on a little farm."[1]

Israel has always been a little player on the world's stage, and not just because it's about the size of New Jersey. It's small in every way, like comparing a family's few tomato plants in the backyard to the large corporate farms of our day. The Gospel writers knew this. None of them held to grand

1. Michener, *Source*, 480.

29

notions of Israel's place within the vast Roman Empire. After the Romans destroyed the Temple in Jerusalem in the year 70 CE, the four Evangelists started to write Gospels, Mark first, and later Luke and Matthew, with John bringing up the rear. All these writers knew how the Jewish religion stood in the grand scheme of things, and its sibling as well, the Jesus movement. The followers of Jesus didn't even show up on the radar of the emperors, not even a blip.

Fast forward some 250 years, and the Emperor Constantine grants legal status to the Christian movement, which by the end of the fourth century was the official religion of the Empire. After that, and perhaps ever since, Christians in many places have tended to equate the Christian tradition with grand schemes, when in reality Christianity has pretty much always remained a blip on the screen. Or to keep the agricultural metaphor going, a "little farm."

Only, as the character Yigal reminds his comrades, it is *God's* little farm; and this diminutive scale appears to have been part of God's agricultural scheme all along. What I mean is that the "bigger is better" philosophy so eagerly embraced by Christians since the time of Constantine may well reflect Madison Avenue marketing more so than Jesus' way of suffering, the *Via Dolorosa*.

My thesis, then, is fairly simple and straightforward, namely that the preaching that helped spread the Christian movement down through the centuries has proven to be modest but effective, changing and shaping the lives of those who hear the gospel proclaimed, often in unnoticed and unheralded ways. Or to put it another way, Christian preaching regularly yields a crop that is sufficient enough to put food on the table, but rarely impressive enough to contact the folks at *Guinness Book of World Records*. You've seen those pictures of pumpkins weighing in at 900 pounds; that is not the kind of crop that preaching produces, not usually. The preaching of the gospel works, but much more modestly than we might have hoped or imagined. And ironically, as we will see, this is one of the things most right about preaching today.

PARABLES ON PREACHING

In order to explore this idea of preaching producing a modest bumper crop, I want us to consider a cluster of three seed parables in the fourth chapter of Mark's Gospel: the Sower (4:3–9, 13–20), the Seed that Grows, (4:26–29), and the Mustard Seed (4:30–32), all of them with implications for preaching. Here's why I say that.

After Jesus tells the parable of the Sower, his disciples ask for some interpretive help. Without his assistance, they don't get what he's saying, which will be pretty much true of them throughout this Gospel. So Mark tells us Jesus offered an interpretation, an explanation that begins with these words, "The sower sows the word" (Mark 4:14). That is our first interpretive clue. When the parable begins, "A sower went out to sow" (Mark 4:3), what is implied by that action is the preaching of the word. Preaching is what this parable is about. And that is the case for all three of these parables because at the conclusion of the seed parables, the Gospel writer tells the reader, "With many such parables he spoke the word to them" (Mark 4:33).

These three parables, then, are not just about the reign (or kingdom) of God; they are about the preaching of Jesus who went about proclaiming that reign. These stories have something to say not just *about* the "word" that gets preached, but the *preaching of that word* itself.

Before we look at each of these parables in particular, a brief review about parables in general would be helpful, since they are not as simple as some people think. The British scholar C. H. Dodd's famous definition of a parable begins, "At its simplest, a parable is . . ." followed by a lengthy and labyrinthine description, forty-one words in all. I am reproducing it here in its entirety, although there are two facets in particular that we will want to note. More about those facets shortly, but for now Dodd's definition:

> At its simplest the parable is a metaphor or simile drawn from nature or common life, arresting the hearer by its vividness or strangeness, and leaving the mind in sufficient doubt about its precise application to tease it into active thought.[2]

Dodd's many words remind us of the complex nature of parables. To simplify the complexity, there are two features worth noting: 1) parables are glimpses into normal everyday life, at least in terms of first-century customs in the Mediterranean world; and, 2) they are also shocking, containing a detail or two that would have seemed patently absurd to Jesus' listeners and readers of the Gospels. As we consider the three seed parables in Mark 4, we will try to isolate features that made perfect sense to those first-century listeners/readers as well as what caused shock, all in order to gain insights into what's right with preaching today. We begin with the parable of the Sower.

2. Dodd, *Parables*, 5.

BUMPER CROP OR NOT?

In the very first written Gospel we read the very first parable of Jesus, the one about a sower. Most of us likely know the basic plot, even if we sometimes blend Matthew's and Luke's versions of the parable into Mark's, thus obscuring Mark's own emphases.

As Mark tells it, some of the sower's seed falls on the path, some into rocky ground, some among thorns, and some into fertile soil. Birds devour the first seeds, the sun scorches the ones on rocky ground, and the thorns choke out the others. But Mark's Gospel tells us the seed that falls into the good soil "brought forth grain, growing up and increasing and yielding thirty and sixty and a hundredfold" (Mark 4:8). So many wonderful words to describe the results we expect when thinking about the gospel and Christian preaching: *growing, increasing, yielding.* This is precisely what we want the preaching of Jesus (and by extension, the preaching in our churches today) to be and do. In a phrase, we crave amazing results, a Miracle-Gro kind of garden.

But what about Jesus' original hearers and Mark's original readers? Did they have such expectations? Is that how they would have experienced this parable? To get at the answers to these questions and more, we need to consider what aspects of this parable made perfect sense to first-century folks and what absolutely shocked them. Not surprisingly, because parables are slippery like riddles, scholars do not always agree on such matters. Would sowers, for example, be so reckless that seed fell everywhere? Even if it *fell* into all those questionable places, wouldn't the seed have been *planted* in the good soil rather than just falling? Who can say whether this made sense or was part of the shock? However, what is clearly consistent with farming then (and now, for that matter) is that some of what is planted yields a return and some of it does not. This is the law of the land.

The real crux of the matter, however, comes in the description of the crop yield, "thirty and sixty and a hundredfold." Such numbers sound impressive. But did they sound that way to Jesus' hearers, to those followers who later read Mark's Gospel? Was a hundredfold an impressive number or not?

For many decades now biblical scholars, C. H. Dodd among them, have viewed this parable as celebrating how small beginnings yield impressive endings.[3] Such an approach makes for uplifting sermons, how God is at work in the world to do amazing things. But not all scholars agree with this

---

3. Dodd, *Parables*, 146, refers to "an excellent harvest." See also Scott, *Hear Then the Parable*, 356–58, who names C. H. Dodd, Joachim Jeremias, and Amos Wilder as proponents of the parable stressing an abundant harvest.

approach, and the reasoning of these other interpreters is quite convincing. Scholars as diverse as Klyne Snodgrass and Brandon Scott, who can sometimes be miles apart in their interpretations, point to the story of Isaac's field in Genesis 26:12 where a hundredfold harvest clearly signals the blessings of God, yes, but not a super-abundant harvest. When ancient writers wanted to exaggerate a harvest, they more often used figures such as a thousandfold, even a million-fold or more.[4] Scott summarizes, "In the end the harvest is ordinary and everyday." But he adds, "In failure and everydayness lies the miracle of God's activity."[5]

This first of the seed parables teases us into imagining a world in which the preaching of the word works, even if in less than spectacular ways. The harvest is a sign of God's blessing, but no one will be blown away by the results. Still, preaching works, because sometimes a seed falls into receptive soil. That is something we should celebrate.

Barbara Brown Taylor's own spiritual journey is a good example. Before she became a popular preacher and spiritual writer, someone else shared the gospel with her. She was a sophomore in college when, out of the blue, two bold coeds knocked on her dorm room door, wanting to talk about her relationship with God. She wasn't interested, but being a mannered southern girl she listened anyway. The two young women explained the good news of the gospel, then asked if she wanted to pray to receive Jesus into her heart. She had no interest in such things, but again her manners kicked into gear, so she said, "Sure."

After the prayer, the coeds excused themselves and left her alone. Of that encounter she writes, "It is still hard for me to describe my frame of mind at the time. I was half-serious, half-amused. I cooperated as much out of curiosity as anything, and because I thought that going along with them would get them out of my room faster than arguing with them."[6] Shortly after the girls left, still trying to make sense of what had happened, Taylor went for a walk, only to discover the world had changed. Everything looked different, felt different. "Was it a conversion?" she writes. "All I know is that something happened, something that got my attention and has kept it through all the years that have passed since then. I may have been fooling around, but Jesus was not."[7]

When preachers sow gospel seeds, it is often as reckless as the sower in Mark's account, seeds falling into all sorts of soils, some of it more receptive

4. Snodgrass, *Stories with Intent,* 155; and Scott, 355–58.
5. Scott, *Hear Then the Parable,* 362.
6. Taylor, *The Preaching Life,* 104.
7. Taylor, *The Preaching Life,* 105.

than others. Think about what happens in churches on any given Sunday, some of the worshipers hanging on every word coming from the preacher's mouth, others trying to stay awake, and everything in between. Even when the preaching of the good news takes root, the harvest is not a huge one. But neither is it an inconsequential one since the categories of size and significance should never be confused.

But what about the other two parables in Mark's cluster? Do they lead to similar conclusions? We turn now to the second of those, the seed that grows.

WHAT KIND OF FARMER DO WE HAVE HERE?

Ambiguity is part and parcel with the parables of Jesus, since as Dodd demonstrated, they are like riddles, teasing listeners into active thought. That said, this might be the most ambiguous parable of them all, and not just among these three, but of all the parables of Jesus. Since it is shorter than the Sower parable, and with no explanation offered, here it is in full:

> The kingdom of God is as if someone would scatter seed on the ground, and would sleep and rise night and day, and the seed would sprout and grow, he does not know how. The earth produces of itself, first the stalk, then the head, then the full grain in the head. But when the grain is ripe, at once he goes in with his sickle, because the harvest has come. (Mark 4:26–29)

Any questions? Yes, of course we have questions, lots of them. It is the only parable in Mark's Gospel not to appear elsewhere in some form or another. Matthew and Luke, both of whom worked from Mark's account, refuse to touch it. Bernard Brandon Scott calls it a "curiosity item."[8] That's an understatement.

The ambiguity and resulting difficulties of interpreting this parable remind me of those word problems in eighth-grade algebra, the ones that didn't seem to offer enough information for solving. "Two trains leave the same station traveling on parallel tracks, headed to the same city. If the first train leaves at 8:00 AM traveling 65 mph, and the second leaves at 10:00 AM traveling 90 mph, at what time will the second one catch the first?" Seriously? This can be solved? Doesn't the station print a schedule so we don't have to work this out ourselves?

In terms of the parable, couldn't Jesus have been clearer with this story? Mark says Jesus told a parable about someone scattering seed, how it

---

8. Scott, *Hear Then the Parable*, 363.

grows even while the man sleeps, eventually leading to harvest time. What are we to make of that? If this has something to say about God's reign among us, what exactly is the message? At least some of those algebra problems included answers in the back of the book; we are offered no such clues with the parables. We seem to be on our own.

Of course, that's not quite right, because in addition to the Spirit's guidance, there are biblical scholars who pay attention to details many of us might miss without such guidance. In some ways, it's like those algebra problems; you have to break it down one piece at a time. As we do, we will want to pay attention again to aspects that would make perfect sense in the first-century world and those that would be perceived as odd.

Unlike the parable of the Sower, this person is described not as a farmer at all, but simply as "someone." Maybe that explains his lack of agricultural expertise since the text says in terms of the seed's growth, "he does not know how" that happens, and his method is described as scattering, not sowing. This man sleeps every night and gets up every morning. Other than the initial scattering, that's it. Some interpreters point to another slippery aspect of this parable, namely how the subject keeps changing. It appears at first to be about the one scattering, then switches to a focus on the seed itself, and finally points us toward the ground upon which it is scattered.

Some scholars believe the real key to interpretation might be one little word in the Greek text, one that gets translated "of itself." The text says, "The earth produces of itself." The one word in Greek is the word from which we get *automatic* in English. What, then, are we to make of this approach to horticulture, the earth producing of itself?

The Greek word is used elsewhere in the Bible, in Greek version of the Old Testament, the Septuagint, for example, when God tells Joshua how the city of Jericho will be destroyed, the walls will fall "of themselves" (Josh 6:5).[9] Something similar happens in Acts 12, when an angel helps Peter escape prison, only to encounter a locked gate. But when Peter and the angel approach it, the gate opens "of itself" (Acts 12:10). Some scholars refer to this as the divine passive, a verb without a stated subject or actor; so naturally it must be the work of God.

In Mark's parable there is nothing whatsoever in the man's technique that could point to his labors, or experience, or expertise. He is just a "someone," whose method of farming is "scattering," and who follows that up with sleep. Nothing is said of his tilling, carefully planting, watering, or ever weeding. And yet when the time is right for harvesting, he reaps. That's because the earth produces "of itself," the silent hand of God at work.

---

9. Scott, *Hear Then the Parable*, 368.

Remembering this parable isn't ultimately about farming but the preaching of the gospel, what might we learn from it? Is the Spirit's blessing upon Christian preaching *automatic*? What about the part preachers play? The congregation's part? This parable does not address these matters, or maybe more precisely it addresses them by omission.

Clearly the parable of the Growing Seed goes to great lengths to stress a harvest that does not depend on the one who scattered the seed. Similarly, Paul tells the believers at Corinth that while God's work in a person's life takes a village, how he planted and Apollos watered, he concludes, "but God gave the growth. So neither the one who plants nor the one who waters is anything, but only God who gives the growth" (1 Cor 3:6–7).

It's generally regarded unwise to form a theology of anything based on one or two passages of Scripture, and that would certainly be the case here as well. While Paul's assessment of our place in the process seems a bit harsh, adding up to nothing, and this parable says not a word about a farmer's work, this stress fits nicely with the distinction theologians make between divine initiative and human agency. While a number of biblical passages elsewhere emphasize our partnering with God, this particular parable stresses *God's* actions behind the scenes, downplaying *our* part as humans. If the parable of the Sower says that despite our haphazard scattering, there is a modest harvest, this parable accentuates the work of God in the process. We cannot for a moment take credit.

Fred Craddock, whom we are honoring in this collection of essays, was fond of making this point when he did workshops with preachers. He would describe the preparation required to be a good preacher, the hard hours of work required each week to put sermons together. He would also emphasize the need for a measure of humility. He'd say something like, "When you're a minister, you get up every day and, as you're heading out the door, you say to yourself, 'I am a minister of the gospel, called by Jesus Christ, supported by God, and led by the Spirit.' Then you put on your hat and say, 'Here goes nothing!'" After sharing that, he would look out on all those ministers and ask, "Do you have a hat?"

Still, I wonder if it would be pushing this parable too far to suggest that even when our sermons are less than polished, when our technique is as sloppy as the man in Jesus' story, still the harvest is automatic? Maybe, and yet God works through all kinds of sermons, and occasionally in spite of some of them. What preacher hasn't experienced God working in amazing ways through a sermon that felt flat to the one proclaiming it? That seems to me to be at least one possible lesson from the parable of the Growing Seed. And that leads us to the last of three parables, the Mustard Seed.

HOW BIG DO MUSTARD BUSHES GET?

It's probably safe to say that while most every churchgoer, minister and laity alike, have heard about mustard seeds, very few have ever held one in their hands. They are tiny seeds, of course; we know that. But given how often they show up in the Gospels (in versions of this parable as well as other passages in which Jesus compares it to how much faith is required to move mountains), it would be easy to combine all those accounts, put them in the blender, and make a Gospel smoothie out of them rather than hear Mark's version of this parable on its own. We begin, therefore, with the parable itself, the very next words in Mark 4 after the parable of the growing seed. It reads as follows:

> He also said, "With what can we compare the kingdom of God, or what parable will we use for it? It is like a mustard seed, which, when sown upon the ground, is the smallest of all the seeds on earth; yet when it is sown it grows up and becomes the greatest of all shrubs, and puts forth large branches, so that the birds of the air can make nests in its shade." (Mark 4:30–32)

Scholars have noted for a long time that mustard seeds are not the "smallest of all seeds," even if they are tiny. If you stood in front of a congregation, pinching a mustard seed between your finger and thumb, no one even on the first row would be able to see it. They are that small.

Traditionally, the parable has been interpreted to stress the dynamics of small-to-large, that while the reign of God may not have appeared like much at first, it was destined to become something grand. But what if this interpretation and the accompanying dreams for the reign of God are more influenced by Constantinian dreams than reality?[10] What if we have yet again misread a parable?

The key to an alternative reading in this case rests with an Old Testament allusion here that lurks beneath the surface of this parable. When Jews dreamed of what life would be like when the Messiah came, one of the more common images was that of the great cedars of Lebanon. For example, in Ezekiel 37:23 God is described as taking a sprig from a giant cedar, one that "will produce branches and bear fruit and become as a noble cedar and the birds of every wing will nest in it." This reference certainly appears to lie behind the parable.

10. For those unfamiliar with this allusion, Constantine was the Emperor of Rome in the fourth century who converted to Christianity and legalized the religion. By the end of the century Christianity would become the official religion of the Roman Empire. While these moves put an end to persecution, they also contributed to a merging of church and state, so to speak. They became one and the same.

Jesus' parable not only uses a mustard seed instead of a cedar, but as the parable goes on to say, when it grows up it becomes "the greatest of all shrubs." Shrubs? The greatest of all *shrubs*? Matthew and Luke, both of whom worked from Mark's Gospel, were clearly not impressed with such an image, their versions resulting in trees (Matt 13:31–32; Luke 13:18–19), not shrubs, even if that is what mustard seeds do indeed become, shrubs. If you wanted to plant one in your yard, you wouldn't need to borrow your neighbor's truck to get it home from the nursery. The mustard seed becomes a mustard bush. Period.

It was the New Testament scholar Robert Funk who back in the early 1970s referred to this parable as a kind of burlesque, poking fun at overly zealous messianic expectations, Israel's longings to be one of the great world powers.[11] Even with this more subdued reading of the parable, we should not overlook two features of the mustard bush Mark describes. He calls it "the greatest of all shrubs," one with branches large enough that birds "can make nest in its shade," perhaps a sign of God's reign providing for all of creation.[12] While not the impressive cedars of Lebanon, Snodgrass reminds us we should not be fooled by what appears unimpressive. He writes, "The kingdom, which has already begun with Jesus, does not come with a glorious bang and the defeat of Rome; rather, it comes unexpectedly, almost unnoticed."[13] But still it comes, with room enough for all us birds.

Recalling that the parable isn't really about gardening but the preaching of the word, we see again that preaching works, even if in less than impressive ways. If the edicts of Rome's emperor were announced with trumpet fanfare, "the voice of God in Jesus was not a shout," but a whisper, as Fred Craddock notes.[14] So soft was the voice of God in Jesus that people could even miss it. All these years later, the sound of our own preaching is just that, a whisper; but it is a whisper that echoes down through the centuries, people still finding comfort and guidance, nesting in the shade of Jesus' words.

The writer Frederick Buechner's own story is a good example. Beloved by clergy and laity alike, and nominated for a Pulitzer Prize for one of his novels, the story of Buechner's own religious conversion under the preaching of George Buttrick continues to amaze me. He tells different versions in his writings, but the basic plot is as follows. He was a struggling young

---

11. Funk, "Looking-Glass Tree."

12. See Scott, *Hear Then the Parable*, 385, who offers a lengthy footnote on this aspect of the parable.

13. Snodgrass, *Stories with Intent*, 225.

14. Craddock, *Preaching*, 57.

writer, living in Greenwich Village, and with nothing much to do on Sunday mornings. He'd heard that George Buttrick, the famed preacher at Madison Avenue Presbyterian Church down the street from him, was a gifted and literate preacher, sprinkling his sermons with lines from Shakespeare and Milton.

So Buechner went one particular Sunday in 1953, and there came one particular phrase that caught his ear and more than that, his heart and soul. George Buttrick was known not just for his literate sermons but also for messages in response to current events that had people talking. The day Buechner attended, the event in the news was the coronation of Queen Elizabeth. Buttrick's text was from the Gospels, the story of Jesus tempted in the wilderness and yet refusing the crown that Satan offered. He declared that even though Jesus refused that crown, he is still crowned in the lives of those who believe and that this coronation takes places "among confession, and tears, and great laughter." In his memoir *The Sacred Journey* Buechner writes, "It was the phrase 'great laughter' that did it, did whatever it was that I believe must have been hiddenly in the doing all the years of my journey up till then."

The really crazy part, if conversion isn't crazy enough, and by just two little words, is that according to Buechner, that little phrase wasn't in the preacher's manuscript but had been ad-libbed on the spot. Someone sent him a copy of the sermon later and the words "great laughter" were noticeably absent.

I later discovered a copy of that sermon in a used bookstore, except with the words "great laughter" in the text. When I shared that with Buechner, he had no explanation. Were the words ad-libbed? Were they added later? It remains a mystery, but one Buechner feels no compulsion to resolve since, as he notes in his memoir, "On just such foolish, tenuous, holy threads as that, I suppose, hang the destinies of us all."[15]

When I sent him a copy of the book with that Buttrick sermon in it, Buechner wrote a personal letter, recalling that sermon so many decades earlier. Near the end of that letter, he writes, "Even the words about 'great laughter' were just words. And yet, for me, they were, well, whatever they were—a river of grace that for all its twisting and turning and seasons of nearly drying up has carried me on through all these years."

Whatever dreams we may have had regarding the church and her preaching, that the planting of gospel seeds would somehow astound the masses, that has not been the case for the most part. In his fascinating book, *Waiting for Gospel*, the Canadian theologian Douglas John Hall reminds us

15. Buechner, *Sacred Journey*, 109.

just how post-Constantinian this world really is, citing the fact that recently in his own Montreal there were fifty cathedrals for sale, and this in a city that at one time considered itself a bastion of Christianity. He acknowledges the situation may be less dire here in the States, but his point merits reflection.[16]

What conclusions, then, might we draw overall? What is right with preaching if the results are less than impressive as some people measure success? Permit me some final reflections.

PREACHING AND GOSPEL SEEDS

Just prior to the three seed parables in Mark's Gospel, we read the context for Jesus sharing them, how he began to teach the crowds by the shore of the Sea of Galilee. Of that setting, Mark writes, "Such a very large crowd gathered around him that he got into a boat on the sea and sat there, while the whole crowd was beside the sea on the land" (Mark 4:1). Are we as readers to hear the parables that follow as some sort of contrast, that while there may be great crowds here at the beginning of his ministry, it will not amount to all that much in the end? Or is the contrast stressing that while Rome catered to the elite of society, Jesus' ministry is among the outcasts since these crowds would represent the ordinary folks in the first-century Mediterranean world?

It is clear in the rest of Mark's Gospel that Jesus' ministry will be less than impressive compared to Rome's rulers and elites. When Jesus hosts a banquet, it will be among society's riff-raff, the menu some meager bread and fish, the venue a wilderness, while Herod and the elites of his court will feast in style in one of his palaces. But of course Herod's feast ends in the death of John the Baptizer, whereas Jesus' feast brings life in the form of food to eat for those who follow him.

Similarly, Jesus spends most of his ministry in the bedraggled villages of Galilee, places so small you might miss them if you blinked. When he finally enters Jerusalem, his entry is anything but triumphant, even if that's what we usually call the Sunday before Easter. He does not ride into the city mounted on a white stallion, troops and trumpets signaling his importance. Instead, he clip-clops into the Holy City on a donkey, his followers a motley crew if ever there was one. It's almost embarrassing, but that is Mark's point. The ministry of Jesus is impressive to those who get it, not to the whole world, and certainly not to those who think they control the world.

---

16. Hall, *Waiting for Gospel*, 58–59. He makes this same point in some of his earlier works, although this particular book is probably more accessible for laity than his hefty theological tomes.

The same can be said for the preaching that will occur in his name down through the centuries.

Throughout the history of Christianity, most of the church's preaching was not like the Billy Graham crusades of the 1950s and '60s, thousands packed into stadiums and buses waiting for the masses that will inevitably come forward for the altar call. Yes, Christian preaching has had its great awakening moments when the Spirit of God moved in dramatic ways, with thousands brought to faith, but the Sunday-after-Sunday grind in which ministers speak the gospel is more the norm, people being shaped by a lifetime of hearing the word preached. Yes, there are moments when one sermon, one message, even two little words makes a difference. But in some ways the experiences of Frederick Buechner and Barbara Brown Taylor capture our fancy not just because they're well-known persons; their experiences are rare. Most of what preaching effects happens over a lifetime of Sundays, little moments here and there.

The prophet Isaiah describes the efficacy of God's word with poetic imagery, comparing it to how the rains fall and water the earth. The prophetic imagery of seeds and sowers seems to resonate so closely with the parables in Mark, one wonders if Jesus didn't have this passage in mind. Isaiah writes,

> For as the rain and the snow come down from heaven, and do not return there until they have watered the earth, making it bring forth and sprout, giving seed to the sower and bread to the eater, so shall my word be that goes out from my mouth; it shall not return to me empty, but it shall accomplish that which I purpose, and succeed in the thing for which I sent it. For you shall go out in joy, and be led back in peace; the mountains and the hills before you shall burst into song, and all the trees of the field shall clap their hands. (Isa 55:10–12)[17]

If the rain that snakes its way down the gutters of our houses, emptying into our flower beds, brings forth azaleas and dogwoods, so does the preaching of the word do its work. Might we hope for more dynamic and gifted preachers everywhere? Better exegesis? Less stale stories and lame jokes? More compelling material? Sure, but don't underestimate what God is doing in little ways all the time. What is most right about preaching is that it works, forming people into God's likeness over a lifetime of Sundays.

---

17. While this passage from Isaiah makes the reception of the word seem automatic, things get much more complicated when it comes to the bigger picture. Mark's Gospel will quote from Isaiah when explaining how parables work, or don't, that there is a hardening of the heart also possible.

A preacher reads her text for the day. She shares some of what she's learned that week. She tells a story about when she was a little girl, daring to set her story next to that of the Scriptures, much the way Jesus talked about farming having something to say about God. She works hard on the wording, practicing on Saturday night in the little sanctuary while others are out on the town. And in the morning she says her prayers just before it's time to preach, a kind of fingers-crossed hope that God will once again show up and breathe through her words. (It's like putting on a hat before heading out the door.) And God does blow upon her words, much the way God breathed through the writer of Mark's Gospel and the way God has been breathing through preachers' sermons ever since. In that sanctuary one person will be bored to tears, as the saying goes, while another will shed a few tears as his heart is touched. Another will laugh at something the preacher says, a form of "great laughter," something about God's presence among us. People will thank her at the door, then pile into their cars, debating where to go for lunch. "What about that place with the blueberry pancakes?"

Is a Sunday morning like that a sign of a harvest few pay attention to? Maybe. But as Fred Craddock himself noted, the fact that some hearts will be opened and others closed signals that preaching actually works. He writes, "Quite consistently, the scriptures declare that presenting the word of God effects a decision to accept or to reject."[18] In the end, the gospel will have been preached, and there will be a harvest, a modest bumper crop.

Most days, I believe that. Or I try to believe that, but as a preacher I often have my doubts. Several years ago now, I took one of our children to visit Princeton, one of the universities on her dream list of schools. The first night there we went for coffee across from the campus, my daughter reading about the school, and me finishing up Anne Lamott's book *Plan B*. At one point Lamott tells the story of a rabbi who was fond of telling his students that if they studied Torah, it would put Scripture on their hearts. When asked why *on* their hearts and not *in* their hearts, the rabbi replied, "Only God can put Scripture inside. But reading sacred text can put it on your hearts, and then when your hearts break, the holy words will fall inside."[19]

I put the book down, took a sip of my hot chocolate, and picked up a copy of *The New York Times* sitting on a nearby table. The cover story was about a judge, Joan Humphrey Lefkow, whose husband and mother had been assassinated a few weeks earlier in retaliation for a sentence she had rendered. It was the kind of story that kicks you in the stomach. Caring for her four daughters, trying to cope, hiding under police protection.

---

18. Craddock, *As One*, 16.

19. Lamott, *Plan B*, 73.

Then, near the end, this one amazing line, of how Judge Lefkow was finding strength in a sermon she heard years ago at Saint Luke's Episcopal Church in Evanston, Illinois.

As a preacher I had two thoughts at that very moment, the first, that I could use the rabbi's line and the Lefkow story in a sermon some time. The word was on her heart all those years, and then when her heart broke, God put it inside her. People's hearts are always breaking, and preachers are always looking for good stories. That's another thing, I suppose, right with preaching today, preachers finding stories so they might speak to people's needs.

But I don't think that is the weightier insight, because my second thought was, *That's hard to believe, drawing strength from a decades-old sermon she recalled. No way.* I know, I'm one of those preachers who plants seeds most every Sunday, but we're all just preaching. We're just sharing some biblical insights, just telling some good stories. Hopefully paying attention to the rules of rhetoric. But drawing strength from something one of us said years earlier? Really?

Yes, really! Taylor, Buechner, Lefkow, and many others testify to this simple yet profound truth: On God's little farm there will always be a bumper crop, a modest bumper crop; but a sufficient crop nonetheless. This is one of the things most right about preaching.

BIBLIOGRAPHY

Buechner, Frederick. *The Sacred Journey*. San Francisco: Harper and Row, 1982.
Craddock, Fred B. *As One Without Authority*. Rev. ed. St. Louis, MO: Chalice, 2001.
———. *Preaching*. Nashville: Abingdon, 1985.
Dodd, C. H. *The Parables of the Kingdom*. New York: Charles Scribner's Sons, 1961.
Funk, Robert W., "The Looking-Glass Tree Is for the Birds." *Interpretation* 27 (1973) 3–9.
Hall, Douglas John. *Waiting for Gospel: An Appeal to the Dispirited Remnants of Protestant "Establishment."* Eugene, OR: Cascade, 2012.
Lamott, Anne. *Plan B: Further Thoughts on Faith*. New York: Riverhead, 2005.
Michener, James. *The Source*. New York: Random House, 1965.
Scott, Bernard Brandon. *Hear Then the Parable: A Commentary on the Parables of Jesus*. Minneapolis: Fortress, 1989.
Snodgrass, Klyne R. *Stories with Intent: A Comprehensive Guide to the Parables of Jesus*. Grand Rapids: Eerdmans, 2008.
Taylor, Barbara Brown. *The Preaching Life*. Cambridge, MA: Cowley, 1993.

"THINK ABOUT IT"

A Remembrance of Fred

M. Eugene Boring

When I first met Fred at registration for the fall semester of 1953 at Johnson Bible College—now Johnson University—we were both beginners. I was beginning my freshman year and he was beginning his first semester of college teaching, just having completed his seminary degree. He was only seven years older than I, but he was "Professor Craddock." It could not have entered my mind that, apart from my immediate family, no one on the planet would have a greater influence on me, just as it would have been beyond imagining that a few years later we would be fellow students at Vanderbilt—he finishing his PhD, I just beginning—and that he and I would be friends and faculty colleagues for a dozen years at Phillips Graduate Seminary in Oklahoma.

Young as he was, we were all impressed with the breadth and depth of knowledge evident in Professor Craddock's teaching. Not only the solid content, of which there was plenty (I still have the class notes), and the intensity of conviction, but the non-dogmatic method, the encouragement to think over options and decide critical issues for ourselves. He had not yet begun the revolution expressed for the first time in *As One without Authority*, and "inductive method" is a phrase we only heard years later. Of course there were expectations; words needed to be spelled correctly, sentences needed good grammar, and Greek vocabulary quizzes had no discussion questions. But we typically heard from him not, "This is the way it is," or, "This is what you should do," but, "Think about it." Of course we respected Professor Craddock—in those days it went with the territory—but we learned that he

44

respected us, trusted that the informed decisions we made were right for us, at least at that stage of our lives.

I had come to Johnson to become a congregational pastor. Fred was serving as part-time minister of a church in the neighboring county while teaching at Johnson. He considered the preaching ministry as needing and deserving the best we could offer. He did not encourage those sophomores who saw themselves as becoming too intellectually advanced for the local church to do advanced study and become a professor. I had come to Johnson to become a congregational pastor, and was challenged by Professor Craddock's expectations of what this required.

At Johnson I had several courses with Professor Craddock, including Homiletics, New Testament Greek, Shakespeare, Milton. He also offered an elective on Romans, which I took my junior year. Among my teachers, I have had some great New Testament professors, including Leander Keck (also Fred's mentor at Vanderbilt), Joachim Jeremias, Ulrich Luz, Georg Strecker, and Hans Conzelmann. But so far as life-impact is concerned, Fred's course on Romans was a game-changer, the most important academic course in my life.

From age twelve, I had been a member of a warm-hearted county seat church in Maryville, Tennessee, that communicated the reality of Christian faith and loving service to me and my family, especially during hard times. But the theology I heard from the pulpit, virtually the only preaching and approach to the Bible I had been exposed to before going to college, emphasized that if we tried really, really hard to do what the Bible says, God might accept us. In Fred's Romans class, for the first time the gospel of grace became real to me. I became acquainted not only with Romans, Paul, and the New Testament from a new perspective, but with Barth's commentary on Romans, and with the wider world of biblical scholarship. Scales fell from my eyes.

About my junior year, Fred inquired in an after-class conversation whether I had considered doing graduate work and teaching in a college or seminary. I responded that I was headed for the pastorate, my calling and first love, and saw no way to combine the two. His gentle, three-word, non-pushy response: "Think about it."

FINDING FRED CRADDOCK

A Remembrance of Fred

Audrey Ward

"Back on that East Tennessee farm my brothers, sisters—and maybe a few neighbor kids—liked to play hide 'n' seek. Little as I was, I could find a perfect place to hide: under the front porch step. Fit right in. So well, in fact, I'd think, 'They'll never find me here—*they'll never find me here!*' And then after some time passed, 'They'll never find me here.' So I'd stick out a foot, hand, or an elbow.

Now what did I want?"

(Long pause while he tapped his finger on the pulpit.)

"I wanted what every person in this room wants." And after a moment longer, while looking around at us in the congregation, he left the pulpit.

That was the first Craddock story I remember that gripped me so entirely I couldn't relate it to anyone else for a long time without my voice cracking. Fred told the story at the Pacific School of Religion's Earle Lectures in Berkeley, in January, 1989.

But that was not the first time I'd heard his voice. The year before, milling around before dinner at a week-long preacher's conference in Pennsylvania, my United Methodist clergy colleague with whom I'd traveled from California, said in a shushed voice, "It's Fred Craddock!"

I shrugged, "Never heard of him."

"*Really?*" she shot back in a voice that implied I must be an ascetic just emerging from my cave.

This particular conference center prided itself on a healthy menu: no fats, no meats, no sugar. After dinner, as the slightly unsatisfied diners drifted away, the man my friend pointed out earlier said with a sigh, "I always think you should have just a little chocolate after dinner. You know? Like a miniature Snickers bar . . ." My friend and I sped into town straightaway and made sure we had a supply of miniatures from that day forward.

Dr. Craddock taught me to do a first person sermon during those days, as "overheard. Fix a point beyond the audience, or set up a person not present to whom you're speaking. Direct address of the congregation is overrated, especially in first-person preaching." He said everything one needed to know in few words, and that made his advice entirely portable.

The last worship time of that week, Friday morning, I was sitting in the back row when he slipped in and sat beside me. He had an air of sheer pleasure about life. It floated around him. Even when nothing appeared funny, you'd end up in a riff of stifled laughter.

As he held the song book and we joined in the music—he, singing slightly off key—it seemed perfectly reasonable that this was no ordinary preaching teacher, but a friend for life.

Twenty-five years later, I was at Christ Church, Oxford, in that august dining hall where noted ancient scholars, politicians, and historic clergymen seemed to lurk everywhere. Next to me sat a Lutheran professor of theology from Canada; across, was a bishop from New Zealand; on his right, a Metropolitan Community Church pastor from Los Angeles, and on my left, a Baptist minister from Raleigh, North Carolina. We were talking about preachers, unsurprisingly, and I related the Craddock "Hide 'n' Seek" story I'd heard him use in Berkeley during Earle Lectures. It was with me still.

Following closely was a favorite Craddock tale told by the Lutheran; then came the Los Angeles pastor's contribution; after that, the Bishop's remembered encounter with Craddock's preaching, and finally, the Baptist from the South. As far apart as we were in geography, and very likely, as different as we were in theology, Dr. Craddock's modest narratives knit us together.

When I wrote Fred on hotel stationery as I recuperated in Cotswalds from the strenuous Oxford study days, this is what I said:

"At first, as each told a story they had heard from you, I sensed your spirit there at our table. But as the stories continued, it dawned on me that each re-teller of the stories had so internalized your stories that they had become personally and intimately embedded in his or her own life. Each still attributed to you the story, but the details of the story had somehow also become intensely personal and even owned. It enlarged the sense of connection we all experienced, and a greater Spirit hovered around us, lifted us, and even taught us."

We had, each of us, been found, in a humble, simple, and profound story that we each carried in our memories from God's man, Fred Craddock. What a man.

— 3 —

SEEING THE WORD

The Sermon as Image

Barbara K. Lundblad

"It is better to have a child's eye than an orator's tongue."[1] Some people might imagine that Fred Craddock wrote those words because he didn't fit anyone's image of a great orator, including his own. "I wasted several years trying to be a drum and a trumpet," he said, "until I finally accepted the fact that I was at best a piccolo."[2] We think of Craddock as a master storyteller and he surely was. But he was also a gifted *seer*—not someone who predicts the future but someone who *sees*. He was talking about paying attention, looking at things the way a child does. If you've walked with a young child in a park or down a city street, you know what Fred meant. A piece of discarded chewing gum on the sidewalk is worth investigation. A fallen leaf becomes a boat in a pond. A two-block walk can take a very long time if you're paying attention.

What would it mean to *see* a sermon? I don't mean a video sermon or a PowerPoint sermon—though digital imagery can be part of this conversation. What I mean is paying attention to a visual image in a biblical text and framing the sermon to make that image come alive. Listen to the text—not only to hear the words but to see them. "*Biblical* preaching asks not only what the text says but *how* it says it. Instead of moving away from the Bible

---

1. Craddock, *As One Without Authority,* 80.
2. Craddock, "The New Homiletic for Latecomers," 16.

to enliven your preaching, move in closer and see how the Bible does it."[3] When the biblical text speaks through a visual picture, tend to that picture in crafting the sermon. The preacher asks the question poets ask: What is this image like? What do people know that is like yeast leavening the dough? What is like a pot shattered or a scroll sliced and thrown into the fire in Jeremiah? What is like twelve baskets of food left over after a hillside feast?

People who regularly preach children's sermons often use physical objects to get a message across. "I'm going to cut this apple open. Look! There's a star inside." Adults often remember the children's message rather than the sermon. What would it mean to begin a sermon holding a water jar: "Why would a woman leave her water jar at the well when she came to get water?" The sermon moves on from that question, recalling the story of Jesus' encounter with the Samaritan woman in John 4. This text may shape a narrative sermon, but with the eyes of a child we see that water jar the woman left behind and the sermon takes shape around that image. The preacher may hold that empty jar, turn it around or set it down, then pick it up again. What does it mean to leave something behind when you are grasped by something more life-giving? Perhaps the sermon ends in silence with that empty water jar sitting on a stand in the middle of the chancel. Perhaps that water jar will be filled with wine or juice at the communion table. Hopefully people will leave worship with that visual image in their memories, wondering what they could or should leave behind to make room for Jesus' life-giving water.

We live in a visual culture. Advertisers know the power of visual images: the Nike swoosh gets our feet moving; the Cialis couple sitting side by side in bathtubs is charged with sexual innuendo; the red circle says "Target" without any words. Long before television ads, the biblical writers knew the power of images to evoke meaning. We remember texts from the prophet Ezekiel for their powerful visual images: dry bones rattling to life or water flowing out under the temple door. The prophet tells stories to set up these images but it's the visual pictures that call the stories to mind.

"The work of preaching is an act of imagination," writes Walter Brueggemann, "that is, an offer of an image through which perception, experience, and finally faith can be reorganized in alternative ways."[4] Visual images can transform how we have always viewed the world. Frederick Douglass knew the power of images—specifically, photographs. He was the most photographed person in the nineteenth century, sitting for more portraits than Abraham Lincoln. He used portraits of himself to change the way viewers saw black people. David Brooks explains:

3. Craddock, *Craddock on the Craft of Preaching*, 41.
4. Brueggemann, *Cadences of Home*, 32.

In almost all the photographs, Douglass is formally dressed, in black coat, vest, stiff collar and bow tie. He is a dignified and highly cultured member of respectable society . . . With these portraits, Douglass was redrawing people's unconscious mental maps. He was erasing old associations about blackness and replacing them with new ones . . . He was creating a new ideal of a just society and a fully alive black citizen, and therefore making current reality look different in the light of that ideal.[5]

Images in the sermon will usually be set within a story. The preacher will not simply say "stones" but will tell the story of Joshua commanding stones to be carried from the Jordan River. These stones, set up as a monument, will beckon questions later on: "When your children ask in time to come, 'What do these stones mean to you?' then you shall tell them that the waters of the Jordan were cut off in front of the ark of the covenant of the Lord" (Josh 4:6b–7a). The children's question becomes our question in the present: What do these stones mean? Spinning off of the biblical image, what "stones" are part of people's lives? Those stones, too, will be set within stories. The preacher's goal is to help people *see* the stones. The picture needs to be particular, not general. We don't see generalities or universals: we see the cornerstone of this church building from 1929 or the heart-shaped stone picked up on vacation years ago. The stones evoke memories.

Years ago at a Presbyterian worship conference the planners placed twelve huge boulders outside the church doors. When worshippers entered they couldn't miss the big pile of stones. "What do these stones mean?" they wondered, whether they used those exact words or not. Those who knew their Bibles might have said to themselves, "Ah, Joshua 4." They were right. That was the text for opening worship, followed by a different stone text on each of the following days. As the week went on—without being coaxed or directed—people added stones to the monument. Children brought stones shaped like footprints. Someone painted a rainbow stone, hoping for the day when the church would accept the ministry of gay and lesbian people. Joshua's stones not only had a past, they had a present and a future.

An image sermon may circle around in a spiral rather than traveling in a straight line. Movement through time isn't as important as in a narrative sermon. But there will be movement. Neither preacher nor listeners stay in one place. The preacher stands looking from one angle, then another and another, inviting listeners to look from these different perspectives. If there are several images in the biblical text it is usually more effective to focus on one image rather than all of them. Too many images will muddle the field

5. Brooks, "How Artists Change the World."

of vision and listeners may miss the image all together. We will consider three different situations where an image sermon can be a good choice: 1) when the biblical text contains a strong visual image; 2) when an image could make an abstract concept real; and 3) when a narrative text includes a compelling visual image.

AN IMAGE SERMON ON AN IMAGE TEXT

On the First Sunday of Advent in Year A of the Revised Common Lectionary, the first reading is from the second chapter of Isaiah: "The word that Isaiah, son of Amoz, saw concerning Judah and Jerusalem" (Isa 2:1). That's a strange way to talk! We would expect the text to say, "The word Isaiah *heard*," or, "The word Isaiah *spoke*." But in this verse Isaiah *saw* a word from God. What does it mean to see a word? For those who follow the lectionary cycle of readings, the season of Advent Year A offers four Isaiah texts with many compelling visual images: swords turned to plowshares, a shoot growing from a stump, animal adversaries lying down side by side, the wilderness blossoming, waters flowing in the desert, lame people leaping, and a pregnant woman who will bear a son as a sign to the king who refused to ask God for a sign. How can people see these images?

What does an image sermon look like? How is it structured and how can it move? Consider the reading from Isaiah 11:1–10, the text for the Second Sunday in Advent. There are many images in this text and it's difficult if not impossible to preach on all of them. The following sermon was preached years ago when I was pastor of a small congregation in New York City, and was revised later to be preached on the radio. The sermon takes into account an awareness that Advent can be a difficult time for many people. The Advent season marks the calendar time between Thanksgiving and Christmas, a time when we're aware of loved ones who are no longer with us. There was an empty chair at the Thanksgiving table. Some people who long to have children feel the pain of these Advent Sundays awaiting the birth of a child. For some, New York City was not yet home. They missed a place faraway that held memories the city didn't yet offer. Many people in the congregation longed for assurance that their faith had not died in the midst of these losses. The first verse of Isaiah's text seems written in bold letters: "A shoot shall come out of the stump of Jesse, and a branch shall grow out of his roots" (Isa 11:1). This text includes many other images: the wolf living with the lamb and the leopard lying down with the kid, the cow and the bear grazing together, a nursing child and a toddler playing unharmed near poisonous snakes. But an image sermon cannot deal effectively with all those images. The preacher must trust that there will be another opportunity to preach on images of the peaceable kingdom, but that will be a different sermon. Every text has a surplus of meanings but this doesn't mean that one sermon can engage all this abundance!

This sermon on the first verse of Isaiah 11 is an example of how an image sermon might be structured. Along the way some phrases are printed in italics to indicate how the central image is woven throughout the sermon. After some background on the historical meaning of the stump, the sermon moves on to look at the image from three different angles. What is like a shoot growing from a stump? Each answer comes in the form of a story but the focus of each story is a visual image that presents a new way of seeing the shoot growing from a place cut off. The sermon begins with the biblical image . . .

A SAMPLE IMAGE SERMON ON ISAIAH 11:1-10

"There shall come forth a shoot from the stump of Jesse . . ." Thus speaks the prophet Isaiah and we usually go on without stopping to argue. "'But, wait,'" I cry, 'it cannot be. For I have seen the stump, clean cut off.'" We count the rings, you and I. Such an old tree, we say, too bad it had to go after standing so long in our yard, shading our parents and our grandparents before us. Now we sit on the stump, waiting for the school bus, or for a car to pull into the long driveway. The stump is solid, smoothed by the saw that severed it from all its branches, from the last traces of green. We sit on the stump waiting. But we do not expect the stump to grow. Not even one tiny shoot. The stump is dead. The prophet had warned us it would be so:

> The LORD enters into judgment
> with the elders and princes of his people:
> "It is you who have devoured the vineyard;
> the spoil of the poor is in your houses.
> What do you mean by crushing my people,
> by grinding the face of the poor?"
> says the LORD God of hosts. (Isa 3:14–15).

This word had come from God: the tree must be cut down. Severed. The tree, the people. Both will be clean cut off. And yet, another word comes from the very same prophet: "A shoot shall come out from the stump of Jesse . . ." Can we even imagine such a thing? Can we dare to believe the prophet's word as we sit on the stump, waiting?

Sometimes, if I close my eyes, I have glimpses of such a promise. Memories of something growing where nothing should. Perhaps you, too, have seen such a word.

First Angle: Equivalent Nature Image

It has now been three years since they built the new police station in our neighborhood. Each time I walked by the construction site, I stopped to watch. "They'll never finish this," I said to no one but myself. For Manhattan is a mighty rock. Beneath the Empire State Building and Rockefeller Center, all rock. Rock so strong it can support the towers and tenements, the miles of subway tunnels, and millions of people coming and going. Such rock does not give in easily. I watched them try. Their machines were huge, hulking jackhammers bigger than a city bus. Up, up they lifted the hammers, then down on the rock with a deafening crash, but barely a dent. Day after day, they went at it until finally cracks appeared on the surface. This same rock runs through the park up the hill from the church, jutting up in oversize boulders along the pathways. Would-be mountain climbers practice on the sheer cliffs, pretending that upper Manhattan is the Tetons. Strong as iron, the rocks stand like sentinels over the Hudson River. Rocks that make a mockery of jackhammers. And yet, I have seen something else along the path: a tiny seedling pushing out into the sunlight. *A tender shoot* no bigger than my finger breaks through the rock without a jackhammer. There are, I know, scientific explanations why such a thing is possible, yet each time I see it, that *tiny sprig of green* seems something of a miracle. Perhaps you've seen it, too. A blade of grass so stubborn it breaks through the concrete sidewalk, growing precisely where nothing was supposed to grow.

Second Angle: Equivalent Human Image

Or maybe you have seen something else—not a rock or a tree, but a sight more fragile still. There is a man on my street, a man I've known for years. We often met in the early morning at the newsstand. Last year, his wife died. Forty-two years together diminished to loneliness. He no longer came to the newsstand. I watched him walking, his head bowed, his shoulders drooping lower each day. His whole body seemed in mourning, *cut off* from me and others on the street. I had grown accustomed to saying, "Good morning," without any response. Until a week ago. Before I could get the words out, he turned to me, "Good morning, Reverend. Going for your paper?" He walked beside me, his face alive, eager to talk. He seemed transformed. I could not know for certain what brought the change that seemed so sudden. For him, it probably hadn't been sudden at all, but painfully slow. *Like a seedling pushing through rock toward the sunlight.* Perhaps there were rational explanations, yet he appeared to me a miracle.

Third Angle: Equivalent Communal Image

Sometimes we decide too soon where things can grow. "Surely not there!" we say. The *rock is too hard*, the light too dim, *the stump too dead.* Yet, the sidewalk has begun to crack. *The man cut off by sorrow has lifted his face to the sun.* There are times when we assume that whole groups of people cannot grow or thrive. Across the Hudson River from Manhattan, within almost a stone's throw of the Statue of Liberty, Jersey City clings to the river's edge. My friend Ruth grew up there in the 1930s. She said the statue looked so close that she and her cousins tried to walk there until the river was up to their necks! She also said it wasn't so bad growing up as a black person in Jersey City. If you were light enough and straightened your hair, you could get a good job at the telephone company—which is what her mother did. Every Saturday afternoon, Ruth and her mother Mabel got all dressed up. They put on their best clothes, fit for the finest party in town. But they didn't even go out the door. They put two chairs out onto the fire escape, opened the windows wide, and tuned the radio to "Saturday Afternoon at the Metropolitan Opera." There they sat for the rest of the afternoon, listening to the opera not from the first balcony but from the fire escape. Mabel knew most of the arias by heart and sang along with her favorites. Ruth came to know them, too, by the time she was in junior high. Once Mabel overheard some white folks say that black people just couldn't understand opera. She told that story and laughed until tears ran down her cheeks, often breaking into an aria! And she surely was pleased when Marian Anderson sang on the steps of the Lincoln Memorial. Some of the executives at the phone company didn't expect much to grow in that part of Jersey City. But some people are stubborn; you can push them down, you can put all kinds of obstacles in their way, and yet, *they push through the sidewalk, they break through the rock where jackhammers failed, and they sing from the fire escape for all in the streets below to hear.*

I cannot tell you how it's possible. I can only tell you that I've seen it and I know it's true. Perhaps, somewhere along the way, they heard the prophet speak and said, "Yes, I believe that word!" In the heart of exile, they trusted the promise. "A shoot shall come out from the stump of Jesse . . ." That small sign spoke hope to generations. "Oh, it seems hopeless, children," they said, "but God hasn't given up on us. People may sit on us *like an old, dead stump but something's already starting to grow.*" With that *powerful, tender shoot growing* in their hearts, they laughed and sang songs the slave owners never understood. "Children's songs," their masters muttered as they heard the refrain across the fields. "Pharaoh's army got drowned, Oh, Mary, don't you weep." They kept on singing through days of slavery and out onto the fire escape where nothing was expected to grow.

Reprise of the Text and Pastoral Connections

"A shoot shall come out from the stump of Jesse, and a branch shall grow out of Jesse's roots." How could people believe Isaiah's word in the midst of judgment? Who could imagine anything growing as they sat on the stump of utter despair, counting the rings of the past? You have sat there, haven't you? Perhaps you're sitting there now at that place where *hope is clean cut off,* where loss and pain have deadened your heart. God's Advent word comes now to sit with you. This word will not ask you to get up and dance. The prophet brings a small vision, not a mighty oak or even the stump restored as it had been. Only this: *a shoot shall begin to grow.* It may seem so tiny, so insignificant that we dismiss it with a cynical smile. "It's nothing," we say, for we have grown accustomed to the dead stump. We have convinced ourselves that any faith we once had is now a relic of the past—perhaps as far back as the twelfth or thirteenth ring of our lives.

No doubt the people of Isaiah's time shook their heads at the prophet's words. They were not naïve. The signs of ruin and desperation were all around them. Hope was a relic to be buried with the throne of David. The nation would never rise again, and they were right in that. The prophet did not promise that the stump would be restored to the tree it had been. *The shoot that was growing, the branch coming out of Jesse's roots would be different from what they knew.* Some heard this small vision and scoffed. Who could find hope in such a small sign? But a few heard and believed. They no longer saw only the stump, but the tender green shoot growing. They cherished that vision even though they couldn't be sure what it would grow to be. All they knew was that God was bringing forth life and hope where death and despair had been. They believed this shoot would grow in spite of evidence to the contrary. It would grow out of the very pain of the past. That pain would not be denied, nor ever really go away. But it would not be the final word. The tender shoot would grow out of the very place cut off. It would seem fragile, yet tenacious and stubborn, growing where nothing should grow. *It would grow within the heart of a man overwhelmed with loss until one morning he can look up again and tip his hat. This fragile plant will grow in the hearts of a people told over and over that they are nothing. Though the pain and anger do not go away, they believe God's promise is stronger than the so-called owners of this world. The plant will grow and break through places where jackhammers fail. It will sing on the fire escape and on the steps of the Lincoln Memorial.*

This promise will grow in you, too, and in me. Precisely in that place that seems cut off from hope. We may long for a bigger sign, a mighty cedar instead of a tiny shoot. But what if we can see it? What if we dare admit that even the smallest sign of life from a stump is a miracle? Perhaps then we will *tend the seedling* in our heart, the place where faith longs to *break through the hardness of our unbelief.* God comes into this Advent time and invites us to move beyond counting the rings of the past. We may still want to sit on the stump for a while, but perhaps we will dare to believe that *a green shoot is springing up* where nothing was supposed to grow. It is springing up in you, just when you thought hope was impossible.

When I preached that sermon in Advent long ago I had set a stump on the steps of the chancel. After the sermon ended, before I sat down, I placed a small green plant on top of the stump. We all sat together in silence before singing, "Lo, how a rose e're blooming, from tender stem has sprung . . ."

Each sermon in the season of Advent Year A can lift up the images in the Isaiah texts. Invite artists to create banners or weavings. Invite children to paint the peaceable kingdom. Use email, a bulletin insert, or the congregation's Facebook page to invite people to respond to a question before the Third Sunday in Advent: "Where have you seen the wilderness blossoming?" The answers to that question will be different in New York City than in rural Iowa where I grew up.

AN IMAGE SERMON ON A NON-IMAGE TEXT

Not every Scripture text paints visual pictures, but it is possible to preach an image sermon on a non-image text. This can be especially helpful when the text is abstract or hard to grasp. In a sermon titled "Telling the Truth," John Vannorsdall worked with texts from Ezekiel and Mark. God sent the prophet Ezekiel to people who had grown stubborn, saying: "Whether they hear or refuse to hear (for they are a rebellious house), they shall know that there has been a prophet among them" (Ezek 2:5). In Mark 6 Jesus has been rejected after preaching in his hometown. He tells the people, "Prophets are not without honor, except in their hometown, and among their own kin, and in their own house" (Mark 6:4). Both texts are hard-hitting and listeners could easily resist hearing these messages. Who wants to be compared to stubborn people who refuse to hear God's word? Is the preacher claiming she or he is a prophet? Aware of this likely resistance, Vannorsdall began his sermon with a whimsical story that sets up a non-threatening image: an old, rusty car that didn't pass inspection.

> So I went to the hardware store and bought some cookie sheets, a pop-rivet gun, body solder, and spray paint, and spent a day cutting, riveting, soldering, and sanding. "Good job," said the inspector. I thought so myself. I now have this fantasy that year by year, as the body rusts away, I will buy more cookie sheets and pop-rivets until I have replaced the whole body. All the people in the town will point when I drive past and say to their out-of-town relatives, "That car is made completely of cookie sheets." But I know it will never happen. The rust and rotting rubber are everywhere . . . Another year, perhaps two, and time will have its victory. When fantasy faces rust, it's the rust that prevails.[6]

In the sermon that follows, Vannorsdall challenges the church to tell the truth: "cookie sheets and pop-rivets will work for a short time, but a temporary patch will not stop the rust that is deep at the heart of things."[7] He brings back the image of that cookie-sheet car as a thread to tie the sermon together. Rather than scolding listeners, he stands with them, preacher and people hearing the prophet's challenging words together. The image of that rusty car carries through to the very end.

> But if the church will attend to its total ministry, dare to look beneath the cookie sheets, to look at the world as Christ dared to look at the world, and to tell the truth about what it sees, then, whether anyone hears or refuses to hear, at least people will know that a prophet has been among us. Which is why, rejected by his own, Jesus nevertheless went through the villages teaching. To honor Jesus for this faithfulness means that the church, in its own time, must do the same. Do it wisely, patiently, and certainly humbly, but do it with clarity and firmness. Much more than an old car is at stake.[8]

Sometimes a biblical text is so familiar that it's hard to hear the words anew. On Pentecost Sunday the reading from Acts 2 contains memorable

6. Vannorsdall, "Telling the Truth," 9.
7. Vannorsdall, "Telling the Truth," 9.
8. Vannorsdall, "Telling the Truth," 12.

images—tongues as of fire and rushing wind—plus Peter's powerful sermon about the Spirit's outpouring on all flesh. The Spirit empowered disciples who had never been to college to speak so people from all over the Roman Empire could understand them. You may have preached on this text every year for twenty years. How could an image that's *not* in the text help you and the congregation hear this text anew?

In her book *Encountering God,* Diana Eck shares something she discovered about medieval churches. The heavenly scenes painted on the great domes of some churches not only inspired devotion, but disguised discreet trap doors. Those doors covered small openings that were cut through the roof. During a worship service on Pentecost some daring folks climbed up on the roof to open the little doors. They released live doves that swooped over the congregation. At the same time the choir broke into the whooshing and drumming sounds of a holy windstorm. That wasn't all. After the doves and the wind, bushels of rose petals showered down on the congregation like tongues of fire. Those openings to the sky in ancient churches were called "Holy Spirit Holes."[9] Diana Eck longs to expand these Holy Spirit holes beyond medieval churches:

> We need these Holy Spirit holes. Our churches need these sky-ward openings to the wind-rush of God . . . Holy Spirit holes would be perpetual reminders to both the prophetic and the Pentecostal movements in our churches that our knowledge of God is not complete. They would ceaselessly remind us that no image or icon, no petal or flame can domesticate God's Spirit. Its symbolic images, like the dove and the wildfire, are images of utter freedom.[10]

Focusing on the image of Holy Spirit holes, the preacher might explore what holes or openings are needed in each person's life to make room for the Spirit. What Holy Spirit holes are needed in our congregation? Where have we become so protective of our worship that there isn't any room for children who may make a little noise? Can the Holy Spirit squeeze between our bricks and mortar to open us to new neighbors whose race or culture is different from those of us inside the walls?

9. Eck, *Encountering God,* 130.
10. Eck, *Encountering God,* 130.

AN IMAGE SERMON ON A NARRATIVE TEXT

Many of the most familiar biblical texts are narratives: God calls Abraham and Sarah to go to a land they've never seen; Jacob wrestles with a stranger at the Jabbok river; David takes Bathsheba because he wants her and has her husband killed in battle; a poor widow feeds Elijah her last morsel of bread; Mary and Joseph go to Bethlehem at the emperor's edict; Jesus heals a bent-over woman on the Sabbath; a Canaanite woman teaches Jesus she deserves more than crumbs; Philip baptizes an Ethiopian eunuch on a desert road where there shouldn't be any water—so many stories within the larger frame of what we call "God's story." Taking a cue from the narrative shape of the biblical text, preachers often preach a narrative sermon, bringing listeners into the biblical story as the sermon unfolds.

Most of Jesus' parables have a narrative shape. In these parables, movement is key. A son demands from his father his share of the inheritance and leaves home. He spends it all, ends up tending pigs, and returns to his father who runs to embrace him even before the rebellious son can stammer his confession. But some of Jesus' parables paint pictures that are more important than the story line: "The kingdom of heaven is like a mustard seed . . . the smallest of all seeds, but when it has grown it is the greatest of shrubs and becomes a tree, so the birds of the air make nests in its branches" (Matt 13:31–32). The visual picture of a tiny seed becoming a tree is the focus rather than the narrative movement of the father forgiving his prodigal son or the Samaritan stopping by the roadside to care for a wounded stranger. Jesus wants us to *see and remember the picture* of the mustard seed tree.

Some biblical narratives include compelling visual images that can become the sermon focus. The story of Rahab in Joshua 2 is a dramatic story of intrigue, deception, courage, and an outsider's faith. A sermon on this text can follow the narrative arc of the biblical story, being intentional to connect that story to the lives of listeners. Two Hebrew spies come to Jericho to assess the city's fortifications. They stop at Rahab the prostitute's house—that seems to be her name: Rahab-the-Prostitute. She lives inside the wall of Jericho, in that space between insider and outsider. The spies decide to spend the night. The text actually says, "they lay there"—perhaps mixing business with pleasure. When the king sends messengers to search her home, Rahab hides the spies on her rooftop to save them. She lies to the messengers: "Yes, some men came here, but they've gone. Perhaps you can catch them if you hurry!" She is no fool. She learned long ago not to trust every man who came to her house in the city wall. So she asks them for a sign that she and her household will be spared when Jericho is attacked. They tell her to tie a crimson cord in her window. She let them down by a rope from her window in the wall. "Then she tied the crimson cord in the window" (Josh 2:21b).

This captivating story can surely be preached as a narrative sermon, finding ways to connect the ancient story with present circumstances: who are the insiders and who are the outsiders? But the preacher can also shape the sermon with the final visual mage in mind: the crimson cord in the window, red as the blood on the doorpost that saved the Hebrew slaves from the angel of death. This is the image you want people to see and remember. The sermon moves toward that red cord. The text has not only a history, but also meaning in the present. There is a message in the red cord for this time and place. Perhaps the sermon might end like this:

> Don't overlook *the red thread* in the window. *The red thread* is woven throughout the tapestry that tells God's story. Without it, some might see the Bible as a story of conquest and holy war. But *the red thread* draws us to the window where we must see Rahab's face. She bids us be attentive to those who live in the margins of life: those who live in the walls of the city, under its bridges and in the doorways. She pleads with those who claim to conquer any land in the name of God, for she knows that the Lord is God of heaven and earth and will not be held captive by any nation.
>
> Whenever anyone speaks of "collateral damage," Rahab begs us to see human beings. She cannot undo the past but if she could, she would tell all her neighbors to tie a crimson cord in their windows. Still she sits at the window in her beloved Middle East. Can you see *the red thread* at the window, the window between insiders and outsiders? Between those who have been promised the land and those who already live in the land? The news is often too terrible for us to bear. Many have given up hope all together. Many see only enemies and a thirst for revenge. But still Rahab is there at the window. *The red thread* must not be forgotten. It is a sign of life saved in the midst of holy war, a blood-red sign tying Hebrew to Canaanite, binding insider and outsider together.[11]

When I preached this sermon I placed a red stole inside the pulpit where no one could see it. At the end of the sermon, I unfolded the stole so it hung down over the pulpit in plain sight. No more words were needed to say, "Remember the red thread."

Even if the biblical text is primarily a narrative form, pay attention to what you see in the text. An image we *see* can help us *hear* the text in a new

11. Lundblad, "Remember the Red Thread."

way. The crimson cord is such an image, and so is the water jar left at the well noted earlier as a focal point for the narrative in John 4. Matthew 14 sets two images side by side: the head of John the Baptist on a platter and twelve baskets of food collected after Jesus fed "five thousand men, besides women and children" (Matt 14:21). Matthew wanted these two stories to rub up against each other. We see two different banquets with two very different leftovers: the first image is gruesome and deadly, the second is abundant and life-giving. These contrasting images so close together challenge us to ask: How is Jesus' kingdom banquet different from Herod's banquet of empire? Reading narrative texts with our eyes wide open often reveals meaning we didn't hear—or see—before.

IS AN IMAGE SERMON MORE EFFECTIVE WITH PICTURES ON A SCREEN?

"Never! There will never be a screen in this sanctuary!" some say. "Of course!" others respond. "Pictures help words come alive—and help listeners pay attention!" Advocates for electronic digital images claim these pictures are like stained-glass windows that taught past generations to visualize biblical stories they couldn't read for themselves. Projected visual images seem like a natural fit for preaching image sermons. Many people are visual learners. Some people in the congregation have never learned to read and words alone may miss them. Children can remember a picture even if they're too young to understand all the preacher's words.

Projected visual images can help people see something they've never experienced in their own lives. Returning to the season of Advent, imagine a sermon on Isaiah 35 with its bountiful images: "The wilderness and the dry land shall be glad, the desert shall rejoice and blossom; like the crocus it shall blossom abundantly, and rejoice with joy and singing . . ." (Isa 35: 1–2a). This hope-filled passage interrupts grim pictures of judgment and ecological destruction. In many ways this chapter seems to be a word out of place and some scholars believe it was written at a time later than Isaiah 1–39. However this chapter ended up here, we can be grateful for a word out of place, not only in the historical setting, but also in our own lives. We, too, long for a word out of place to disrupt despair and fear. Again, the preacher asks the question poets ask: What is this like? What is like the wilderness blossoming? How can the desert rejoice and sing? People who live in or near the desert will say, "I've seen it!" They know the wonder of that season when everything that looked dead and drab comes to life in vivid colors. Cacti blossom abundantly and the landscape becomes a multi-colored impressionist painting. But for those who have never seen such a thing, a picture on the screen can make that image real. The biblical writer must have seen this miraculous sight when the desert was transformed into the garden of Eden. Using Internet resources, such as doing a Google image search, it's possible to find many visual images of deserts blooming.

Yet the biblical image is about more than the natural world revived and vivified. What is like the wilderness blossoming in your community beyond the world of nature? In an urban setting it's possible to see a vacant lot transformed into a community garden. Can you see it? People in the neighborhood came together to clear a vacant lot once strewn with crack vials, beer bottles, and piles of trash. Now elders and grade-school kids are working together weeding rows of string beans and carrots. Walk around almost any city and you can take pictures of these wonderful gardens. How can the wilderness be transformed where you are? Send teams of people out into the community to photograph images of transformation. Perhaps confirmation students can be invited to create a visual collage of these images. The preacher can also expand people's vision beyond the immediate community. Can you see it? On the screen is a picture of lush rice paddies in Cambodia. Not too long ago, nothing grew in these fields except danger and death. Land mines littered the ground and one false step meant death to a child or amputation for an adult. In 1996 land mines killed over 43,000 people in Cambodia. Because of the work of dedicated de-miners funded by churches and governments, that number was reduced to 286 by 2010. By now that number is probably even less. The once-deadly fields are singing for joy. There are other images that move the focus from the natural world to transformation in people's lives: the power of Black Lives Matter in response to police killings; the lesbian couple dancing down the steps of the courthouse after their legal marriage; the broad smile of an athlete in the Paralympics. Look around! Where do you see the wilderness rejoicing where you are?

Projected images can provide a road map to help the preacher move the sermon along. Each new picture marks a place on the map and provides a kind of visual outline. Picture the desert blossoming. Picture the city lot transformed into a community garden. Picture deadly Cambodian rice fields green with life rather than death. One picture is enough for each move in the sermon. Too many images will be overwhelming. Preacher and listeners are apt to get lost. The Isaiah 35 text can keep returning as a thread to tie the sermon together.

While many people will *see* the sermon more clearly through digital images, there are pitfalls to projecting pictures on the screen. Once an image is projected it becomes frozen. The image on the screen becomes *the* way to imagine a shoot growing from a stump. Perhaps it's the difference between radio and television or between reading a book and seeing the movie. Hearing a preacher describe an image leaves room for imagination, but once the image is on the screen, imagination takes a back seat. Images can be culturally exclusive, leaving out different races, cultures, ages, genders, and classes of people. Do all hopeful pictures feature young children while images of despair and loneliness focus on older people? Years ago a bulletin cover from the Lutheran church publishing house featured the skyline of New York City on the cover with the text: "What does it profit you to gain the whole world and lose your soul?" People in our little congregation took offense at the assumption that our city was synonymous with unfaithfulness and greed.

Preachers always need to ask, "How will this image connect with these listeners?" Of course that question should be asked whether the image is described by the preacher's words or projected on the screen. If the sermon looks at a biblical image from three different angles, it's important to create pictures that will reach different listeners within the congregation. Familiar images will have people nodding their heads—they've seen the gnarled tree the preacher described and they'll remember the sermon whenever they pass that tree. Some images are strange and may have people scratching their heads. Like the photographs of Frederick Douglass, some images will challenge people to reconsider stereotypes and assumptions.

Fred Craddock urged us to pay attention, to see with the eyes of a child and to hear a biblical text with our eyes as well as our ears. "*Biblical* preaching asks not only what the text says but *how* it says it."[12] If the text paints a visual image, how can we help people see that image in their lives? If the text is a theological concept that's hard to grasp, is there an image that can make something abstract more tangible? If the biblical text is a narrative do we see something we didn't notice before that gives the text new meaning? Every sermon will not be an image sermon. Neither will every sermon be a narrative or a parable, a teaching or a celebration. One of the things that's right about preaching today is that we have permission to explore many different sermon forms. When we consider the wild variety of biblical texts—narratives, parables, exhortations, letters, songs, poems, prayers, visual images—there is no reason for every sermon to have the same shape. There is no reason for preachers or listeners to ever become bored. "The word that Isaiah son of Amoz *saw* concerning Judah and Jerusalem" (Isa 2:1). How can we help people see the word that Isaiah saw?

---

12. Craddock, *Craddock on the Craft of Preaching*, 41.

BIBLIOGRAPHY

Brooks, David, "How Artists Change the World." http://www.nytimes.com/2016/08/02/opinion/how-artists-change-the-world.html?r=0.

Brueggemann, Walter. *Cadences of Home: Preaching among Exiles.* Louisville: Westminster John Knox, 1997.

Craddock, Fred B. "The New Homiletic for Latecomers: Suggestions for Preaching from Mark." In *Preaching Mark's Unsettling Messiah,* edited by David Fleer and Dave Bland, 14–29. St. Louis, MO: Chalice, 2006.

———. *As One Without Authority: Essays on Inductive Preaching.* Enid, OK: The Phillips University Press, 1974.

———. *Craddock on the Craft of Preaching.* Edited by Lee Sparks and Kathryn Hayes Sparks. St. Louis, MO: Chalice, 2011.

Eck, Diana L. *Encountering God: A Spiritual Journey from Bozeman to Banaras.* Boston: Beacon, 2003.

Lundblad, Barbara. "Remember the Red Thread." Unpublished sermon. Calvary Episcopal Church, Memphis, Tennessee, Lenten Preaching Series, 2003.

Vannorsdall, John. "Telling the Truth." In *Sermons from the Lutheran Series of the Protestant Hour, February 23–March 30, 1986,* Office of Communications, Lutheran Church in America.

THE DAY I PREACHED
BEFORE DR. CRADDOCK

A Remembrance of Fred

Bill Briley

I WOULD PREACH TO LARGER GROUPS BUT NEVER TO ONE MORE INTIMIDAT-ing than the group I faced on August 26, 1975. I had been invited by a planning committee to be the preacher for a retreat that would kick off the school year for Phillips Theological Seminary. It was the beginning of my third year in seminary. One hundred fellow students and all of my professors would make up the community of worshippers at Red Rock Canyon. I can't believe I said "yes."

By that time I was taking every course available taught by Dr. Craddock. My father was a minister and I had patterned sermons after his style until I read Dr. Craddock's books and took his classes. His preaching touched my soul and brought the gospel to life for me. I longed to communicate in a similar fashion.

While I prepared for my Red Rock sermon, I reflected on an experience with a family in my student church who had taken me fishing. I borrowed a lure that I inadvertently threw over the branch of a willow tree while standing in the water. My attempt to retrieve the lure involved a climb up the tree, wiping out the branches that turned out to be rotten, before making a huge splash as I fell into the pond. My host and I met face to face as he peered over the side of the boat and I came bobbing to the surface with some minor scratches down my arms.

I included the story in my sermon, using the story to illustrate extravagant love as I recalled the woman in Mark 14 who anointed Jesus with expensive ointment. I believed our seminary community of faith and the congregations we served needed us to love as extravagantly those we were called to serve. The cost of my effort to retrieve a wayward fishing lure for my friend—a little flesh and blood—was nothing compared to all that our Lord had given.

Dr. Craddock had a part in the service and we were seated beside one another in the front row. I cannot even explain how nervous I was to preach that day. I had labored over the message, creating the nest in which I hoped to lay the gospel egg with relevance, humor, and genuine hope. I had skipped some small group activities earlier in the day just to find a quiet spot to practice preaching through the message several times. Then came the moment of truth.

To preach a sermon in a class to fellow students was intimidating enough. To preach to all your peers and professors who were experts in all things theological and homiletical was beyond frightening. I had to trust what they had been teaching. I had to believe that even this community of faith would be sustained by grace and needed to rely upon the extravagant love of God to energize us and to direct us in the coming year.

I preached. They listened. They laughed. It got quiet. The Holy Spirit seemed to be at work. I finished and sat down. What I remember most about that experience was how Dr. Craddock worshipped with me. His face showed me that he was open to hearing what I had to say. More than that, his expressions gently told me that he understood what a challenging task this was for me but that it was being received with grace. Spoken in love, received in grace—such could be the preaching environment when God's people come together to worship.

After the service, one classmate told me how he felt God's Spirit to be powerfully present. Another just wanted to know how scary it was. A third didn't like the story as well as I had hoped; comparing my experience on a fishing pond to that of Jesus on the cross was a bit presumptuous. Dr. Craddock was kind and commented on what an extraordinary story it was.

As a master storyteller, Dr. Craddock more than any other human being brought the biblical story to life for me. I saw him at a convention after my parents had passed. I told him that for years I had identified him and my parents as the three persons in the world who had most shaped me. With them gone, I was going to look up to him more than ever. He had the same kind of look on his face that he did when I preached before him. Spoken in love, he received most graciously.

PASSING ON THE ITCH

Remembering Fred

André Resner

FRED WAS GRACIOUS IN OFFERING ME AN EVENING TO VISIT. IT WAS COOL that fall. We were out on the deck in rocking chairs. After some small talk to catch up, we sat mostly in silence. It was still and the deer didn't seem to notice us.

I had been a student of Craddock's work since Tom Long assigned Craddock's *Preaching* in my introductory preaching class at Princeton Seminary in 1985. It had just come out and Tom's *Witness of Preaching* was still four years away from appearing in print. Although I enjoyed Fred's writing, I became fascinated by Fred's preaching. In 1989, I began roundtable discussions of Fred's theoretical work in PhD seminars with fellow students Alyce McKenzie, Cleo LaRue, Scott Black Johnston, and of course, our pedagogical mentor, Tom Long. But it was Fred's preaching, his actual sermons, that gripped me most.

Everywhere Fred would go and speak he was, of course, swarmed, both before and after he spoke. When he came to Abilene Christian University in the early 1990s where I was a newly appointed assistant professor of preaching, I hoped to be able to spend some alone time with him, but it was not to be. Every minute he was there was taken. I observed from a distance. It wasn't until my visit with him at Cherry Log in 2014 that I got to spend any one-on-one time with him. For me it felt so long overdue.

AR: "Thank you, Dr. Craddock, for what you've done for me in your work."

FBC: "Now, now, call me Fred, we shouldn't stand on formalities, *Dr. Resner* (sly grin). And if you've been helped by my work, then I'm grateful."

AR: "I wonder if you can identify what prompted you to do what you did. Most historians of homiletics recognize you and your work as one of the watershed moments in homiletical theory and preaching practice."

FBC: "It's not a new idea, I know, but when I look back on it now I was only trying to scratch an itch that wouldn't go away, like a nagging feather under your nose . . ."

AR: "Who would you like a conversation with if you could have it?"

FBC: "It may sound surprising, but I'd like a chat with Karl Barth. I like Barth, I really do. Brilliant man. Genius. But the gospel is not something that is hermetically sealed away from life and its messiness. It doesn't get dropped from the sky like food from a plane in a war zone. It is gospel precisely because it intertwines with the messiness of our world and our lives and somehow makes a difference—*the* difference—in somebody's world and outlook for the future. From what I see in many of Karl's sermons, he knows this, but his sermons and his systematics seem to me to be two trains passing in the night."

AR: "How exactly did you develop your theory?"

FBC: "It's no big mystery, really. I guess I just wrote it down. My musings. My wrestling. My scratching around. And if it helped someone else, that's a bonus. As a professor you know that the greatest gift of the job is that we get to think out loud until we understand what we think. Same with writing. We write down what we think we think, then we redline the stuff that doesn't work. Keep the rest. Hope it works. I'm grateful for the itch. Maybe that's the way God gets things done in this world. Putting a feather under our nose or behind our ear, provoking us to bat at it or relieve the irritation, and in the process, *voila*! Maybe.

I think Karl Barth must have been afraid of the messiness. I don't know why. He had to know it, feel it, have seen it throughout his life. It was all around him in those awful decades of the early and mid-twentieth century."

A long interlude followed as the light on the horizon ebbed away. The temperature was dropping fast. Fred asked in a sort of side-glancing way, "What do you plan to do next?" "Drive home, I guess." "Well, that's good. You can't stay here, but that's not what I meant. With your work. With your life. With your calling. What are you going to do? I'm interested . . . And about staying here? I was joking. If you need to stay over, we'd be thrilled to have you stay."

I didn't know that this was the last time I would see Fred. That this was the last question he would ask me. But now I think about it every day. What am I going to do? Fred's interested. Damn feather . . .

— 4 —

THE ROLE OF THE PREACHER'S EXPERIENCE
IN THE SERMON

Alyce M. McKenzie

IN THE EARLY 1990S, I SAT AT TABLE IN A CONFERENCE ROOM ABOUT TO
present a paper based on my recently completed doctoral dissertation on
preaching biblical wisdom literature. The setting was a workgroup session of the Academy of Homiletics, the international guild of teachers of
preaching. I sat at the table, the sheets of "Proverbs as Subversive Wisdom
for Preaching," stacked neatly in front of me. I was to be the first presenter
of the session. I remember looking up from my paper to see Fred Craddock
walk into the room and take his seat at the conference table. I remember
placing my hands flat on the table so their shaking would be less obvious.
Though I had never formally studied with Fred, one of the brightest lights
in the homiletical firmament, I had read his numerous books and many of
his articles and played his sermons as models in my preaching classes at
Princeton Theological Seminary.

I made it through offering the synopsis of my paper. In the discussion
that followed, this renowned author and preacher offered positive, encouraging comments much appreciated by a young scholar. Looking back, I realize I need not have been quite so anxious at his presence. He had come, he
told me later, because he was drawn to my topic. It makes complete sense
that he would have an affection for proverbs. They are a genre that owe
their existence to inductive reasoning trained on daily experiences. They

71

are conclusions arrived at through the observation of specific details of everyday scenarios in human and natural life. They are not only an inductive, experiential genre; they are an egalitarian genre. Sages aren't the only ones who can collect and coin proverbs. Everybody is called to exercise the habit of close observation of daily life that leads, with divine guidance, to wisdom.[1]

Søren Kierkegaard, Fred's favorite philosopher, is purported to have said, "Life can only be understood backwards; but it must be lived forwards." In looking back at my twenty-five-plus years of writing, teaching, and preaching, I realize that my work has many threads in common with Craddock's. The focus of my research for the first twenty years of my career was on biblical wisdom literature: a decidedly inductive, experiential genre. Following that, I turned my attention to what preachers can learn from the way novelists create imaginative worlds from the alchemical reaction between their inner experience and their contextual crucible.[2] This was an interest Craddock shared, in his conviction that good preaching had much in common with short stories.

Not only my writing, but also my teaching has been indebted to Fred's inductive methods, from guiding introductory students in how to approach a text for preaching to helping them shape a coherent, compelling sermon. This essay focuses on just one of Fred's many contributions to "what's right with preaching today," his legacy, not only to my ministry, but to the lives of a multitude of grateful students, colleagues, and congregations. That contribution is his legitimizing of the explicit use of the preacher's personal experience in preaching. This may be one of the best strategies for twenty-first century preachers to reach those who have a passion for sharing vignettes from their own experience on social media, but little use for God and church.

To quote the lyrics of a classic country music song, Fred's influence has been "gentle on my mind," from the very beginning of my call to preach.[3] But to tell that story, we must go back several decades. In the early 1970s I was sitting in church in New Cumberland, Pennsylvania, the small town on the Susquehanna River where I grew up. I was listening to three-point sermons, which, though they had their moments, often left me wondering two things: "Where is the preacher in the sermon? And, when life is so interesting, why is preaching often so boring?" As a self-absorbed adolescent,

1. My dissertation was published with the title *Preaching Proverbs: Wisdom for the Pulpit*.

2. See McKenzie, *Novel Preaching*.

3. "Gentle on My Mind" was written by John Hartford in 1967 and has been covered by numerous artists since then, most notably Glen Campbell.

my concerns and thoughts were focused largely on myself and on my own experience. What was often missing for me was a sermonic connection between Scripture and that experience. Thinking back, that may have been because the connection between the preacher's experience and Scripture didn't shine through the sermon very brightly.

The preacher was, no doubt, only following the advice about preaching he had learned in seminary. "Don't talk about yourself." Karl Barth's view that "The word of God makes its own hearing!" affected the teaching of preaching in seminary and college classrooms of the day.[4] Preachers were instructed that congregational analysis is not necessary. The preacher's background and personal stories were not relevant. Worse, they were disruptive and distracted from the message of the sermon. But that brand of preaching wasn't speaking to me. I didn't have words to express what was lacking then. But I realize now what I needed in order to hear the good news. It was for someone to legitimize the use of the preacher's personal experience in preaching as part of a bigger picture of honoring human experience in the whole preaching enterprise. That someone was about to come to my aid.

As my adolescent self was sitting in church, New Testament scholar and teacher of preaching Fred B. Craddock was writing his groundbreaking work *As One Without Authority*. It is not surprising that this work emerged at the beginning of the authority-challenging 1970s. It was a critique of the top-down model of the authority of the preacher and the preacher's message and the form it most often took, namely a deductive offering of conceptual information, typically broken into three points. Craddock's work instigated what is called the "turn toward the hearer," and away from propositional, predictable sermons. The movement that followed came to be called "the New Homiletic," a turn toward narrative, inductive preaching.[5]

Craddock would have said that the reason I found the sermons of my teen years boring was because they did not take seriously the everyday, mundane experiences of the preacher as a reader of the text or of the people as the hearers of the sermon. If he had been sitting next to me in the pew, I can imagine his scrawling notes on his bulletin (in our pre-texting world) and passing them to me. They would say, "Where is the adventure? Where is the congregational participation?" For him the underlying question was, "Why should preachers domesticate the exciting process of biblical exegesis for preaching into three points and a poem? He regarded much traditional preaching as akin to the preacher going on the whitewater rafting trip of

4. The image of the preacher created by this perspective is what Thomas G. Long in his book *The Witness of Preaching*, 24–25, calls "the herald."

5. See Lowry, "The Revolution of Sermonic Shape."

biblical interpretation and bringing the congregation back a keychain. He wanted to take the congregation along on the trip!

I begin my Introduction to Preaching classes by telling students I'm going to teach them the answer to a question. I have them repeat after me: "At least one." Then I teach them the question: "How many points should a sermon have?" Craddock believed that one was better than three, likening three-point sermons to three pegs on a pegboard with little relation to one another. That one theme should be the destination of the sermon, not the starting point. The inductive preaching he modeled moved the theme sentence from the top of the first page to the bottom of the final page of the sermon manuscript. He wanted the sermon to be a journey in which listeners were active participants, not a foregone conclusion, a destination that had not included a trip. If he had his way, my adolescent self, rather than being a passive recipient, what he called a "javelin catcher" for the preacher's ideas, would have been an active participant in the process. The preacher would have entered into the experiences of the congregation through empathic imagination and their concerns would have shaped the theme and form of his sermons.

Fred Craddock's contribution to "what's right with preaching today" is not limited to good advice on sharing personal stories in sermons, though he does offer some of that in his 1985 textbook titled *Preaching*. His desire to bring the preacher's life experience into play went way beyond the sharing of autobiographical anecdotes in sermons. His inductive approach, outlined in *As One Without Authority*, grew out of a profound honoring of human experience with implications for how we understand the way we process life and gain insight, the process of exegesis, the nature of Scripture as word of God, the identity of the preacher in relation to the hearers, and the shaping of the sermon.

Craddock joined other philosophers, theologians, and biblical interpreters in honoring human experience as the arena wherein biblical, theological insights arise, not just the place where they are applied. We experience life inductively, not deductively, according to Craddock. Specific experiences yield general insights. This understanding challenged the then-current approach to biblical exegesis for preaching. The traditional view was that the preacher goes to a text and discerns its universal, objective meaning. He then applies that meaning, often broken into three points, to listeners' lives through illustrations and anecdotes. Craddock exposed the illusion that an interpreter can discern the objective, universal meaning of the text, as if it was something that floats above his or her own experiences of life. Taking his cue from theologian and New Testament scholar Rudolf Bultmann, he understood that there is no understanding without pre-understanding, that everyone brings their social location, prejudices, preferences, and priorities to the act of interpretation. There is no way the preacher's life experience can help but affect what he or she discerns as the "objective" meaning of a text. For this reason, I tell my Introduction to Preaching students to begin in front of the text with existential questions, to move into the text to literary and theological questions, and only then to move behind the text to historical and social contextual questions.

A beautiful prayer many preachers pray before they preach is, "Lord help me to get out of the way of your word." There is wisdom in leaving our ego at the door. But a prayer Craddock would like better is this: "Lord, help me to put everything I am and have experienced in the path of your Holy Spirit as I come to Scripture listening for your presence and guidance."

For Craddock understands Scripture as word of God in terms of divine self-communication that desires dialogue, rather than static content that demands assent. The word of God is located in movement, in communication, in conversation between Scripture and church. Craddock is indebted to the "new hermeneutic" movement of Lutheran theologian Gerhard Ebeling and others, who insisted that texts don't just want to say something, they seek to do something, to have an impact on readers. Craddock makes the same claim for sermons based on biblical texts. His understanding of the word of God as contained in Scripture has to do with potentiality, not with actuality. A text, then, is not content awaiting application to experience, but a dialogue partner waiting for engagement with a reader and a community.[6] This doesn't mean that the interpreter imposes contemporary concerns on the text. For Craddock, as he expounded in his *Overhearing the Gospel: Preaching and Teaching the Faith to Persons Who Have Already Heard,* the process of overhearing precedes that of hearing. The preacher brings to bear scholarly skills at historical and literary analysis. It is as if she put a glass to the door to overhear what may have been the concerns of the author in his time and place and seeks to then hear how those concerns might be heard in her time and place.

The authority of the preacher for Craddock does not derive from his or her being the ultimate, authoritative source of universal truths. Rather, authority moves in the direction of authenticity. The preacher is one who comes to Scripture from a ground of shared experiences with the congregation. "Preaching brings the scriptures forward as a living voice in the congregation."[7] For that voice to be heard, the preacher must first have listened, both to Scripture and to the experiences of his or her people.

---

6. Craddock, *As One Without Authority,* 132–33.

7. Craddock, *Preaching,* 7.

"Listeners participate in the sermon before it is born. The listeners speak to the preacher before the preacher speaks to them. The minister listens before saying anything. Otherwise, the sermon is without a point of contact, whatever may be the general truth of its content."[8]

The preacher is, like the congregation, one who is also discerning God at work in her everyday experiences. In her exegesis and preaching, she models that discernment process for the congregation to equip them to discern God at work in their everyday lives.

Much of my own work has focused on the wisdom literature of the Bible, and on the role of the preacher as sage, seeker, and teacher of wisdom. Craddock's inductive method mirrors the approach of the sages of Israel, including Jesus. They train their senses on human interactions and the natural world, discerning patterns of behavior and consequences. They coin proverbial wisdom sayings, partial generations to be placed in new situations with which they are an apt fit.

"A soft answer turns away wrath, but a harsh word stirs up anger" (Prov 15:1).

"Like clouds and wind without rain, so is one who boasts of a gift never given" (Prov 25:14).

I have coined a term for this habit of attentiveness. I call it the "knack for noticing." It is much like the *lev shomea,* the "discerning mind," or the "listening heart" Solomon asks for from God in 1 Kings 3:9.

My model for the preacher as sage has much in common with Craddock's preacher who asks for ears to listen for God. Craddock's preacher operates like proverbial wisdom, moving from specific observations to more general insights. The preacher as sage models for the congregation the habit of hyper-attentiveness to where God is at work in what I call the inscape (inner life), the landscape (community and congregational context), and the textscape (the world of the text in context). She models the fruits of that habit, as she grows in wisdom and discernment. The sage's authority comes from his trust in God the giver of wisdom and his lifelong habit of seeking that which is already his.

Craddock's honoring of human experience in the exegetical process, exegesis both of the congregation and the text, affects how he views the identity of the preacher and the nature of the sermon. The preacher is first a listener and only then a speaker. The sermon is a dialogue rather than a monologue. The final area of preaching affected by Craddock's honoring of human experience is the shape of the sermon. He resisted the common homiletical habit of "laying a grid over the message, alien to it and rising

---

8. Craddock, *Preaching,* 25.

from another source."[9] Given his belief that we experience life inductively, Craddock believes this is how listeners should experience a sermon. For him, beginning with the conclusion, without giving listeners a chance to anticipate it or experience what led up to it "goes against the currents of everyday experience." Craddock asserts that deduction is a crime against the normal currents of life.[10] A sermon should be, like life, a journey, not a destination. He sought to lead people from to a point where they can draw their own conclusions, not hand one over before the journey ever begins.[11] Craddock intended sermons to live on and to shape the experiences of listeners after the preacher leaves the pulpit, "so that the congregation cannot shake off the finished sermon by shaking the minister's hand."[12]

Throughout the 1980s and 1990s, other preachers and teachers of preaching suggested variations for the experiential, inductively shaped sermon. Eugene Lowry, a jazz pianist and homiletician, applied Aristotle's dramatic theory for twentieth-century preaching, moving from "oops, to ugh, to aha, to wheeee, to yeah!" Henry Mitchell, in his *Celebration and Experience in Preaching,* demonstrated the cross-cultural power of the classic African American sermon as, "start low, strike fire, end high." David Buttrick said a sermon should have "moves," in his *Homiletic: Moves and Structures.* Canadian homiletician Paul Scott Wilson's *Four Pages of the Sermon* argues that the sermon should work from trouble in the text to trouble in the world to good news in the text to good news in the world. Patricia Wilson-Kastner, Episcopal priest and homiletics professor, in her book *Imagery for Preaching,* offered a model of Ignatian meditation as the form of the sermon's preparation and plot. Enter into the story with an intention, ask for God's grace, experience the story, and give thanks for the resulting insight.

I've used all of these homileticians' methods in my teaching and preaching, aware of their debt to Craddock's insight that effective preaching requires an honoring of human experience.

CONDITIONS FOR SHARING PERSONAL EXPERIENCE

Craddock rightly recognized that, since the preacher's personal experience is going to be at play no matter what, and since it is integral to discerning

9. Craddock, *Preaching,* 189.

10. Craddock, *As One Without Authority,* 63.

11. Craddock, *As One Without Authority,* 146.

12. Craddock, *As One Without Authority,* 158.

the sermon's message in dialogue with the text, we had best harness it in the service of the gospel. I have come to believe that the preacher's experience with God can be a compelling invitation to listeners' experience of God. As long as it is based on thorough exegesis of the text and of the congregational context.

Lutheran preacher and teacher Richard Thulin wrote a now classic book in 1989, in which I see some of Craddock's influence, *The "I" of the Sermon*. Thulin asserts that the preacher's authority is, at least in part, a personal authority.

> What catches the ear and urges response is the voice of a living witness. What is needed is the voice of one who can speak to the accuracy of what he or she speaks. Not because it has been read somewhere or because it has been overheard, but because it speaks the truth about one's own life and because it speaks the truth from the details of one's own life. It is a voice of conviction supported by a life story.[13]

THE NEED FOR THOROUGH EXEGESIS OF THE BIBLE

Craddock shared his own life stories in such a way that biblical, theological truths emerged in the course of their telling, intertwined with images, themes, and plot lines of the biblical text. In this way his homiletical approach mirrored the inductive process by which we gain wisdom from daily living. In his sermon "Speak Up and Be Quiet," he begins with the account of his first day of first grade. In "At Random," the sermon theme emerges out of two boys arguing in a parking lot.[14] "Grace and Disgrace" begins with the scene of Saul in the tent of the Witch of Endor. He quickly connects it with scenes from everyday life in which people who were so high have been brought so low.[15]

But since not everyone (myself included!) was or is Fred Craddock, sharing personal stories in inductive preaching could deteriorate into the preacher standing up front with hands in pockets meandering from anecdote to anecdote. Craddock imitators sometimes bypassed the exegetical depth that characterized Craddock's preaching, missed the scriptural intertwining and ended up sharing sermon-length personal stories with, at best,

13. Thulin, *The "I" of the Sermon*, 14.

14. Craddock, *The Cherry Log Sermons*.

15. "Grace and Disgrace" was preached at Chautauqua Institute on July 25, 1995.

vague connections to scriptural, theological themes. It is to his credit that he himself foresaw this danger and warned against it: "The most important single contributing factor to consistently effective preaching is study and careful preparation. This must be said repeatedly in considering inductive preaching because the method itself can so easily degenerate into casual conversation with the congregation."[16]

THE NEED FOR THOROUGH CONGREGATIONAL EXEGESIS

Amen to Craddock's insight that the preacher's use of personal experience must not only interact at a profound, sustained level with the biblical text, it must also connect with the congregational context! Otherwise, sermons, week in and week out, can reflect the preacher's concerns to the exclusion of the congregation, what one wise retired United Methodist Bishop told me he calls, not homiletics, but "I–meletics." Like the sermons I heard for several months as a regular attender at a church whose pastor's default theme was, "How to deal with difficult people." After the third or fourth sermon on that topic, I began to wonder if he was talking about me!

I first met my husband when, years ago, I preached a sermon at a church in Pennsylvania. On the way out the door, most people simply say, "Enjoyed your sermon." Not this young man. He offered me unsolicited sermon critique. So, obviously, I had to marry him to ensure the continuation of this weekly homiletical dialogue! These days, he rarely offers unsolicited comments, but recently I pressed him for his opinion on a line of thought I was considering for an upcoming sermon. Finally, I wore him down. He said, "It seems like you are making a point that is only significant to you." To which I replied, "Well, that's just your opinion!" But, just in case, I moved on to another theme. Because that's the last thing I'd want people in the congregation thinking while I was preaching!

Craddock's antidote to overly subjective preaching was to listen carefully to the congregation, to their needs for challenge, and not just for commendation. He was never one to give people a palliative message not in keeping with the Christian message of a crucified and resurrected Lord. This syncs with what André Resner has argued in an essay entitled, "At Cross Purposes:"

> The predispositions of our hearers cannot simply be rubber-stamped and, thus, implicitly validated by our capitulation

---

16. Craddock, *As One Without Authority*, 98.

always to starting wherever they happen to be. Where they *"are"*
may be a place at cross purposes with the gospel and the nature
of Christian community . . . [P]reachers must examine their
persons and message, within their various communities from
the vantage point of the cross, i.e. the message of preaching. It is
not a static message. It is one constantly being discovered anew
both within God's self-giving ways which are depicted within
the scriptures and within God's self-giving ways revealed within
human experiences.[17]

Contemporary preachers need to be careful that their choice of personal stories and sermonic themes are not idiosyncratic and by making sure
that they exegete their congregations as fully as they do their own experiences and the text. Craddock pointed toward this necessity. Others in the
field, notably Nora Tubbs Tisdale, in her *Preaching as Local Theology and
Folk Art,* outlined a process for congregational exegesis. She insisted that it
is as crucial as textual exegesis if we are to preach sermons that don't just get
something said, but also get something heard. Despite Craddock's insistence
that exegesis is for the community, his method could become unintention-
ally individualistic, and ultimately, universalize the preacher's interpretation
in a manner similar to the three-point sermons he was criticizing. The "New
Homiletic" later criticized itself for times when, despite Craddock's warning that inductive preaching should undertake in-depth scriptural study, its
preaching reduced the gospel to experience, usually that of the preacher![18]

LISTENERS HAVE CHANGED SINCE THE 1970S: ADAPTING OUR OUTDATED ASSUMPTIONS

Fred would have been the first to encourage preachers today to cast off
outdated assumptions about their listeners' needs. We cannot assume the
common ground between our life experiences and competencies and those
of our listeners that preachers did a generation ago. We cannot assume that
listeners share the preacher's faith, knowledge of Scripture, and theology, or
share a habit of making ongoing narrative sense of their lives, connecting
disparate events along some sort of coherent plot line.

Some listeners today may be indifferent to faith and the church. They
are likely to be biblically and theologically uninformed. They are often

---

17. Resner, "At Cross Purposes," 72. See Resner's book-length treatment of the cru-
ciform person and message of the preacher in *Preacher and Cross.*

18. Key figures in the New Homiletic critique their own contributions to preaching
in a collection of essays entitled *The Renewed Homiletic.*

unpracticed in making sense of the disjointed events of their daily lives. Discovering these features of our twenty-first century listeners is part of our congregational, cultural exegesis for preaching today. In my view these realities should encourage preachers to include more deductive elements in their sermons than Craddock did throughout the last quarter of the twentieth century.

I am convinced that the theological and biblical illiteracy of our day means that many listeners will need more explicit help than Craddock's method offered at making connections between the Bible and life. In his book *Overhearing the Gospel: Preaching and Teaching the Faith to Persons Who Have Already Heard,* Craddock applied to North American pulpits in the last quarter of the twentieth century the insights of Danish philosopher Søren Kierkegaard. Kierkegaard's nineteenth-century context was one in which the content of the Christian message was known, but not inwardly appropriated.[19] Today, we cannot be so confident that the content is known, much less appropriated.

The prevalence of biblical, theological illiteracy means that inductive, subtle sermons may not be the strategic form of choice to reach a congregation. To set one's life in the context of a text at the end of a subtle, inductive sermon may require more basic biblical knowledge than many people today possess. I preached a sermon as a guest preacher recently on the sacrifice of Isaac. I ended it with a question related to how listeners felt about the story's ending. A woman on the way out enthused: "I can't wait until your sermon next week when you tell us what happened to that poor boy. This is going to be a very interesting sermon series!" The only thing was, I wasn't coming back next week!

Another reason we may need to move in a more deductive direction in sharing our personal experience in sermons is that not everyone has the basic narrative skills needed to connect Scripture with their lives. Craddock's homiletic, and that of the New Homiletic as a whole, was based on the assumption that everyone was in the process of making a coherent narrative out of the many and varied events of their daily lives. In an article entitled, "Out of the Loop," Thomas Long argues that, given our fast-paced, hand-held-device–driven culture, many people may have lost both the will and the skill to follow a biblical story and connect it to their own lives without more deductive assistance. They may be more inclined to live from episode to episode of their daily lives and need the preacher's help connecting the dots by setting them more explicitly within a larger sacred story.[20]

19. Craddock, *Overhearing the Gospel,* 83.
20 Long, "Out of the Loop," 126.

Not only do sermons today need to be more deductive, but they may need more didactic substance as well. So a mix of deductive and inductive, didactic and invitational, is called for. This is what Mike Graves is getting at in his recent book *The Story of Narrative Preaching: Experience and Exposition*. Adapting Craddock's respect for experience and narrative for today's preaching, he demonstrates that the skillful interweaving of experience and exposition can touch, not only people's emotions but also their intellects, It can result in sermons that are not only creative but also offer crucial content.

O. Wesley Allen, a student of Craddock's, uses the metaphor of conversation to express his understanding of preaching. He asserts that "human thought constantly mixes deductive and inductive reasoning . . . To be true to the full range of human experience, preachers should be able and willing to use both inductive and deductive approaches in sermons."[21]

Craddock's denunciation of deductive approaches seems overstated in our context. Just because a sermon is didactic and deductive does not make it authoritarian in the way the preacher sees herself and the purpose of preaching. Nor, as Allen points out, is deduction completely at odds with the currents of life. While we experience life inductively, we also employ general insights gained from past experiences as we move forward into new ones. The New Homiletic's disdain for deductive, doctrinal, theological sermons is outdated these days when, for biblically and theologically illiterate listeners, they may be just what the doctor, or the patient, ordered!

CRADDOCK'S LEGACY FOR THE COMPELLING USE OF THE PREACHER'S EXPERIENCE IN SERMONS

Listeners may have changed in some key ways since 1971, but in one way, many of them have not. Many, though by no means all, people are still resistant to top-down propositions from religious authority figures. If Craddock thought preachers and organized religious institutions lacked authority in 1971, what would he think of today!? The recent Pew Research Center statistics on "America's Changing Religious Landscape" show that the number of those who identify as Christians has dropped sharply over the past seven years, while those who list themselves as having no religious affiliation (the "nones") are increasing, and not just in the under thirty-five age group. Persons who, for a variety of reasons, have come to consider religion as irrelevant, do not feel it is a necessary requirement for surrounding oneself with a supportive community or living an ethical life.[22]

21. Allen, *The Homiletic of All Believers*, 73.
22. See http://www.pewforum.org/2015/05/12/americas–changing–religious

Lutheran homiletician David Lose points out that we preach to postmodernists, secularists, and pluralists, each of whom, for differing reasons, is not buying our metanarrative of Creation, Fall, Redemption, and Recreation. Postmodernists aren't buying our claim that God can be known. Secularists aren't buying our claim that daily life is an arena for an encounter with God, and pluralists aren't buying our claim that Christians have a distinctive story of human identity and divine activity in the world.[23]

Our complex twenty-first-century context features people who doubt that everyday experience is a realm where God can be met and known. These same people, despite this skepticism, have a passion for everyday experience, a compulsion to share its stories and scenes in words and in video, on every social media outlet known to humankind. These slices of life range from the humorous to the horrific: from a child singing in his car seat, to a dog helping a puppy down the stairs, to a woman being beaten to death in a street riot. It is, of course, above the preacher's pay grade, as a mere human, to create faith in our hearers. Nevertheless, into this complex context, of skepticism about God and passion for experience, we are called to preach good news, to both invite faith and impart knowledge. Craddock would encourage us to bring our passion for God and our passion for experience, our own and others, together in our sermons.

Look out over the congregation on any given Sunday and see who's there and who isn't there, who's listening and who isn't listening. There is a young woman in church this morning who volunteers at an animal shelter, doesn't know anything about the Bible, and is only in church because her boyfriend's parents demanded they both come to church this morning. There is a man in his forties, recently divorced, who has taken up rock climbing, schedules his drinking around it, and who has formed the impression that the Christian religion is judgmental. She regularly posts stories and pictures from her animal shelter work. He posts pictures of his rock climbing club. She doesn't post pictures indicating the power struggle she experiences with her prospective in-laws. He doesn't post video footage of himself passed out drunk on his couch at 8 AM.

The preacher doesn't know all the particulars of congregation members' experience. But maybe the preacher knows something about conflicts within families, even or especially her own. Maybe the preacher knows something about struggling with destructive habits that threaten his relationships and his career. If the preacher brings his in-depth knowledge of the everyday experiences of the people, along with his own inner life into

---

-landscape/.

23. Lose, *Preaching at the Crossroads*, 6–9.

conversation with a biblical text before he ever steps into the pulpit—maybe he has a chance of reaching our young animal shelter volunteer. If the preacher can share a vignette from everyday life, maybe her own, and show how it reflects and connects to just one glimpse of the larger sacred story, she may have a chance of reaching our alcoholic rock climber.

CRADDOCK'S LEGACY FOR THE COMPELLING USE OF THE PREACHER'S EXPERIENCE IN SERMONS

Years ago, when the school where I teach, which for the purpose of this illustration will remain nameless, was first experimenting with distance learning, I was teaching a class in Houston from a classroom in Dallas. That week the students were preaching their first sermons. They were to have connected their technology so that in the monitors at the back of their room, they saw themselves preaching as they recorded their sermons. Instead, through some unthinkable error, what they saw was me sitting and listening in the classroom in Dallas. I assumed that I was alone and unobserved. Don't judge me. We all act differently when we are alone, or think we are. I suppose seeing me responding to them was the most honest feedback they had ever received before or since. It does make one wonder how listeners would respond to our sermonic stories if they didn't think there was anyone else in the room. I hope not by pencil-twirling, head-shaking, eye-rolling, or, God forbid, putting one's head down on the desk with a groan!

In the course of teaching preaching for twenty-five years, I have heard lots of sermons. In them, I have heard lots of personal stories. Some of them have been effective and compelling. Others . . . not so much. And I have used many personal stories in my own sermons. I admit some have worked better than others. Some have, apparently, not been as humorous or as moving to others as they were to me. In his *The "I" of the Sermon*, Richard Thulin points out that personal stories go wrong when they fall into several all too familiar traps. They can be narcissistic, privatistic, isolationist, trivializing, and/or disproportionate. They are narcissistic when the preacher's motivation for telling the story is to draw attention to herself. They are privatistic when the preacher's stories are idiosyncratic and do not connect with the congregational context. They can be isolationist when they do not connect with Scripture. They can be trivializing when they are not at the same level of *gravitas* as the biblical and theological truth they are intended to illuminate. The preacher equates training his dog to stay off his bed with a rolled up newspaper to God's challenging the Israelites in the wilderness.

She equates a child throwing up Oreo cookies on her father's shoulder and his continuing to hug her with divine, unconditional love.

Stories can also be disproportionate. The common sense principle of proportion says we are to spend the most time and energy on the most important part(s) of the sermon. A story is disproportionate if, for example, the preacher spends the first nine minutes of a twenty-minute sermon on a story about her adorable toddler that is, at best, tangential to the theme of the sermon.

I recently coauthored a book entitled *What Not to Say: Avoiding the Common Mistakes that can Sink Your Sermon,* with John C. Holbert, a homiletical colleague of mine. One chapter I contributed was, "What Not to Say in Stories." It encourages appropriate self-disclosure and discourages inappropriate self-exposure. It includes a lineup of all the usual suspects. Don't tell stories for the wrong reasons. Don't tell the wrong stories. Don't tell stories you don't have permission to tell. Don't tell stories in which you are always the hero or the heroine. Don't tell stories the wrong way.[24] Dr. Holbert and I admit in the preface to our book that many of our examples of what not to say come from our autobiographical experiences!

It occurs to me that I might not have heard (or preached!) some of those personal stories gone bad if I had read Fred a little more carefully. In his book *Preaching,* Craddock offers good advice on anecdotes in sermons. Make sure they carry the freight of the point and are not perceived as silly. Make sure of the emotional nature and load of a story, and time it far enough along in the sermon to have set the context and earned the congregation's trust.[25]

Craddock shares wisdom deeper than tips on how to recount any one specific story within a sermon. He describes four dynamics of the preacher's experience in relation to the congregation's that should characterize every sermon. I've found these to be, not boxes to be checked off, but invaluable reminders in the lifelong journey of preaching. The first dynamic is that of recognition. The preacher needs to have held the text up as a mirror and recognized something about his own life that he can communicate to his congregation. "Since preaching is for the church as well as to the church, since the gospel is from the community of faith as well as to it, the parishioners must recognize in the sermon their own confession of sin and repentance, their own affirmation of faith, their own vision and hope, their own burst of praise."[26] He calls for a mix of the familiar and the new. He recommends

24. McKenzie, "What Not to Say in Stories."
25. Craddock, *Preaching,* 203–9.
26. Craddock, *Preaching,* 159–60.

presenting the new with interest and enthusiasm, never assuming lack of interest on the part of the listeners.[27]

A second dynamic, closely related to recognition, is identification. The preacher has probed human behavior and relationships with perception, holding human emotions up to the light of God's grace. The preacher dares to be specific without being intrusive and draws on realistic scenarios from daily life. The preacher uses the emotional affect appropriate to the story, and an economy of words. If the content has emotional force but is delivered with emotional restraint, it creates a safe space for listening. As much as possible, the preacher should re-experience the sermon material as it is related.[28]

A third dynamic of shared experience in the sermon is anticipation. Given Craddock's respect for the inductive way we experience life, he wants to honor that in the preaching event, not giving away the punchline prematurely, but drawing listeners in as they anticipate the good news.[29]

The fourth and final dynamic is intimacy. Intimacy has to do with the effectiveness of the preacher's sharing of his or her experiences. The preacher needs to be fully present in the moment. In her ministry beyond the pulpit she needs to have created a context of trust and care that is essential to effective speaking and hearing of the gospel.[30] Preachers would do well to revisit Craddock's four dynamics of the preacher's experience from time to time as reminders of the importance of telling the right stories, for the right reasons, in the right way.

In the Introduction to his book *Preaching*, Craddock lays out three key convictions about preaching. They circle like ribbons on a maypole around the topic of the preacher's sharing of his or her experience of God with the congregation in the sermon. One is, as we have already discussed, that listeners are active participants in preaching.

Another key conviction is that all preaching is to some extent self-disclosure by the preacher.[31] I tell my preaching students that we don't always, and shouldn't always, speak specifically about our own experiences, but we can't help but always speak out of them. We do not, however, preach our own experience. We preach our experience with God. Craddock offers this

---

27. Craddock, *Preaching*, 162.

28. Craddock, *Preaching*, 164–65.

29. Craddock, *Preaching*, 167.

30. Craddock, *Preaching*, 169.

31. Craddock, *Preaching*, 23.

word of warning: "If the dimension of self-disclosure moves center stage in the preacher's mind, preaching will wither under the spotlight on self . . ."[32]

A final key conviction is that there is no separating the speaker from the sermon. Fundamental to the effectiveness of the sermon is the trustworthiness of the preacher.[33]

The preacher is to be a person of faith, passion, authority, and grace. Faith makes one believable. Passion makes one persuasive. Authority is that which gives one the right to speak. It is ecclesiastical by reason of ordination; it is charismatic by reason of a call; it is personal by reason of talent and education; it is democratic by reason of the willingness of the listeners to give their attention.[34] "Grace is that which keeps the speaker a listener . . . Grace is the presence of a God who sends rain upon the good and evil and who is kind even to the ungrateful and selfish. The true work of grace in us is to make us gracious also."[35]

A FINAL WORD OF THANKS

When I sat in church as a teenager tuning out the preacher's well-intentioned and earnest sermons, I had no idea that I would be called to preach one day. I have wondered if my adolescent arrogance may be what brought the call upon me! I had no idea at that time how difficult, and yet how joy-filled, preaching and the preaching life would be. But Fred Craddock did. In his writing, preaching, and teaching, he modeled how a person grows in faith and wisdom by listening: to God through Scripture as its light shines upon his own and others' experience. He modeled what it looks like to offer that gift on behalf of God's people.

In his *Overhearing the Gospel,* Craddock suggests we take our cue as preachers from Søren Kierkegaard and his indirect method of communicating with readers. "The communicator is consumed, disappearing to help others become." "While very much involved in the issues of his own existence, he in no way is offering himself as a model or seeking attention whatsoever. His passion, rather, is for enabling the hearer to appropriate the truth."[36]

If I didn't know better, I'd say Fred was describing himself!

32. Craddock, *Preaching*, 23–24.
33. Craddock, *Preaching*, 22–23.
34. Craddock, *Preaching*, 24.
35. Craddock, *Preaching*, 25.
36. Craddock, *Overhearing the Gospel,* 94–95.

If, as Søren Kierkegaard says, "Life can only be understood backwards, but must be lived forwards," then I am grateful that Fred's wisdom on the role of the preacher's experience in preaching accompanies us into the twenty-first century.

BIBLIOGRAPHY

Allen, O. Wesley, ed. *The Renewed Homiletic*. Minneapolis: Fortress, 2010.

Craddock, Fred B. *As One Without Authority*. Nashville: Abingdon, 1971.

———. *Overhearing the Gospel*. Rev. and expanded ed. St. Louis, MO: Chalice, 2002.

———. *Preaching*. Nashville: Abingdon, 1985.

———. *The Cherry Log Sermons*. Louisville: Westminster John Knox, 2001.

Graves, Mike. *The Story of Narrative Preaching: Experience and Exposition: A Narrative*. Eugene, OR: Cascade, 2015.

Long, Thomas G. "Out of the Loop: The Changing Practice of Preaching." In *What's the Shape of Narrative Preaching?*, edited by Mike Graves and David J. Schlafer, 115–30. St. Louis, MO: Chalice, 2008.

———. *The Witness of Preaching*. Louisville: Westminster John Knox, 1989.

Lose, David J. *Preaching at the Crossroads: How the World—and our Preaching—are Changing*. Minneapolis: Fortress, 2013.

Lowry, Eugene L. "The Revolution of Sermonic Shape." In *Listening to the Word: Studies in Honor of Fred B. Craddock*, edited by Gail R. O'Day and Thomas G. Long, 93–112. Nashville: Abingdon, 1993.

McKenzie, Alyce M. *Novel Preaching: Tips from Top Writers on Crafting Creative Sermons*. Louisville: Westminster John Knox, 2010.

———. *Preaching Proverbs: Wisdom for the Pulpit*. Louisville: Westminster John Knox, 1996.

———. "What Not to Say in Stories." In *What Not To Say: Avoiding the Common Mistakes that Can Sink Your Sermon*, by John C. Holbert and Alyce M. McKenzie, 88–102. Louisville: Westminster John Knox, 2011.

Resner, André. "At Cross Purposes: Gospel, Scripture, and Experience in Preaching." In *Preaching Autobiography: Connecting the World of the Preacher and the World of the Text*, edited by David Fleer and Dave Bland, 47–74. Abilene, TX: ACU Press, 2001.

———. *Preacher and Cross: Person and Message in Theology and Rhetoric*. Grand Rapids: Eerdmans, 1999.

Thulin, Richard L. *The "I" of the Sermon*. Minneapolis: Fortress, 1989.

Tisdale, Nora Tubbs. *Preaching as Local Theology and Folk Art*. Louisville: Westminster John Knox, 1997.

THE MOST IMPORTANT THING I LEARNED FROM FRED CRADDOCK

A Remembrance of Fred

Ron Allen

In 1968, I transferred as a sophomore into the College of the Bible, Phillips University, Enid, Oklahoma. The College shared a towering gothic building containing the Graduate Seminary. That year I was absorbed with Greek and Bultmann and other things too wonderful for a nineteen-year-old from the Ozarks. But again and again I heard seminary students in the library whisper a name in reverence: Dr. Craddock. Not "Fred." "Dr. Craddock."

Despite the College of the Bible and the Graduate Seminary sharing the same building, the schedules for the two schools were different, and Bible College students rarely saw seminary students and faculty. So when I heard someone call, "Dr. Craddock," I immediately turned and looked down the long hall. I looked, but I didn't see. His reputation had prepared me for someone six feet tall, 250 pounds, with a voice that could overpower the pipe organ in Bivins Chapel. I literally did not see him in the mix of people down the hall.

The next year, Dr. Craddock was on research leave in Germany. But he came back my last year at Phillips, and that was my first time to hear him preach. There is a reason "the first time I heard him preach" is a trope among preachers. University chapel. Christmas service. Packed. People literally lining the wall and spilling out the doorway.

I was seated in the chancel where I had read the Bible lesson for the service. I could see Dr. Craddock rise, bend slightly, use his foot to slide an empty wooden case for Coca Cola bottles into the pulpit, and step onto the case. A student poet had left several poems on the pulpit. Dr. Craddock opened with what I came to recognize as one of his many signatures—just the right words to begin. "I'd like to thank Pat for leaving all this material." He held up the poems with that classic expression of bemusement on his face. "But I don't think I'll need it." Pause. "The Bible gives us quite enough material for today." Slight pause. "Herod ordered the slaughter of innocent children all around Bethlehem. And Matthew remembered what the prophet Jeremiah had said centuries before. 'A voice was heard in Ramah, wailing and loud lamentation.'" Slight pause. "'Rachel weeping for her children.'" Pause. "Can you hear that?" Little pause "Can you hear the wailing and lamentation?" Bigger pause. "Can you hear Rachel . . . weeping . . . for . . . her . . . children?" Significant pause.[1]

I knew that sermon was special. But, I was nineteen. I had not read a single book about preaching. It was 1970. There were still giants in the land of the pulpit in places like New York and Los Angeles. And, after all, we were in western Oklahoma, where the geography is such that you can barely tell where creation ends and chaos begins. The sermon drew me in, but I did not see the significance of that way of preaching.

A few months later, *As One Without Authority* came out. It was published by a science professor who had a second-hand printing press set up in his garage and who operated under the name Phillips University Press. Some of the pages immediately came loose from the binding. You can understand why I did not see what I was seeing.

To be sure, the content was captivating. I started reading it after supper, and against my genetic tendency to go to bed early, I kept reading into the night. Yet, I had minors in philosophy and speech. I had read Aristotle, both *Rhetoric* and *Poetics*. I liked *As One Without Authority*. "This book is engaging. But I know all about inductive logic."

Sometimes we know what we know, but what we know is not what we think we know.

The most important thing I learned from Dr. Craddock is not inductive preaching or how to tell a story or ending a sermon in such a way as to leave a congregation speechless. The most important thing I learned is to think again about what I think I know. That is not only true of preaching. It is also true of the Bible, and of God.

---

1. I recall this sermon from memory. I can feel that beginning as if I heard it in seminary chapel this morning. The text was Matthew 2:13-23. Matthew 2:18 cites Jeremiah 31:15.

"FORM SHAPES THE LISTENER'S FAITH"

A Remembrance of Fred

Margaret Moers Wenig

I NEVER STUDIED WITH FRED CRADDOCK, BUT MY STUDENTS ARE INTRO-
duced to his teaching every year. In the years when publishers used to come
to the annual meeting of the Academy of Homiletics, their tables overflow-
ing with luscious resources, I'd spend hours looking through their displays
and buy an armload of books. One was Fred Craddock's *Preaching*, published in 1985. Half of the pages of my copy are dog-eared. Underlinings
and marginal comments abound. (Be reassured, you who write, edit, and
publish books: They matter! Hundreds of people you've never met may
read and be influenced by them.) Among the lessons Fred Craddock taught
me and a quarter-century of my students at Hebrew Union College–Jewish Institute of Religion in New York, are these: "Form shapes the listener's
experience of the material," and "[f]orm determines the degree of participation demanded of the hearers."[1] Though these lessons were not part of the
homiletical training I received in rabbinical seminary, I eventually heard
those lessons echoed by many others in the field of (Christian) homiletics. Fred Craddock, however, added this, and this lesson I have not heard
echoed nearly enough:

> Form shapes the listener's faith . . . Ministers who, week after
> week, frame their sermons as arguments, syllogisms armed for
> debate, tend to give that form to the faith perspective of regular
> listeners. Being a Christian is proving you are right. Those who
> consistently use the "before/after" pattern impress upon hearers

1. Craddock, *Preaching*, 173–74.

that conversion is the normative model for becoming a believer. Sermons which invariably place before the congregation the "either/or" format as the way to see the issues before them, contribute to oversimplification, inflexibility and the notion that faith is always an urgent decision. In contrast, "both/and" sermons tend to broaden horizons and sympathies but never confront the listener with a crisp decision. Form is so extremely important. Regardless of the subjects being treated, a preacher can thereby nourish rigidity or openness, legalism or graciousness, inclusiveness or exclusiveness, adversarial or conciliating mentality, willingness to discuss or demand immediate answers.[2]

BIBLIOGRAPHY

Craddock, Fred B. *Preaching*. Nashville: Abingdon, 1985.

2. Craddock, *Preaching*, 173.

— 5 —

ONE THING RIGHT ABOUT PREACHING IS THE WAY OUR TEACHING AND LEARNING CONTEXTS CHALLENGE GROWTH

Debra J. Mumford

INTRODUCTION

WHEN I WAS ASKED BY THE EDITORS OF THIS BOOK TO THINK ABOUT WHAT is right about preaching, I remembered the many contexts within which I have been challenged to learn and grow even as I was trying to teach and inform. Students, preachers, homiletical colleagues, and scholars from other disciplines have all pushed me to new research, writing, and teaching trajectories. Each context has challenged me with insights and questions. They have pushed me to think deeply about how best to deal with topics like anxiety, race, and the role of the Holy Spirit in preaching. They have solidified the importance of story and compelled me to examine my own theology around health and healing.

TEACHING PREACHING IS A TWO-WAY STREET

In my introductory preaching class I ask of the students: "What do you like most and least about preaching?" What many of them like most is that preaching actually matters. They know that when preaching is done well and effectively, it has the ability to positively affect lives. When prompted, they can each easily recall at least one sermon that impacted their lives in meaningful ways. I am encouraged by the healthy respect the students have for the potential of the preaching moment.

At the same time, this healthy respect for preaching gives birth to what students like least, namely the fear and anxiety of actually doing it. Students are afraid that their preaching will not honor God. They are afraid that with all of the responsibilities that come along with day-to-day ministry they won't have adequate time to prepare meaningful and effective sermons. They are afraid that their delivery will be flat and ineffectual. They are also afraid of the ways their bodies react physically in the preaching moment.

The anxiety that students feel when confronted by the demands of preaching pushed me into an initial research trajectory. I was not unaware of this issue, having had to deal with my own anxiety, but encountering student anxiety as a teaching assistant in graduate school, I was inspired to write my first paper for the Academy of Homiletics, the annual professional conference for teachers of preaching, on preaching and anxiety. Overcoming anxiety in order to perform well in preaching is an important part of the learning process for preachers. A performance-in-preaching class I took with Jana Childers helped me understand that preachers can learn a lot from music and theater performance studies about controlling the often crippling effects of anxiety when facing the preaching moment.

As it relates to both preaching and musical performance, performance anxiety has three components: physiological, cognitive, and behavioral. The physiological component is exhibited through difficulty concentrating, loss of appetite, increased heart rate, shortness of breath, dizziness, shaking knees and hands, and sweaty palms.[1] These physiological symptoms may interfere with performance by making it difficult for the performer to control parts of the body (such as hands) and breathing. Cognitive symptoms of anxiety include fear of making mistakes, feelings of inadequacy, and worrying about what could happen. Behavioral symptoms include not being able to do things which would otherwise happen naturally. For example, older professional musicians are better able to cope with stress than younger performers. As musicians age and gain more experience, they develop strategies for coping with anxiety. Mastery of tasks and anxiety are related. If the task is simple or well learned so that the correct responses are dominant, then an audience enhances task performance. However, if the task is poorly learned so that incorrect responses are likely to be dominant,

---

1. Miller, "A Discussion on Performance Anxiety."

then an audience inhibits task performance. In either case, the audience enhances the dominant response.

Childers helps preachers understand the importance of well-developed, positive, dominant responses when recommending rehearsal and application of oral interpretation guidelines. Rehearsal leads to internalization, which can enable the preacher to mentally recreate story in the preaching moment while also enabling the preacher's muscles to resonate with the words being shared.[2] Her oral interpretation guidelines include: not automatically pausing when encountering commas or quotation marks, using emphasis strategically to convey meaning, and employing pause to group related thoughts together and to give listeners time to absorb the message.[3] In addition, Childers contends that by taking the time to internalize the sermon, the preacher then enters into a process of "dialogue, discovery, and synthesis" with the text.[4] The result is a sermon that reflects the voice and life of the text as fully as it reflects the voice and personality of the preacher.

Other recommendations in my paper included: prayer and meditation, deep breathing exercises, calisthenics, and eating natural beta blockers (such as bananas, potatoes, white beans, raisins, raw spinach, almonds, walnuts, citrus fruits, pomegranate, and orange juice). These all help address the physiological symptoms of anxiety. I also made commonsense recommendations such as wearing comfortable clothes and shoes when preaching and arriving early to the preaching engagement to allow time to gain composure and centering oneself for the task as hand.

I thought I had addressed the subject well and quite thoroughly. However, it was in the small group of seasoned homileticians who gathered when I presented my paper that I was told I missed something, something big. Anxiety about preaching has one key difference from anxiety of musical or theater performance: the God factor. Preachers have the unwieldy task of speaking on behalf of God. People gather week after week in villages, small towns, and big cities around the world in eager anticipation of hearing a word from God. They expect to hear messages that speak to the situations and circumstances of their lives and help them to navigate challenges that come their way. The enormity of the task of speaking on God's behalf produces a type of anxiety that is very different from music or theater performance anxiety. Anxiety as it relates to preaching includes the fear of speaking words that people then choose to live by. How daunting is that?

2. Childers, *Performing the Word*, 92.

3. Childers, *Performing the Word*, 81–86.

4. Childers, *Performing the Word*, 95.

I was reminded by some more senior members of the guild that having anxiety about preaching is good and healthy. Anxiety about preaching can be evidence that the preacher understands the consequential nature of her task. When preachers acknowledge and even embrace their anxieties, then they can develop strategies for using their anxieties to develop strong and compelling sermons. As a result, in addition to internalizing the sermon preachers may be compelled to start their exegetical work early and space it out over a week so their sermons will have more theological depth and they will have more time to select fitting and relevant illustrations.

A PEDAGOGICAL LACUNA ONLY THE HOLY SPIRIT CAN FILL

An interaction that I have had with students that sparked another significant research and teaching trajectory for me occurred in my first year of teaching at Louisville Seminary. I thought I had developed a solid syllabus. I had included all of the methodologies, tools, and structures that I thought would help prepare preachers to preach the word of God effectively and responsibly. I had included voices of homileticians who represented racial, ethnic, and gender diversity. I had included details about each assignment so that all of the students would be clear about my expectations of them in the course. I had chosen local pastors to work with me who were experienced and good exemplars of the art of preaching. I thought I had thought of everything.

On the initial day of my first introductory preaching class, a student who grew up in the Church of God in Christ raised her hand after I had reviewed the syllabus for the semester and the agenda for the day. The question she asked has shaped every preaching class I have taught since. She asked respectfully, "Dr. Mumford, I don't see anything about the Holy Spirit on the syllabus. Don't we need the Holy Spirit in preaching?" Talk about a "come to Jesus" moment. In all of my preparation, I had overlooked the Holy Spirit. In graduate school I had read James Forbes's *The Holy Spirit and Preaching*. But perhaps somewhere between defending my dissertation and preparing my first syllabus, I had unconsciously demoted the Holy Spirit to implicit status rather than elevating it to its rightful explicit and primary eminence. That encounter with a student years ago, along with many encounters since, continually reminds me that my preaching courses should always acknowledge the importance of the Holy Spirit for sermon development and delivery. That encounter also never lets me forget the importance of the Holy Spirit in my own preaching and preparation.

For James Forbes, Godly preaching is impossible without the Holy Spirit. When Forbes uses the term *anointing* he defines it as *empowerment*.[5] When empowered by the Spirit of God, all believers become more effective in their ministries.[6] He argues that the presence of the Holy Spirit provides wisdom and knowledge of human situations and circumstances while also providing believers with the power to facilitate abundant life. In addition, those who are confident of the power of the anointing working in their lives will have more confidence that their ministries make a difference in the lives of God's people than those without the anointing.[7]

Building on Forbes's work in his book, *Spirit Speech: Lament and Celebration in Preaching*, Luke Powery posits that there are five manifestations of the Spirit that provide a Spirit-sensitive theology of preaching: celebration, lament, grace, unity, and fellowship.[8] Celebration in preaching is a gift of the Spirit that provides the congregation with the assurance of grace. The practice of celebration imbues listeners with hope both inside and outside of worship.[9] Celebration and lament are intricately linked through human suffering. By naming pain and reclaiming memories, listeners begin the journey to healing, wholeness, joy, and hope. When space is made for lament in preaching, hearers begin to believe that their tomorrows can be better than today. In addition to grace being manifested in the preaching moment through celebration, the grace of God is also revealed through the preacher who engages in thorough sermon preparation.[10] The Spirit of unity is manifested in preaching when the preacher is guided by love in everything she does and says.[11] Through the power of the Spirit of fellowship, God's new social order can be revealed in preaching. The anointed preacher exposes death in all of its manifestations and casts demons out of ecclesial, political, and social institutions.[12] Forbes and Powery remind us all to invite the Holy Spirit into every part of the sermonic process: inspiration, conception, development, rehearsal/internalization, and delivery.

5. Forbes, *The Holy Spirit and Preaching*, 44.

6. Forbes, *The Holy Spirit and Preaching*, 50.

7. Forbes, *The Holy Spirit and Preaching*, 50.

8. Powery, *Spirit Speech*, 117.

9. Powery, *Spirit Speech*, 33.

10. Powery, *Spirit Speech*, 49.

11. Powery, *Spirit Speech*, 75.

12. Powery, *Spirit Speech*, 88.

TURNING EXEGETES INTO PREACHERS:
ENTER CRADDOCK

Another encounter with a different set of students sent me scrambling to discover a pedagogical cure. In my first years of teaching preaching in Louisville, I noticed that many of my students who hailed from mainline white Protestant churches had a unique challenge: they mistook lecturing for sound preaching. Most were bright, eager, and committed to sound biblical exegesis. When I introduced them to an approach to weekly biblical exegesis that was logical and easy to follow, they embraced it with minimal pushback or objection. They also appreciated being introduced to structures that would enable them to organize their sermons in ways that the people in the pews could easily follow. However, when it came to delivery, they largely used the preaching moment to convey the exegetical information they gathered in their study. They then took a dispassionate stance when delivering the sermon. They exhibited little conviction and enthusiasm for the sermons they worked so hard to develop. After a couple of years of observing this phenomenon, I enlisted the help of Fred Craddock.

In his book *As One Without Authority*, Craddock launched a revolution in mainline Protestant preaching that began with a scathing critique of its status. Craddock contended that preaching had been convicted and sentenced by the court of public opinion and found wanting.[13] Week after week people were being exposed to sermons that conveyed sound theological information but failed to engage the heart and inspire change in the hearers. Craddock believed that some of the fault for the sad state of preaching could be found in, among other things, the Enlightenment. Scientific approaches to biblical studies and theology yielded an abundance of facts and pools of knowledge that preachers felt compelled to share with the listeners. Some preachers saw themselves as transmitters of information about God.[14] They had separated the message from the messenger by believing the method of the delivery did not matter. Rather it was the message that was most important. Craddock strenuously disagreed with this contention when he argued, using the work of Ernst Fuchs, Amos Wilder, and Robert Funk, that "the method is the message."[15] In all preaching, what is preached is at one with how it is preached. Using his signature folksy language, Craddock wrote that, "it is not just the destination but the trip that is important."[16]

13. Craddock, *As One Without Authority*, 3.

14. Craddock, *As One Without Authority*, 9.

15. Craddock, *As One Without Authority*, 44.

16. Craddock, *As One Without Authority*, 44.

Craddock argued that people in the pews were living concrete lives rather than theoretical ones, meaning that preachers could not truly engage people using only abstract, scientific, historical, or theological language. They must use language that connects with the images that shape and define people's lives: images they received from parents, friends, family, teachers, writers, or some combination thereof. Craddock believed that a person can only be changed when current images are replaced with new, more godly ones. And even when people embrace the preacher's new images, old images still linger for a while. Change takes time. According to Craddock, "the longest trip a person takes is that from head to heart."[17]

As it relates to emotion, Craddock contends that many preachers have been educated to regard it negatively. With that in mind, he assures preachers that the presence of emotion is not evidence of a lack of intelligence or a tacit approval of emotionalism. While the appeal to emotionalism is fraught with the potential for dishonesty, deception, and manipulation, the appeal to emotion is an attempt to connect to the lived experiences of the listeners.[18] Therefore, the preacher who is able to engage both head and heart without apology is a preacher who is able to minister holistically to the people of God. Craddock inspired years of scholarship and conversations about the role of story in preaching.

STRETCHING THE STORY IN NEW DIMENSIONS: THE MULTI-CULTURAL CLASSROOM

One place where preachers can continue Craddock's prescription for using story for effective preaching is when helping preachers develop sermons about race. In a class I co-taught in the ACTS Doctor of Ministry program at Lutheran Seminary in Chicago with Dawn Ottoni-Wilhelm, the pastors and preachers in our class had a burning desire to preach culturally relevant and timely sermons that didn't just tickle the ears of their congregations, but that actually inspired social transformation. In June of 2015, our class met just one week after the horrendous Charleston, South Carolina shooting at Emanuel African Methodist Episcopal Church. In the shooting, nine people who had gathered for Bible study were gunned down in cold blood. Dawn and I talked in the days immediately after the shooting about how best to incorporate the shooting incident into our class discussions. However, when we began our class, the students made it abundantly clear that they wanted to think deeply about and be challenged to deliver sermons in light of such

17. Craddock, *As One Without Authority*, 64.
18. Craddock, *As One Without Authority*, 69.

tragedy. It was readily apparent that they were not going to be content with easy platitudes or calls to hold hands and sing "Kumbaya." They expected us to deconstruct the shooting incident and interpret its meaning and impact on prophetic preaching and prophetic preachers. They wanted to unpack the ways that all of us have been shaped and impacted by the ideology of race in various ways. They wanted to be challenged to not just preach a message that comforted those who were saddened by such a tragic loss, but wanted to encourage their congregations to recognize the incipient nature of racial ideology and be charged to dismantle its structures wherever they are found.

But how are preachers supposed to preach about a subject that is as divisive and potentially explosive as race? Perhaps Craddock can be helpful here. Craddock's contention that people can only be changed when their received images are changed into more godly ones is directly applicable to the issue of race. So in addition to reviewing and discussing readings from womanists and Mujuerista theologians, Dawn and I decided to take a different approach to talking about race. We decided to share personal stories about how we each first became aware of the concept of race. Dawn and I each shared our stories first. Then we invited members of the class to share their stories as well. Sharing personal stories allowed us to discuss and explore race from many different perspectives in a non-confrontational way. We encouraged everyone to ask questions after stories were told. By delving more deeply into the stories of other members of the class, the students were able to clarify and deepen their understandings of the impact of racialized ideology. We discussed the challenges of embodying the reign of God in a culture in which people often failed to live up to our highest ideals. Some people reap social and economic benefits from racism. Others are scarred and demoralized by it. None of us has escaped its influence. Through the use of personal stories we were able to begin the process of better understanding and relating to one another.

In his book *Race Talk and the Conspiracy of Silence*, Derald Wing Sue writes that personal stories can potentially unmask the master narrative that we receive in our culture, which informs us: (a) that we are a democratic society; (b) we are a land of good and moral people (c) we value egalitarianism; (d) justice and truth are our core values; (e) equal opportunity and equal access are hallmarks of our nation; (f) discrimination and prejudice of any kind are bad; (g) individual effort and hard work lead to success; (h) race and skin color do not matter; (i) we are a post racial society.[19] In the book, Sue writes that white Americans are taught these values from the

---

19. Sue, *Race Talk and the Conspiracy of Silence*, 38.

moment of their birth. Indeed, most people in our culture hear these values being touted in public spaces such as schools and workplaces. However, there is also a counter-narrative or a hidden curriculum that derives from the same cultural source as the master narrative. In this counter-narrative, some people are naturally less worthy and less deserving of these core values than others. It is the continual rehearsal of the master narrative that does the following for white Americans: (a) assures them that they are fair, good and moral people; (b) prevents them from being conscious of their biases; (c) allows them to live under false deception; (d) maintains their innocence and naiveté; (e) perpetuates the status quo as it relates to race; (f) serves as blinders to keep white Americans from being conscious of inequities that exist for people of color; (g) justifies inaction on their part.[20] Counter-narratives told of the lived experiences of those who experience discrimination and oppression can lay bare the mythology of the master narrative. By sharing our stories and the stories of those who have experienced racism in the preaching moment, we may be able to open the door to dialogue and understanding.

RESEARCH BEGETS RESEARCH: CROSS-DISCIPLINARY CHALLENGES AND GROWTH

Earlier this year I presented a paper on preaching and health at Societas Homiletica, the international homiletics conference, in Stellenbosch, South Africa. During the question and answer period, I was asked, "If it is the will of God that all people experience good physical health, what do you have to say to good and faithful Christian people who experience illness and disease and who do not experience healing?" After the conference I began to wrestle with that question. I sought answers from a number of different theologians and found some of them in the work of disability theologian Nancy Eiesland.

Nancy Eiesland was an ethics professor at Candler School of Theology and a pioneer in the field of disability theology. In her book *The Disabled God*, Eiesland sought to develop a theology of disability that would encourage Christians to embrace their disabled sisters and brothers and welcome them into their faith communities. She argued that if Christians could conceive of the resurrected Christ as disabled because of the impairments of his hands and feet which he suffered on the cross, then new possibilities of understanding the human body in relation to God could be realized. First of all she asserts that the disabled God allows us to redefine what it means

20. Sue, *Race Talk and the Conspiracy of Silence*, 39.

to be whole. The Greek term *hugies,* which is translated as *whole* in some of the Gospels, can mean "to restore to health." Yet, Eiesland argues, though Jesus was physically impaired he was still understood by his followers to be holy and divine. Therefore, Eiesland believes that *wholeness* has more to do with relationships—with God and other people—than bodily perfection. If we apply Eiesland's logic to those experiencing sickness and disease, then someone who has terminal cancer and is in right relationship with God and their neighbors, is indeed whole.

Secondly, Eiesland contends that the disabled God calls upon all Christians to recognize and accept the limits of human physical bodies. Jesus' physical body bore evidence of its limits through impairments acquired through abuse and torture. Eiesland deems acknowledgment of the physical limits of the human body as *liberatory realism.* Liberatory realism is freedom experienced by accepting the reality that all bodies have limits. It is the truth of being human.

Eiesland highlights the disconnect between the idealized bodies that are paraded in advertisements and the real bodies of most of us that fall far short of physical perfection. Attempting to realize the *ideal* body prevents most people from loving and appreciating their bodies just as they are.[21] For Eiesland, when all humans accept the reality that their physical bodies have limits, attention that is now focused on attaining and retaining human perfection can be redirected to issues of justice to insure that all people have access to resources they need to live full lives. Barriers that exclude and humiliate many can be torn down. Hope can be envisioned so that people with bodies outside of the previously accepted social norms will realize that their lives are worth living. Those with conventional bodies may be emboldened to embrace their own bodily limitations by acknowledging that even conventional bodies fail at times. Those with impaired bodies may be emboldened to affirm their own bodies as good, whole and beautiful just the way they are.[22]

Thirdly, Eiesland believed that all human bodies are subject to contingency or chance and uncertainty. As a result, all human bodies come in three forms: temporarily able-bodied, temporarily disabled, or permanently disabled.[23] The temporarily able-bodied are those who have not yet experienced the effects of sickness, disease, or age. She contends that even those who experience good health throughout their lives will, if they live to experience old age, also experience disability to some degree. Her point here is

---

21. Eiesland, *The Disabled God,* 110.

22. Eiesland, *The Disabled God,* 95–96.

23. Eiesland, *The Disabled God,* 110.

that being disabled or sick is not necessarily an indication of lack of faith or being in a sinful state. Rather, physical disability, sickness, and illness are the consequences of being human. Period.

CONCLUSION

I am grateful for the many questions, observations, and thoughts of pastors, preachers, homiletical colleagues, and scholars from other disciplines that have motivated me to dig deeper, research further, or simply reclaim aspects of my tradition that I somehow left behind. Their willing engagement and keen insights give me hope. This is why I believe that one of the things right about preaching in the twenty-first century is the people who commit themselves to increasing their knowledge of preaching and all its various cognate disciplines; those who wish to hone their skills of theological thinking, inquiry, and articulation; those who seek to understand more deeply the relevance of culture and life-circumstances in relationship to the big questions and who make themselves available to the Spirit of God to fully engage themselves in every way imaginable. It is to these people that we commit the future of not only the church—because the impact of good preaching transcends the boundaries of the walls of the church—but also the future of our communities, our nation, and our world. Based on my teaching and learning experiences, our future is bright. Thanks be to God!

BIBLIOGRAPHY

Childers, Jana. *Performing the Word: Preaching as Theatre.* Nashville: Abingdon, 1998.

Craddock, Fred B. *As One Without Authority.* Rev. with new sermons. St. Louis, MO: Chalice, 2001.

Eiesland, Nancy. *The Disabled God: Toward a Liberatory Theology of Disability.* Nashville: Abingdon, 1994.

Forbes, James. *The Holy Spirit and Preaching.* Nashville: Abingdon, 1989.

Miller, Carole B. "A Discussion on Performance Anxiety." *Mostly Wind* (2011). http://www.mostlywind.co.uk/performance_anxiety.html.

Powery, Luke. *Spirit Speech: Lament and Celebration in Preaching.* Nashville: Abingdon, 2009.

Sue, Derald Wing. *Race Talk and the Conspiracy of Silence: Understanding and Facilitating Difficult Dialogues on Race.* Hoboken, NJ: Wiley, 2015.

HE KNEW ME VERY WELL

A Remembrance of Fred

Bill Cotton

ONE DAY I ATTENDED A PREACHING EVENT FOR PASTORS. I WAS THE NEW pastor of a large church that listed great preaching as a first priority. You might say I was a bit up against it. I had been preaching for about twenty-five years and I was tired of my words. The speaker was a little man, almost hidden by the pulpit. After quibbling about the height of the pulpit he said, "I hope you brought your Bibles. If you don't have one they sell them in the bookstore—or the used bookstores have them. If you buy secondhand you can take credit for the underlining." I was now awake and wondering, "Who is this guy?"

What followed was a trip through the Gospels. Here was a preacher who was also a biblical theologian. To this day I do not know what he did, except he changed my life in the pulpit. In Kierkegaardian fashion, he slipped up on my behind side and caused me to rethink who I was as preacher, person, and member of the church. On one occasion pastors were speaking of the loneliness of the preaching life, and Fred responded by asking, "Have you thought about joining your church? You might discover some really interesting people sitting out there who can help!"

I never knew Fred personally. *But he knew me very well.* I keep one of his quotes near my desk. "If you are going to boil water why not make soup," and I am encouraged by one of his confessional comments when he said that he "had preached all of [his] sermons too soon; but Sunday is always coming."

Because of Fred Craddock I had ten wonderful years in that church. He helped me see that sermon preparation and delivery was a rare adventure. And I continue these days in retirement, at age eighty-three, working with Course of Study students, hoping that some of what I learned from Fred Craddock will rub off and their sermons will not be like something that came from Roy Rogers's horse, "Trigger!"—another Craddock line. God bless this good and faithful servant.

THE PROBLEM OF CALFHOOD

A Remembrance of Fred

David Greenhaw

"No farmer deals with the problem of calfhood, only the calf." I remember the day I read this sentence for the first time.

I was serving a country church in central New Jersey. Not a week before, I had left the church late at night, shut out all the lights, and walked across the barely graveled lawn we called a parking lot. With the lights out, it was pitch dark. I had to walk to my car more from memory than from sight. When I reached my car, I looked up and saw a shiny reflection in the deep brown eyes of a cow not more than an arm's length away. I gasped, the cow snorted—what I now believe was her version of a gasp at encountering me face to face. I should have been used to the cows that grazed in the pasture next door to the church. I should have been used to their very bovine presence. But I was face to face with a cow, not a bovine presence, not an abstract encounter between country and city but a cow, a real cow, a brown-eyed cow, a snorting cow—a cow. And face to face with the cow, I was startled in a concrete, non-reducible way.

At the time I first read this sentence about the problem of calfhood in Fred Craddock's extraordinarily important book *As One Without Authority*, my mind was drawn immediately to this, my most recent encounter with a cow. Craddock's point is that preaching must start where people start, in the concrete everydayness of life. Preaching needs to move inductively, Craddock argued, not deductively. From the particular to the universal, not the other way around. If there is such a thing as the problem of calfhood, it comes to a farmer from a problem with one calf at a time. It comes from a real calf. One encountered in the actual flesh. One born to a cow. When

I read this sentence, I got it, I got it because the idea of cows was not an abstraction to me, it was a night in the space we called a parking lot at Centerville Church. It drew to my mind an actual cow.

It was part of the genius of Fred Craddock to know that preaching has to start with the everyday, the concrete, but should not stop there. This is a point often missed in Craddock's work. Craddock starts in the particular but moves to the universal. The idea that simply sharing a thickly described story constitutes preaching the gospel does not find support in Craddock's work. He made the move from a concrete experience to a larger principle or concept applicable beyond the singular experience. If the gospel were only for the singular, it could not be preached; it could only be individually and uniquely experienced. But the gospel *can* be preached; it can transcend individual unique experience to form the community that is the church.

The wisdom of engaging listeners with radically particular stories of everyday occurrences was Fred Craddock's forte. But never be fooled; in his folksy way, he moved from a particular instance to a larger truth. Fred Craddock turned preaching on its head by urging induction instead of deduction. He shaped subsequent preachers by having them change the direction of thought, from universal principles illustrated in particular cases, to particular situations to universal principles. It was a great move forward for preaching and for me it started in a gravel parking lot, face to face with a cow.

FRED SAID "YES"

Remembering Fred

Jimmy Mohler

WE MET OFTEN. I SEIZED UPON MANY OPPORTUNITIES TO HEAR DR. FRED Craddock speak. There was a tent revival staged by Covenant Christian Church. I was there. Pastors happy for this Saturday afternoon opportunity to hear Fred asked our host, Pastor VerBurg, "How did you get him to come to this experimental event at this small church in Cary, North Carolina?" VerBurg's response: "I asked him. He said, 'yes.'"

When Fred spoke at the Week of Compassion breakfast at the Kansas City General Assembly, I was there. He declared to those gathered that they had a 6:30 in Cherry Log, Georgia, but that it was in the evening. Yet Fred said "yes" to Johnny Wray's invitation.

When he spoke at the Spirit Fest in Kansas City, I was there. I asked if I could meet with him. He said "yes." I asked if he would write the introduction for *Compassion Corner*, a booklet I had put together as a devotional fundraiser for Week of Compassion. He said, "Thanks for asking." Then he said, "Yes."

When he spoke at the installation service of a pastor in Washington, DC, I was there. Problem was, the newly hired minister left town (and quit the church) shortly before his installation service. Fred came anyway. He had been invited. He said "yes." Even though the need had changed, Fred spoke in a manner that addressed the new need. In similar fashion, even though the need had changed, he preached to his Cherry Log congregation the Sunday after 9/11/2001 in a manner that addressed the new need. On the night Dr. Martin Luther King, Jr. had been killed, Fred learned about

The turn to the listener in the late twentieth and early twenty-first centuries has proven to be one of the most significant and transformative developments in preaching. As the field of homiletics has learned to attune its ears to the role of sermon listeners as never before, preachers and those who study their sermons have recognized the decisive role that listeners play in the preaching moment.[2] There would be no hearing if there were none to hear—and those who listen are instrumental to what is received, interpreted, understood, embraced, and/or rejected in the preaching moment. For centuries, the onus of responsibility for what was heard in preaching lay with the preacher. But as many people in the pew tuned out or turned away from the church and as others asked for more relevant or relatable sermons, preachers realized that hearing the gospel not only depends upon those who preach (Rom 10:14b) but those who listen: they not only need to account for their congregants' concerns and contexts but to listen to them, to welcome and invite their participation in the preaching moment, so that God's word might facilitate a hearing.

In the 1970s, Fred Craddock was among the first Eurocentric preachers and scholars in North America to recognize that preaching encompasses not only listening to God's word but also to God's people.[3] Moving from *deductive approaches* to sermon design (beginning with general truths culled from Scripture and then offering "applications" of them) to *inductive approaches* (beginning with the particulars of human experience and moving toward a general truth or conclusion), Craddock assumed that listeners are not only intimately involved in sermons but ultimately responsible for what is heard and understood in the preaching moment.[4] His confidence and trust in those who listen to Sunday morning sermons meant that he respected their need to discover for themselves what sermons have to offer and he trusted them to understand and determine their significance. Craddock respected "the hearer as not only capable but deserving the right to participate in that movement" in preaching that is akin to a conversation whose participants do not know where it will lead or conclude.[5] His

2. Surveys exploring "the turn to the listener" include Allen, "The Turn to the Listener," and Rietveld, "A Survey of Phenomenological Research of Listening to Preaching."

3. As described later in this chapter, other preachers and preaching traditions had already developed highly responsive means of interacting with sermon listeners in the preaching moment and/or worship (e.g., African American preaching, Anabaptist worship services, women preachers). Since these were afforded less attention in mainstream, male-dominated circles of discourse and mainline publications of the same period as Craddock, their contributions have only recently come to our attention.

4. Craddock, *As One Without Authority*, 54–57.

5. Craddock, *As One Without Authority*, 62.

profound respect for sermon listeners has helped preachers and teachers of homiletics to understand that the inductive process preachers undertake when they search the Scriptures during their weekday study may be retraced on Sunday mornings as they accompany their listeners along a similar journey of discovery.

In identifying with sermon listeners, Craddock in many ways continued the interests of the great American preacher Harry Emerson Fosdick, whose preaching ministry at the Riverside Church in New York City and through numerous nationwide radio sermons focused on the problems and struggles of his listeners, a form of preaching that has often been described as "counseling on a group scale."[6] Fosdick helped the church to attend to the questions, concerns, hopes, and fears of congregants and their neighbors by addressing the difficulties they encountered in daily living. Like Fosdick, Craddock realized the importance of sermons that explore the needs and struggles of people in the pews. Both preachers were also expert in relating their listeners' concerns to Scripture. Their sermons were fully immersed in the Bible, drawing from its breadth, length, height, and depth as a necessary partner in theological reflection and our encounter with God's living word among us.

Craddock's further contribution was to insist that listeners be considered not only through addressing their particular problems, needs, and interests in conversation with Scripture but in the very formation of the sermon itself; that is, he proposed an approach to sermon design that echoes the preacher's own experience of exploring biblical texts and topics in search of what they might mean for listeners. Craddock insisted that "the method is the message . . . *how* one preaches is to a large extent *what* one preaches," and "is probably a clearer and more honest expression of [the preacher's] theology than is the content of [the preacher's] sermons."[7] Craddock proposed that during the preaching moment, listeners enter a journey of discovery, probing biblical texts and current issues inductively so as to "complete the sermon" for themselves.[8] The preacher would then accompany and guide listeners without exercising "imperialism of thought" or demanding a particular destination but humbly trusting that listeners will draw their own conclusions and derive applications that are important for their lives.[9]

---

6. Tisdale, "Preachers for All Seasons," 70–72.

7. Craddock, *As One Without Authority*, 52–53.

8. Craddock, *As One Without Authority*, 64.

9. Craddock, *As One Without Authority*, 65, 57.

In his later writings, Craddock also acknowledged a frequent criticism of his work; namely, his assumption that listeners are able to recognize or understand the biblical allusions and theological themes they hear from the pulpit. In response, he reaffirmed his belief that people hear in gospel preaching what they inherently recognize and yearn to hear, "a word for which we had waited and listened"—or what he described as the experience of the gospel being "twice-told" in the ears of listeners.[10] But Craddock also offered a correction to his earlier thinking, acknowledging that there is indeed "an informational dimension to Christian preaching" that must be taught lest "references and allusions to the historical content of the faith are lost on the hearers."[11] Craddock wondered if he had abdicated too much authority to the listeners' role by "relocating the authority in the ear of the listener more than at the mouth of the speaker," sometimes accommodating cultural movements at the expense of the gospel's counter-cultural assertions.[12]

Less obvious to Craddock but equally consequential to his approach was the homogeneity that he assumed among sermon listeners, as if all who preach and listen share the same perspective, worldview, and an interchangeability of human experience and understanding.[13] Churches in early twenty-first century North America (and many other global contexts as well) are increasingly aware of the diversity of perspectives, experiences, and interpretive lenses that are cut and polished through very different economic circumstances, racial, ethnic, class, and gender identities, sexual orientations, life experiences, geo-political movements, and myriad other differences among us. Prior to the development of the New Homiletic that Craddock is credited with having inspired, many non-Eurocentric preaching traditions had long incorporated listeners' participation in the preaching moment as well. Among these, African American preaching has

10. Craddock, "Preaching," 68.

11. Craddock, "Preaching," 68. Theologically, Craddock insisted that "because Christian faith is centered on incarnation—and, simply put, incarnation means God within history," preachers are responsible for teaching some of the times, dates, places, biblical characters, and events that inform the historical content of faith.

12. Craddock, "Inductive Preaching Renewed," 46. For a more thorough critique of the general "turn to the listener" in homiletics, see Lose, "Whither Hence, New Homiletic?"

13. See, for example, Craddock's assumption that there is "a ground of shared experience" among sermon listeners: *As One Without Authority*, 58. His confidence in the preacher's ability to know and speak on behalf of listeners is evident in asserting that, "Before the first word of the sermon is spoken, the preacher has a clear idea of the listeners' posture of mind and heart in relation to the message to be delivered," *Preaching*, 188.

long accounted for and actively incorporated listener participation and response. In the words of homiletician Dale Andrews, "Whether one refers to induction, narrative preaching, story-telling, phenomenological experience, the preaching event, a happening, an encounter, a movement, hearer participation, hearer response, or the exigency of contemporary language and immediate experience, the new homiletic mirrors long established black preaching traditions, not to mention others."[14] Despite the regrettable homogeneity of most congregations, those who gather for worship across North America are slowly (or in some cases, suddenly) becoming aware of diverse sermon listeners and preaching traditions that may help the church realize the breadth and depth of the gospel speaking through people and places, situations and settings, that are as different as they are beloved of God.

Following the trajectory of Craddock's influence, at least three developments in the turn to the listener have emerged in the last decades of the twentieth century and opening decades of the twenty-first, all of which have greatly enriched preachers' engagement with sermon listeners and have brought to our attention the need for diverse voices and perspectives in preaching: innovations in the formfulness and artistry of sermons (including narrative preaching and the contributions of a wider range of preachers and scholars among people of color, diverse gender and sexual orientations, etc.), empirical studies of sermon listeners (not only in the US but around the world), and recent interest in conversational preaching.

INNOVATIONS IN SERMON FORMS AND ARTISTRY

The New Homiletic that arose in the US during the 1970s (primarily among Eurocentric mainline scholars and preachers) was in large part a response to a new understanding of the eventfulness of preaching and how listeners may be accounted for in the preaching moment.[15] Chief among those who

14. Andrews, "New to Whom?," 3.

15. The "New Homiletic" arose in response to the "New Hermeneutic" developed by Gerhard Ebeling (the University of Zurich) and Ernst Fuchs (the University of Marburg) after World War II. Ebeling and Fuchs developed a theology of speaking that emphasized the "eventfulness" of preaching (*Sprachereignis* or *Wortgeschehen* as a language event that not only communicates faith ever anew as divine word and Holy Spirit encounter changed situations), a revitalized understanding of the relationship between the form and content of sermons, and a greater concern for sermon listeners than was previously conceived. During a research sabbatical at the University of Tübingen, Germany, Craddock studied the works of Ebeling and Fuchs, which contributed greatly to his first book, *As One Without Authority*. For a fuller explication of the influence of the New Hermeneutic on the New Homiletic in North America, see

led and contributed to this movement, Craddock's turn to the listener radically reconsidered the formfulness of preaching (i.e., the design and internal movement of sermons) in order to better meet the perceived needs and desires of sermon listeners. He and many other preachers turned from rationalistic and linear approaches to sermon design that outlines correct beliefs or "points" derived from Scripture (e.g., traditional and deductive modes of preaching) to more inductive, narrative, and literary-artistic sermons that they hoped would more fully engage listeners in the preaching moment. In terms of what Augustine identified in the early fifth century CE as the three primary purposes of preaching (i.e., to teach, delight, and persuade),[16] the preoccupation of the church in North America during the last few decades has been to delight sermon listeners through innovations in sermon forms and artistry.

At its best, this has meant a radical reconsideration of how listeners perceive or participate in the preaching moment. More than entertainment or the preacher trying to endear him- or herself to listeners, the turn to the listener has resulted in a radical reconsideration of how to render sermons more "hearable," accessible, relevant, and attractive to people whose interests and attention we hope to engage—including the ways sermons are formed and the literary artistry with which they are composed and delivered.[17]

Perhaps no development in the formfulness of sermons during the past few decades has been as recognizable and far reaching as the emergence of narrative preaching forms. In the same year that *As One Without Authority* was released, Stephen Crites published his essay "The Narrative Quality of Experience."[18] Identifying the inherent story-like movement of our lives from moment to moment, day to day, year to year, Crites describes the narrative nature of our experience as events in time with beginnings, middles, and ends. Similarly, Scripture itself follows an overall narrative structure that moves from creation to fall, redemption to apocalyptic expectation.

Randolph, *The Renewal of Preaching*, and Ottoni-Wilhelm, "New Hermeneutic, New Homiletic, New Directions."

16. Augustine, *On Christian Doctrine*, 136.

17. At its worst, preoccupation with sermon forms and rhetorical artistry may contribute to preachers' concerns for entertaining their listeners rather than stimulating their intellectual curiosity, understanding of Scripture, and deepening their spiritual maturity and relationship with God. Among the most egregious abuses are the manipulation of peoples' feelings and attitudes, seeking listeners' favor and approval rather than focusing on substantial matters of faith and the Bible's challenges to preachers and congregants alike. As noted earlier, Craddock also voiced concern for preachers' abdicating their authority (and, we may assume, their responsibility) for identifying the counter-cultural claims of Scripture. See "Inductive Preaching Renewed," 46–47.

18. Crites, "The Narrative Quality of Experience," 291.

Recognizing that sermons also follow this kind of movement by incorporating introductory moments, the development or body of the sermon, and a conclusion of some kind, homiletician Eugene Lowry argued that sermons are also events-in-time that unfold like "a plot (premeditated by the preacher) which has as its key ingredient a sensed discrepancy, a homiletical bind," so that "the preacher's task is to 'bring the folks home'—that is, resolve matters in the light of the gospel and in the presence of the people."[19] According to Lowry, anticipation is key to this process as each step in the sequence of sermon development moves from expectation to fulfillment.[20]

Amid homiletical interest in the story-like movement of sermons, Ronald J. Allen has identified four related but different approaches to sermons that have emerged in the latter decades of the twentieth century which may be described as "narrative preaching."[21] First, a sermon may be *a story in and of itself* from beginning to end, incorporating a plot (i.e., a sequence of events), characters, and setting, without offering commentary or interpretation on the part of the preacher.[22] Second, a sermon may *move in a story-like manner* that is not a single extended narrative but arranged in such a way that it is heard or followed as one would experience a story (e.g., Lowry's five-step method). Third, Allen notes that narrative preaching is sometimes associated with "*story theology*" as, for example, when preachers tell stories and sometimes offer reflections on them and at other times allow

---

19. Lowry, *The Homiletical Plot*, 12, 20. Lowry's five-step method of sermon design includes: 1) upsetting the equilibrium of listeners by introducing a conflict or tension, whether "life-situation, expository, doctrinal, etc. in content" (an "itch waiting to be scratched"), 2) complicating this problem by delving more deeply into the opening tension so that the congregation will more carefully and critically explore its nature, 3) offering a clue to the resolution of the problem, tension, or question that is based upon a "gospel insight" or new understanding, 4) expanding on the implications of this insight by helping the congregation to imagine its implications for their lives, and 5) anticipating the future consequences as listeners consider what is expected or possible in light of what they have heard. Throughout, the preacher is to enjoin listeners on a journey that begins with a problem and moves them toward a solution that brings new understanding, action, and/or relationships with God and others.

20. Lowry, *The Sermon*, 18. Lowry also explored six identifiable types or models that arose out of the New Homiletic, including: the inductive sermon, story sermon, narrative sermon, transconscious African American sermon, phenomenological sermon, and conversational-episodal sermon.

21. Allen, "Theology Undergirding Narrative Preaching," 27–29. See also Robinson, ed., *Journeys toward Narrative Preaching*.

22. An example of this is Willis's sermon, "Noah Was a Good Man," in Lowry, *How to Preach a Parable*, 42–49. Lowry presents this sermon as an example of "Running the Story"—in this case, the biblical story is the basis for the entire sermon as it is retold and expanded upon by Willis.

stories to speak for themselves.[23] Finally, postliberalism in preaching has invited preachers to clarify Scripture's claim upon listeners' lives so that the sermon *draws them into the world of the biblical narrative.*[24] The emphasis in this approach is not primarily the interpretation of scripture, "but to narrate the congregation into the larger and ongoing biblical story."[25]

One of the most consequential contributions to the turn to the listener was developed by David Buttrick, whose landmark text *Homiletic: Moves and Structure*, focuses on the formation of communal consciousness in the preaching moment.[26] Buttrick's work develops a method of sermon design intended to move the entire congregation along a plot-like structure that connects Scripture and listeners in a dynamic relationship. According to Buttrick, preaching is "story transformed" as it "constructs in consciousness a 'faith-world' related to God . . . a story with transcendent dimension."[27] Recognizing that communal consciousness develops more slowly than individual consciousness, Buttrick proposes the sequencing of sermon parts or "moves." He operates with a "camera model" of human consciousness, with each move providing a particular element in the sequence (or a "point of view") rather than a static presentation of cognitive points.[28] Perhaps more than any other homiletician of the late twentieth century, Buttrick understood that worshipping communities are formed in faith at least in part by the practice of sermon listening.

Buttrick has also helped preachers grasp the role of image and metaphor in our encounter with divine mystery and revelation. Because preaching "is concerned with bringing Presence to consciousness" and bringing into view "unseen reality," sermons "will, of necessity, dabble in metaphor, image, illustration, and all kinds of depiction."[29] As such, "Inescapably, preaching is a work of metaphor."[30] Through analogy, metaphor, illustrations, examples, images, and myriad other artistic means, preachers may

23. Allen points to the work of Song, *The Believing Heart*, and Song, *Tell Us Our Names*.

24. Campbell, *Preaching Jesus*.

25. Allen, "Theology Undergirding Narrative Preaching," 28.

26. Buttrick, *Homiletic*.

27. Buttrick, *Homiletic*, 11.

28. Buttrick, *Homiletic*, ch. 2. In ch. 3 Buttrick describes how each move is to be introduced, developed (by various means), and brought to closure before offering a transition to the sermon's next move (developed in greater detail in chs. 6 and 7).

29. Buttrick, *Homiletic*, 113. Buttrick goes on to say, "After all, preaching is preoccupied with Christ who comes to us as story, and as a living symbol; thus, preaching is bound to tell stories and explore images."

30. Buttrick, *Homiletic*, 113.

invoke Christ's presence in the preaching moment and seek the reconciliation of our stories and lives with God's life revealed in Scripture and Christ's Spirit moving in the world among us.

The turn to the listener engendered greater appreciation for and interest in what stirs listeners' imagination and engagement with sermons in worship. This continued to develop among preachers and homileticians who explore literary artistry to better meet, inspire, and challenge sermon listeners. Mirroring the interests of literary criticism (the "New Criticism") of the 1970s, many homileticians cultivated greater interest in poetry, psalms, and other biblical genres, with attention given to literary and rhetorical forms as these create expectations on the part of listeners. The goal of these, according to homiletician Thomas G. Long, is that preachers may "say and do" in their sermons what biblical texts "say and do" in their literary settings.[31] Charles Rice helps preachers to understand that the arts can provide more than illustrations for sermons and that sermons themselves may be works of art that embody creative elements of interpretive expression.[32] And Thomas H. Troeger describes how "godly wonder" may be reborn through attention to the place of beauty in worship and preaching.[33] In *The Preaching Life*, Barbara Brown Taylor describes the church's central task as "an imaginative one . . . in which the human capacity to imagine—to form mental pictures of the self, the neighbor, the world, the future, to envision new realities—is both engaged and transformed."[34] In her thoughtful and creative representation of biblical stories and images, Barbara Lundblad helps preachers encounter the timeliness of biblical texts.[35]

---

31. Long, *Preaching and the Literary Forms of the Bible*, 33. In this book, Long carefully examines how the literary form and dynamics of biblical texts should impact sermons created from those texts. In many ways, this work builds on Long's exegetical method outlined in his text *The Witness of Preaching*, where he not only directs preachers to identify a discrete *focus* for each sermon but a *function*; that is, to be clear from the outset what the sermon intends to *say* as well as what it intends to *do* in the lives of its listeners (how the focus/message is to impact listeners). He goes on to explain that the focus and function should arise directly out of the preacher's encounter with the biblical text, be related to each other, and be clear, unified, and relatively simple (108–16).

32. Rice, *Interpretation and Imagination*, and *The Embodied Word*.

33. Troeger, *Wonder Reborn*. See also Troeger, *Imagining a Sermon*, and more recently, Troeger's focus on the "end" (i.e., purpose) of preaching as prayerful communication with God, often through poetic expression (based on this 2016 Lyman Beecher Lectures): *The End of Preaching*.

34. Taylor, *The Preaching Life*, 39. Taylor's published sermon collections have also provided inspiration to many preachers. For example, *God in Pain*.

35. Lundblad, *Marking Time*.

Women preachers have long been attuned to their own life experiences and those of their listeners as touchstones of divine-human encounter. With the ordination of women across many denominations in the mid to late twentieth century, the field of homiletics has come to recognize some of their distinct contributions, including the use of personal stories, images, and the impact of personal experience in exegeting biblical texts, as women preachers often seek interpersonal connections with listeners.[36] Christine Smith has helped raise the church's awareness and appreciation of women's insights, perspectives, and stories, as well as the inclusion of diverse people and perspectives in preaching.[37] Anna Carter Florence has explored the testimonial nature of women's preaching and Lisa Thompson draws from the deep well of the spirituality of black women to empower and guide preachers' creative connections with sermon listeners.[38] Collections of women's sermons also recognize the diverse ways that women preachers develop connections with their listeners.[39]

The field of homiletics has also become increasingly aware of and informed by African American homileticians whose work recognizes the history and development of rhetorical artistry and innovations in African American preaching. Cleophus LaRue has examined the communicative power and artful language of black preaching as it offers purpose and guidance for black communities of faith through the ages.[40] Frank Thomas develops Valerie Bridgeman's poetic sermonic form and draws from performative and poetic expressions of black music and poetry (e.g., Hip Hop) to explore new horizons of literary and rhetorical artistry among rising generations of preachers today.[41] Among emerging generations, numerous African American homileticians such as Kenyatta Gilbert and Donyelle

36. For a summary of these influences and studies of women preachers in late twentieth century North America, see Zink-Sawyer, "A Match Made in Heaven," ch. 3.

37. Among the many important and influential texts related to women's preaching that have arisen in recent decades are several exploring the formfulness of preaching, diverse images, and the need for different perspectives and stories in preaching Smith, *Weaving the Sermon* and *Preaching Justice*.

38. Florence, *Preaching as Testimony*. Thompson, *Ingenuity*.

39. Among sermon collections, see Mitchell and Bridgeman Davis, eds., *Those Preaching Women*, and Childers, ed., *Birthing the Sermon*.

40. LaRue, *I Believe I'll Testify*.

41. Thomas, *Introduction to African American Preaching*, chs. 3 and 4, and Bridgman, "Celebration Renewed," 75. Also, Thomas's formative work *They Like to Never Quit Praisin' God* builds on the work of Mitchell, whose *Black Preaching* outlines the contributions and contours of black preaching as an art. In *Dem Dry Bones*, Luke Powery studies how African American spirituals provide inspiration and guidance for preaching about hope in the midst of death and despair.

McCray and Latinx homileticians such as Jared Alcántara, Tito Madrazo, and Alma Ruiz explore and develop the biblical, theological, spiritual, and rhetorical dimensions of preaching that help deepen and expand our understanding of situational contexts.[42]

EMPIRICAL STUDIES OF SERMON LISTENERS

The turn to the listener is most explicitly undertaken in numerous empirical studies of sermon listeners around the world, each of which has enhanced our understanding of the needs and perceptions of listeners. With a sense of urgency for relating preaching to people in worship and other public settings and to better address their questions, needs, and interests, recent developments in the empirical study of listeners has spanned Europe, the US, and other nations and continents.[43] Beginning in the late 1970s and early '80s, phenomenological studies of sermon listeners in Europe focused on diverse populations. Johannes Sterk's sociological study of 1,231 German Catholics in 1975 uncovered a correlation between a positive evaluation of the sermon and higher levels of church involvement on the part of the listener.[44] Initially inspired by studies of the mass media, in 1983 German researcher Karl Daiber, et al., conducted an extensive study of over 6,000 listeners and 200 preachers in the Evangelical Lutheran Church of Germany. Working from a model of informational transfer from speaker to listener, their research assumed that misunderstandings and differences between listeners and speakers are hindrances to be overcome.[45] These early approaches suggested that it is possible to break through listeners' consciousness and better direct their hearing by seeking to reduce "noise" so that information may arrive in an undisturbed manner to its recipients.[46] They did not, however, consider the active participation of sermon listeners in the preaching moment as co-creators of meaning or agents who identify, shape, and imagine new applications of what they are hearing.

In the early 2000s, Ciska Stark surveyed 246 listeners and their preachers in the Netherlands. Her research did not identify one type of sermon as

42. See Gilbert, *Exodus Preaching* and *A Pursued Justice;* McCray, *The Censored Pulpit;* Alcántara, *The Practices of Christian Preaching;* and Madrazo and Ruiz, "Preaching from Sanctuary."

43. Portions of this summary are informed by Rietveld, "A Survey of Phenomenological Research of Listening to Preaching," and Gaarden's research summary in *The Third Room of Preaching,* ch. 1.

44. Sterk, *Preek en toehoorders,* 89, 218.

45. See Piper, *Predigtanalysen.* Also, Daiber, *Predigen und Hören.*

46. Ringgaard Lorensen, *Preaching as a Carnivalesque Dialogue,* 68–69.

more effective than others but offered three key observations, namely: that churchgoers come to church to meet God (i.e., they have religious, spiritual, and/or transcendent motives); they expect to hear an encouraging exposition of Scripture and to receive inspiration from it; and, more than 50 percent of the respondents identify preaching as central to worship.[47] Another Dutch researcher, Hanneke Schaap-Jonker, conducted 460 surveys and a few qualitative interviews of sermon listeners from three Dutch Protestant congregations.[48] She describes the process of meaning construction among sermon listeners as a process of relating (*What does the sermon have to do with me?*), focus (*What was the sermon about?*), dialogism (*What do I think of that?*), and actualizing (*What does the sermon mean to my own situation?*). Theo Pleizier's qualitative interviews of sermon listeners in the Netherlands identify three stages of sermon listening: when listeners open themselves up to hearing what is said, when they dwell in the sermon (experiencing, perceiving, and identifying with what is preached), and when faith is actualized (i.e., in "illuminative moments" during the sermon as well as the continuing effects of remembering what was preached).[49] In Plezier's study, sermons are aesthetic as well as functional and he offers a metaphor of preaching as a "temporary house for kingdom citizens."

Research into sermon listeners has also flourished in Nordic countries.[50] Homileticians in Denmark have offered several important empiri-

47. Stark, *Proeven van de Preek*. Stark identified six dimensions of sermons (i.e., sermon, listener, biblical text, preacher, liturgical context, ecclesial sociological context, and the work of the Holy Spirit) and offered a taxonomy of preaching based on two sets of variables (i.e., "text driven" and "application driven").

48. Schaap-Jonker draws on the object relations theory of British psychoanalyst Donald Winicott and Ana-Marie Rizutto's theory of God images as key to her analysis. Schaap takes three psychological variables (i.e., the listener's God image, affective state, and personality) to explore how meaning is shaped when hearing the sermon. See Schaap-Jonker, *Before the Face of God*.

49. Based in Grounded Theory, Pleizier's doctoral research and thesis has since been published. Pleizier, *Religious Involvement in Hearing Sermons*.

50. Nordic countries include Iceland, Greenland, Finland, Denmark, Sweden, and Norway. A Swedish survey conducted in 1999 by Hans Almer identified different concepts of preaching among listeners and preachers. Almer, *Variationer ava predikoup-pfattningar i Svenska kyrkan*. Another Swedish homiletician has studied listeners of sermons in Madagascar: Austnaber, *Improving Preaching by Listening to the Listeners*. In Finland, a study of nine different listeners in 2003 who heard the same sermon explored similarities and differences in listeners' reception. Sundkvist, *En predikan*. In Norway, recent studies of sermon listeners have also included consideration of young people and children attending worship. As of the time of this publication, the Norwegian research project titled, "Forkynnelse for Små og Store," ("Preaching to Young and Old") is being directed by Tone Stangeland Kaufman at the Norwegian School of Theology in Oslo, Norway. Previous Norwegian studies include Fylling, ed., *Hellige ord*.

cal studies of sermon listeners, including that of Marianne Gaarden and Marlene Ringgaard Lorensen, who describe listeners as creators of meaning in dialogue with the sermon.[51] They offer three "modes" in which listeners engage in sermons, viewing preachers as "interrupters" of human consciousness and listeners as the authors and creators of meaning. Gaarden's recently published doctoral dissertation utilizes empirical and theological approaches to sermon listeners to identify how "the encounter between the preacher's outer words and the listener's inner experience brings about . . . a *Third Room* in which the listeners, in internal dialogue, create a surplus of meaning that was previously not present in either the preacher's intent or the listener's frame of reference."[52] In the mid-2010s, Ringgaard Lorensen also conducted field interviews with refugees in the Danish church to assess their perceptions, impressions, and understandings of sermons in worship.[53]

Beyond Europe, Hendrik Pieterse's qualitative study of South African sermon listeners in the early 1990s focused on the impact of different types of congregations and how these ecclesial contexts impact the "homecoming" of sermons; that is, how the ecclesial context of hearing impacts the meaning and application of sermons for their listeners.[54] More recently, Pieterse's work has taken a Grounded Theory approach to sermon analysis of sermons on poverty and directed to "the poor" as listeners.[55] Barend De Klerk's study of "vulnerable listeners" among farm workers in South Africa focused on "what it means to preach to those who are vulnerable and how such preaching can be continued by the hearers."[56] Significantly, South African homiletician Johan Cilliers proposes a more integrative and embodied approach to preaching and sermon reception that provides a welcome counterpart to Western studies of sermon listeners that dwell on listeners' cognitive aspirations and interests (*fides quaerens intellectum*, faith in searching of understanding). Instead, Cilliers approaches the sermon in worship as "immediate participation; as multi-sensory interpretative act;

51. See Gaarden and Ringgaard Lorensen, "Listeners as Authors in Preaching." The authors speak of the sermon as a "polyphonic event" in which different voices participate.

52. Introduction to Marianne Gaarden, *The Third Room of Preaching*.

53. Ringgaard Lorensen, "Preaching as Repetition." Ringgaard Lorensen's study points to the paradox of hope encountered among refugees interviewed in the Church of Denmark.

54. Pieterse, *Gemeente en prediking*. Pieterse's study identifies a "shepherd-flock" hierarchical church, a "body-of-Christ" church whose members often discussed sermons openly, and hybrids of these.

55. Pieterse, *Acta Theologica*, 30(2).

56. Barend J. de Klerk, "Conveyance of Preaching by Vulnerable Listeners."

and as broken presence and celebrated absence."[57] Only very recently have studies of sermon listeners been pursued in Asia, notably in South Korea where interviews of preachers and listeners identified four themes which researchers Hyun Park and Cas Wepener relate directly to the influence of the New Homiletic, namely; the turn from the "herald" to the "pastor" image of the preacher, differences between preachers and listeners in their perceptions of listeners in preaching, strong support for preaching the gospel and God's Word as it is revealed in the Bible, as well as a desire among listeners for sermons that address social and communal/shared aspects of life.[58]

Remarkably fewer empirical studies of sermon listeners have been conducted in the US.[59] Among the most fruitful was the "Listening to Listeners Study" of 2000–2004.[60] Focused in the Midwest, this qualitative study included interviews with 263 laity and their pastors and priests from twenty-eight congregations of diverse Protestant denominations,

57. Cilliers, "Fides quaerens societatum." Cilliers identifies more traditional, western paradigms of fides quaerens intellectum (faith in search of understanding), fides quaerens verbum (faith in search of words), fides quaerens actum (faith in search of acts), fides quaerens imaginem (faith in search of images, symbolic expression), fides quaerens visum (faith in search of concrete visualization, including modern technology), and fides quaerens spem (faith in search of hope), then proposes a more integrative paradigm of fides quaerens corporalitatem (faith in search of embodiment), honoring our bodies as central to what we perceive and experience, including our relationship with God whose incarnation and continued embodiment in the church entails notions of contextualization, immediacy, encounter, embrace, communality, radicalization, and concreteness.

58. Park and Wepener, "Empirical Research on the Experience of the New Homiletic in South Korea."

59. Among the first in the US, Lori Carrell interviewed and surveyed preachers and listeners in the late twentieth century, noting that listeners frequently discuss sermons but rarely do so with preachers. Carrell, *The Great American Sermon Survey*. In comparing and contrasting preachers' and listeners' perceptions, Carrell concluded that sermons are not as effective or dialogical as they could be. The practical suggestions she offers are in tension with her findings that the sermon-as-monologue is an expectation widely shared by both preachers and listeners (141). Not based on empirical research but for the sake of aiding preachers' abilities to better understand their congregants and sermon listeners, Nora Tubbs Tisdale provides guidance for local pastors in studying the congregational context of preaching and the perspectives and needs of their listeners. See Tisdale, *Preaching as Local Theology and Folk Art*. An examination of how preachers may appreciate and address the variety of listeners in congregations according to generations, different modes of mental process, gender, multicultural, and other differences, see Allen and Jeter, *One Gospel, Many Ears*.

60. The Listening to Listeners Study was administered by Christian Theological Seminary, Indianapolis, and its co-directors were Ronald J. Allen and Mary Alice Mulligan, both serving on the teaching faculty of CTS. The Study was supported by the Religion Division of the Lilly Endowment.

geographical locations, and ethnic identities.[61] It was initially envisioned as a way of identifying how congregants perceive of what they hear through three traditional rhetorical categories: *pathos* (emotions), *logos* (logical arguments), and *ēthos* (connections with the preacher). However, it was soon evident that such channels of understanding were not nearly so relevant to listeners' experiences and practices of sermon listening as were other interests and topics that drew them into the preaching moment (see the third book in the series, *Believing in Preaching: What Listeners Hear in Sermons*).[62] Although the most important finding from this study is undoubtedly the remarkable diversity with which listeners engage in sermon listening, it is also significant to note the strong affirmation among listeners for the importance of preaching in worship.[63] Nearly two-thirds of the respondents reported that a major purpose of preaching is to teach congregants about Scripture and how Christian faith relates to daily living and the world we share.

Another important study of sermon listeners in the US was conducted by Karla Bellinger. In *Connecting Pulpit and Pew: Breaking Open the Conversation about Catholic Preaching*, Bellinger builds on her survey of Catholic high school youth and their connection with Sunday preaching as well as her study of Catholic catechetical leaders and their relationship with preaching.[64] Listening to young people in particular, Bellinger notes the importance of building human connections of deep caring between the pulpit and pew, inspiring others to share what they've heard with family and neighbors. Her work does not identify or operate within a specifically

---

61. The four books generated by this study were published by Chalice Press in 2004 and 2005: John S. McClure, Ronald J. Allen, Dale P. Andrews, L. Susan Bond, Dan P. Moseley, G. Lee Ramsey, Jr., *Listening to Listeners* (presenting six slightly abbreviated interviews as case studies); Ronald J. Allen, *Hearing the Sermon* (outlining interviewees responses to the categories of *pathos, logos, êthos*, and embodiment on which the project was originally based); Mary Alice Mulligan, Diane Turner-Sharazz, Dawn Ottoni-Wilhelm, and Ronald J. Allen, *Believing in Preaching* (organized around "clusters" of interest that interviewees named); and Mulligan and Allen, *Make the Word Come Alive* (advice gleaned from sermon listeners for preachers). Others have worked with the data collected in the Listening to Listeners Study in their research and scholarly endeavors: see Little, "God, Authority, and Theological Literacy in Preaching," which builds on her dissertation for the Graduate Theological Foundation, Mishawaka, IN.

62. Allen, Mulligan, Turner-Sharazz, and Ottoni-Wilhelm, *Listening to Listeners*.

63. This is also supported by a recent poll conducted by the Pew Research Center: "Fully 83% of Americans who have looked for a new place of worship say the quality of preaching played an important role in their choice of congregation." See "Choosing a New Church or House of Worship."

64. Bellinger, *Connecting Pulpit and Pew*.

formulated methodology but identifies and develops assessment tools and resources to aid in the improvement of preaching among Catholic clergy.[65]

CONVERSATIONAL PREACHING

One of the most compelling developments in the turn to the listener has been the emergence of conversational preaching. More than the dialogue sermons of the 1960s, conversational preaching recognizes the "embeddedness of preaching within a range of conversations taking place with the academy, congregation, community, nation and across the globe."[66] The reorientation from didactic or dogmatic sermons to sermons that purposefully incorporate listeners' perspectives and invite their internal if not also expressed response to what is heard has signaled one of the most important developments of the turn to the listener in preaching. Theologically and practically, conversational approaches have incorporated listeners' perspectives from conceptualization of the sermon's content to its development, methods of biblical interpretation (e.g., sometimes adopting communal, small group discussions), incorporation of public concerns and allusions/ examples, and means of delivery in worship.

Among the first to identify a conversational approach to preaching, Lucy Atkinson Rose proposed that "preaching's goal is to gather the community of faith around the Word where the central conversations of the church are refocused and fostered. In conversational preaching, the preacher and the congregation are colleagues, exploring together the mystery of the Word for their own lives, as well as the life of the congregation, the larger church, and the world."[67] According to Rose, the *purpose* of conversational preaching is to offer a "wager" or tentative proposal for listeners to consider rather than privileged or authoritative assertions; the *content* of the sermon is to reflect the multivalent nature of our lives and our interpretations of Scripture; sermonic *language* is to be confessional or testimonial and evocative rather than declaratory in nature as it recognizes the limitations of language and the historical conditioning of all biblical interpretations and insights; and the *forms* of conversational preaching favor inductive and narrative designs that foster a partnership between the preacher and congregation,

---

65. For more on Bellinger's tools and resources, see "The Elephant in the Room," and "How's the Preaching?"

66. "Conversational preaching" in McClure, *Preaching Words*, 18.

67. See Rose, *Sharing the Word*, 4.

who are to relate to one another in ongoing conversations in and out of worship.[68]

For preaching traditions that have long assumed or assimilated various means of engaging sermon listeners in the preaching moment, such terms and expectations are not surprising. In many African American preaching traditions, the practice of call and response is integral to the sermon as preachers depend upon worshipers to react with words of encouragement, challenge, and direction in response to the sermon, creating a dialogical relationship between preacher and listeners amid the otherwise monological act of preaching.[69] This time-honored means of engaging one another in the preaching moment builds on patterns of African music as participants offer extemporaneous and/or patterned exclamations in response to what is preached. In many Anabaptist traditions, the work of preaching is shared among several members, and opportunities for congregants to speak out of their experience of the gospel and to expand upon and respond to the preacher's words during worship continues the preaching moment amid the worshiping body.[70] As such, the sermon offered by an individual preacher in Anabaptist worship is not considered a definitive Word of God but the basis of shared admonition and witness as the entire community shares responsibility for interpreting and engaging God's living word and the Spirit of Christ in worship.[71] These long-standing preaching traditions have survived and thrived alongside of, but often at an unseen distance from, mainline preaching forms.

Among Eurocentric homileticians, John S. McClure has explored the practical and theoretical dimensions of taking seriously the role of listeners in preaching. In terms of encouraging and integrating listeners' voices in the conception and preparation of sermons, McClure's *The Roundtable Pulpit: Where Leadership and Preaching Meet* sets forth a collaborative method of sermon preparation that incorporates sermon listeners in roundtable

---

68. Rose differentiates between conversational approaches and traditional, kerygmatic, and transformational approaches.

69. See Crawford, *The Hum.*

70. See Ottoni-Wilhelm, "God's Word in the World."

71. The means of communal sharing in the sermon are varied among Anabaptist communities and congregations with some communities offering time for extended silence immediately following the sermon and some offering brief silence immediately followed by opportunities for congregants to rise and speak a continued word of the sermon (e.g., expanding upon the interpretation of the biblical text, bearing testimony to its meaning and relevance). In Anabaptist faith and practice, this shared responsibility for the spoken word is not offered as disputation or refutation of what has already been spoken since all sharing is believed to be inspired by the Spirit of Jesus Christ.

discussions.[72] Drawing from shared interpretive encounters among congregants and pastoral leaders, McClure does "not suggest that preachers actually hold conversations from the pulpit or that they attempt two or three party 'dialogue sermons'" but "move closer to a model of single-party preaching that includes the actual language and dynamics of collaborative conversation on biblical texts, theology, and life" that have been shared during prior roundtable discussions.[73]

As the church continues to grapple with what it means to be in dialogue with itself and others, homileticians and preachers search for ways of creating sermons that are more conversational in nature. In his introductory-level textbook on preaching, Ronald J. Allen envisions "the sermon as a conversation in which preacher and people search together to interpret our common life from the perspective of the gospel," incorporating the Bible, Christian history and tradition, contemporary theologians, the local congregation, wider culture, the preacher's life experiences, and God.[74] Similarly, O. Wesley Allen considers the church itself as the locus of "ongoing conversations owned by the community" and develops a homiletic that shifts the focus from individual sermons to ongoing conversations in the life of the church.[75] Allen and Allen have also worked collaboratively to explore what it means to preach in a "postapologetic" culture so that preachers may help the church seek "critical reciprocity between the many and varied voices in, around, and outside of the church."[76] Indeed, the global context of today's preaching urges us to reflect critically and cooperatively with theologians, ministers, homileticians, and preachers who will listen anew to the many voices participating in ongoing conversations about preaching.[77]

72. McClure, *The Roundtable Pulpit*.

73. McClure, *The Roundtable Pulpit*, 8. At a more theoretical level, McClure's *Other-Wise Preaching* provides the philosophical underpinnings of conversational preaching through a consideration of homiletic deconstruction (i.e., of the traditional authorities of the Bible, tradition, experience, and reason). Building on the work of Jewish philosopher Emmanuel Levinas, McClure recognizes the rupture that occurs when our efforts to devise systems of sameness or "totality" in preaching are confronted by "face-to-face encounter with other human beings. In this encounter, the glory of otherness interrupts our attempts to cling to sameness . . . and introduces a profound obligation into [our] experience," *Other-Wise Preaching*, 8. Accordingly, conversational preaching as represented by McClure provides a way to incorporate the perspectives, concerns, and insights of others who may not otherwise be considered when preparing and preaching sermons.

74. Allen, *Interpreting the Gospel*.

75. Allen, *The Homiletic of All Believers*, 15.

76. Allen and Allen, *The Sermon without End*, xiii.

77. In Allen et al., eds., *Under the Oak Tree*, the editors invite theologians, ministers, and homileticians to reflect on tasks of ministry (including preaching) as these may

CONTINUING TO LISTEN . . .

With his turn to the listener, Fred Craddock began a conversation between pulpit and pew that continues to the present day. Following his lead, preachers are not isolated ideologues who can pontificate "points" that have little to do with the lives of their listeners, all the while assuming that people will listen in rapt attention. Instead, Craddock helped the church and its preachers to understand the shared nature of preaching so that listeners can experience gospel not above or apart from them but with and among them.

At least two areas of exploration call for our attention as preachers and teachers of homiletics continue to turn our attention to sermon listeners today. First, in a politically and culturally divisive time, while fear runs rampant among us and the rise of populist movements around the world continue to enflame and threaten civil discourse, what does it mean to listen to those with whom we so often radically disagree and how do we do so as preachers and members of the church?[78] Since we can no longer view ourselves in isolation from Christians in other parts of the world, how may the church, its preachers, teachers, and members hear and respect the myriad expressions of faith and practice, of preacher formation and sermon practices that are represented across cultures and continents? What may we learn from one another? With whom will we form partnerships and how will we move forward in faith together?[79]

Amid the challenges and opportunities of this time, there is yet something profoundly moving and life-changing when people gather in the name of Christ to listen to God and one another in worship. In a world increasingly saturated with sound bites and tweets, pixels and pictures, preaching and sermon listening are significant but peculiar acts of devotion. We share and care for the most extraordinary things: ancient texts and stories, words from afar, poetic and musical utterances, assertions of life and death and life beyond death. If we have ears to hear, we may continue to listen.

BIBLIOGRAPHY

Alcántara, Jared E. *The Practices of Christian Preaching: Essentials for Effective Proclamation*. Grand Rapids: Baker Academic, 2019.

---

embody a more robust exchange of faith within and beyond the church.

78. Among those who study preaching in divisive settings and times, see Schade, *Preaching in the Purple Zone.*

79. This has been the ongoing interest of Societas Homiletica, the international association of homileticians, since its inception in the early 1980s. See www.societas-homiletica.org.

Allen, O. Wesley, Jr. *The Homiletic of All Believers: A Conversational Approach*. Louisville: Westminster John Knox, 2005.

Allen, O. Wesley, Jr., and Ronald J. Allen. *The Sermon without End: A Conversational Approach to Preaching*. Nashville: Abingdon, 2015.

Allen, O. Wesley, Jr., et al., eds. *Under the Oak Tree: The Church as Community of Conversation in a Conflicted and Pluralistic World*. Eugene, OR: Cascade, 2013.

Allen, Ronald J. *Interpreting the Gospel: An Introduction to Preaching*. St. Louis, MO: Chalice, 1998.

_____. "The Turn to the Listener: A Selective Review of a Recent Trend in Preaching." *Encounter* 64:2 (2003) 167–96.

_____. "Theology Undergirding Narrative Preaching." In *What's the Shape of Narrative Preaching?*, edited by Mike Graves and David J. Schlafer, 27–40. St. Louis, MO: Chalice, 2008.

Allen, Ronald J., et al. *Believing in Preaching: What Listeners Hear in Sermons*. St. Louis, MO: Chalice, 2005.

_____. *Listening to Listeners: Homiletical Case Studies*. St. Louis, MO: Chalice, 2004.

Allen, Ronald J. and Joseph R. Jeter, Jr. *One Gospel, Many Ears: Preaching for Different Listeners in the Congregation*. St. Louis, MO: Chalice, 2002.

Almer, Hans. *Variationer ava predikouppfattningar i Svenska kyrkan. En fenomenografisk undersökning om predikanter och åhörare*. Lund: Arcis, 1999.

Andrews, Dale P. "New to Whom?" *Homiletix E-Forum*, www.homiletics.org, Academy of Homiletics, Fall, 2006.

Augustine. *On Christian Doctrine*. Translated with an Introduction by D. W. Roberston, Jr. Upper Saddle River, NJ: Prentice Hall, 1958.

Austnaber, Hans. *Improving Preaching by Listening to the Listeners: Sunday Service Preaching in the Malagsy Lutheran Church*. New York: Peter Lang, 2012.

Bellinger, Karla. *Connecting Pulpit and Pew: Breaking Open the Conversation about Catholic Preaching*. Collegeville, MN: Liturgical, 2014.

_____. "The Elephant in the Room: Catechetical Leaders Speak about the Sunday Homily." *Catechetical Leader* 25:2 (2014) 20–24.

_____. "How's the Preaching? Young Listeners Respond." A paper presented to the Word and Worship Seminar. North American Academy of Liturgy, Orlando, FL: January, 2014.

Bridgman, Valerie. "Celebration Renewed: Response by Valerie Bridgman." In *The Renewed Homiletic*, edited by O. Wesley Allen, Jr., 74–77. Minneapolis: Fortress, 2010.

Buttrick, David. *Homiletic: Moves and Structures*. Philadelphia: Fortress, 1987.

Campbell, Charles L. *Preaching Jesus: The New Directions for Homiletics in Hans Frei's Postliberal Theology*. Eugene, OR: Wipf and Stock, 1997.

Carrell, Lori. *The Great American Sermon Survey*. Wheaton, IL: Mainstay, 2000.

Childers, Jana, ed. *Birthing the Sermon: Women Preachers on the Creative Process*. St. Louis, MO: Chalice, 2001.

Cilliers, Johan. "Fides Quaerens societatum." *Verbum et Ecclesia* 30 (1) 50–64.

Craddock, Fred B. *As One Without Authority*. Nashville: Abingdon, 1971.

_____. *Preaching*. Nashville: Abingdon, 1985.

_____. "Preaching: An Appeal to Memory." In *What's the Matter with Preaching Today?*, edited by Mike Graves, 59–73. Louisville: Westminster John Knox, 2004.

_____. "Inductive Preaching Renewed." In *The Renewed Homiletic*, edited by O. Wesley Allen, 41–55. Minneapolis: Fortress, 2010.

Crawford, Evans. *The Hum: Call and Response in African American Preaching*. Nashville: Abingdon, 1995.

Crites, Stephen. "The Narrative Quality of Experience." *Journal of the American Academy of Religion* 39 (1971) 291–311.

Daiber, Karl-Fritz, et al., eds. *Predigen und Hören*. Ergebnisse einer Gottesdienstbefragung—Band 2: Kommunikation zwischen Predigern und Hören. Sozialwissenschaftliche Untersuchungen. München: Kaiser, 1983.

Florence, Anna Carter. *Preaching as Testimony*. Louisville: Westminster John Knox, 2007.

Fylling, Hilde, ed. *Hellige ord i vanlige live: En studie av kirkegjengeres vurderinger av prekener*. Tromsø: Kirkelig Utdanningssenter i Nord, Praktisk–kirkelig årbok, 2015.

Gaarden, Marianne, and Marlene Ringgaard Lorensen. "Listeners as Authors in Preaching; Empirical and Theoretical Perspectives." *Homiletic* 38:1 (2013) 28–45.

Gaarden, Marrianne. *The Third Room of Preaching*. Louisville: Westminster John Knox, 2017. Also forthcoming in paper edition, Eugene, OR: Wipf and Stock.

Gilbert, Kenyatta. *Exodus Preaching: Creating Sermons about Justice and Hope*. Nashville: Abingdon, 2018.

_____. *A Pursued Justice: Black Preaching from the Great Migration to Civil Rights*. Waco, TX: Baylor University Press, 2016.

Klerk, Barend J. de. "Conveyance of Preaching by Vulnerable Listeners—A Case Study of Farm Workers in the Vredefort Dome South Africa." http://www.researchgate. net/publication/277895995.

LaRue, Cleophus J. *I Believe I'll Testify: The Art of African American Preaching*. Louisville: Westminster John Knox, 2011.

Little, Jennifer A. "God, Authority, and Theological Literacy in Preaching." *Encounter* 75:1 (2015) 1–23.

_____. *Power in the Pulpit: How America's Most Effective Black Preachers Prepare Their Sermons*. Louisville: Westminster John Knox, 2002.

Long, Thomas G. *Preaching and the Literary Forms of the Bible*. Philadelphia: Fortress, 1985.

_____. *The Witness of Preaching*. 2d ed. Louisville: Westminster John Knox, 2005.

Lose, David. "Whither Hence, New Homiletic?" A paper given in Dallas, TX, at the Preaching and Theology Section of the Academy of Homiletics, December, 2000.

Lowry, Eugene L. *The Homiletical Plot: The Sermon as Narrative Art Form*. Expanded ed. Louisville: Westminster John Knox, 2001.

_____. *The Sermon: Dancing the Edge of Mystery*. Nashville: Abingdon, 1997.

Lundblad, Barbara K. *Marking Time: Preaching Biblical Stories in Present Tense*. Nashville: Abingdon, 2007.

Madrazo, Tito, and Alma Ruiz. "Preaching from Sanctuary." In *Preaching God in a Fear-Filled World: Proceedings from the Conference of Societas Homiletica*, 119–33. Durham (2018). Forthcoming, Germany: LIT Verlag, 2020.

McClure, John S. *Other-Wise Preaching: A Postmodern Ethic for Homiletics*. St. Louis, MO: Chalice, 2001.

_____. *Preaching Words: 144 Key Terms in Homiletics*. Louisville: Westminster John Knox, 2007.

_____. *The Roundtable Pulpit: Where Leadership and Preaching Meet*. Nashville: Abingdon, 1995.

McCray, Donyelle. *The Censored Pulpit: Julian of Norwich as Preacher*. Lanham, MA: Lexington Books/Fortress Academic, 2019.

Mitchell, Ella Pearson, and Valerie Bridgeman Davis, eds. *Those Preaching Women: A Multicultural Collection*. Valley Forge, PA: Judson, 2008.

Mitchell, Henry H. *Black Preaching: The Recovery of a Powerful Art*. Nashville: Abingdon, 1990.

Ottoni-Wilhelm, Dawn. "God's Word in the World: Prophetic Preaching and the Gospel of Jesus Christ." In *Anabaptist Preaching: A Conversation between Pulpit, Pew & Bible*, edited by David B. Greiser and Michael A. King, 76–93. Telford, PA: Cascadia, 2003.

_____. "New Hermeneutic, New Homiletic, New Directions: An U.S.-North American Perspective." *Homiletic* 35:1 (2010) 11–17.

Park, Hyun W., and Cas Wepener. "Empirical Research on the Experience of the New Homiletic in South Korea." *Verbum et Ecclesia* 37:1 (2016). http://dx.doi.org/10.4102/ve.v37i1.1458.

Pieterse, Hendrik J.C. *Acta Theologica*. Vol. 30:2 (2010) 113–29.

_____. *Gemeente en prediking*. Pretoria: NG Kerkboekhandel, 1991.

Piper, H. C. *Predigtanalysen. Kommunikation und Kommunikationsstörungen in der Predigt*. Göttingen: Vandenhoeck and Ruprecht, 1977.

Pleizier, Theo. *Religious Involvement in Hearing Sermons*. Delft: Eburon Academic, 2010.

Powery, Luke A. *Dem Dry Bones: Preaching, Death, and Hope*. Minneapolis: Fortress, 2012.

Randolph, David James. *The Renewal of Preaching in the 21st Century*. Babylon, NY: Hanging Gardens, 1998.

Rice, Charles L. *The Embodied Word: Preaching as Art and Liturgy*. Fortress Resources for Preaching. Minneapolis: Fortress, 1991.

_____. *Interpretation and Imagination: The Preacher and Contemporary Literature*, Preachers' Paperback Library. Philadelphia: Fortress, 1970.

Rietveld, David. "A Survey of Phenomenological Research of Listening to Preaching." *Homiletic*, vol. 38, no. 2, 2013. http://www.homiletic.net/index.php/homiletic/article/view/3867.

Ringgaard Lorensen, Marlene. "Preaching as Repetition—in Times of Transition." *International Journal of Homiletics* 1:1 (2016) 34–51.

_____. *Preaching as a Carnivalesque Dialogue*. Copenhagen, Denmark: Copenhagen University Press, 2012.

Robinson, Wayne Bradley, ed. *Journeys toward Narrative Preaching*. New York: Pilgrim, 1990.

Rose, Lucy Atkinson. *Sharing the Word: Preaching in the Roundtable Church*. Louisville: Westminster John Knox, 1997.

Schaap-Jonker, Hanneke. *Before the Face of God*. Zurich: Lit Verlaag, 2008.

Schade, Leah. *Preaching in the Purple Zone: Ministry in the Red-Blue Divide*. New York: Rowan & Littlefield, 2019.

Simmons, Martha and Frank A. Thomas, eds. *Preaching with Sacred Fire: An Anthology of African American Sermons, 1750 to the Present*. New York: W. W. Norton & Co., 2010.

Smith, Christine M. *Preaching Justice: Ethnic and Cultural Perspectives.* Cleveland, OH: United Church, 1998.

———. *Weaving the Sermon: Preaching in a Feminist Perspective.* Louisville: Westminster John Knox, 1989.

Song, C. S. *The Believing Heart: An Invitation to Story Theology.* Minneapolis: Fortress, 1999.

———. *Tell Us Our Names: Story Theology from an Asian Perspective.* Eugene, OR: Wipf and Stock, 2005.

Stark, Franciska. *Proeven van de Preek: Een praktisch-theologisch onderzoek naar do preek als Woord van God.* Zoetermeer: Boekencentrum, 2005.

Sterk, Johannes G. M. *Preek en toehoorders: sociologische exploratie onder katholieke kerkgangers in di Bondsrepubliek Duitsland.* Nijmegen: Instituut voor Toegespaste Sociologie, 1975.

Sundkvist, Bernice. *En predikan—nio berättelsert: en studie i predkoreception.* Finland: Åbo akademi, 2003.

Taylor, Barbara Brown. *God in Pain: Teaching Sermons on Suffering.* The Teaching Sermon Series, edited by Ronald J. Allen. Nashville: Abingdon, 1998.

———. *The Preaching Life.* Boston: Cowley, 1993.

Thomas, Frank A. *Introduction to African American Preaching.* Nashville: Abingdon, 2016.

———. *They Like to Never Quit Praisin' God: The Role of Celebration in Preaching.* Rev. and updated. Cleveland, OH: Pilgrim, 2013.

Thompson, Lisa. *Ingenuity: Preaching as an Outsider.* Nashville: Abingdon, 2018.

Tisdale, Nora Tubbs. "Preachers for All Seasons: The Legacy of Riverside's Free Pulpit." In *The History of the Riverside Church in the City of New York,* edited by Peter J. Paris, et al., 55–135. New York: New York University Press, 2004.

———. *Preaching as Local Theology and Folk Art.* Philadelphia: Fortress, 1997.

Troeger, Thomas H. *The End of Preaching.* Nashville: Abingdon, 2018.

———. *Imagining a Sermon.* Nashville: Abingdon, 1990.

———. *Wonder Reborn: Creating Sermons on Hymns, Music, and Poetry.* Oxford: Oxford University Press, 2010.

Willis, Dennis M. "Noah Was a Good Man." In *How to Preach a Parable: Designs for Narrative Sermons,* edited by Eugene L. Lowry, 42–49. Nashville: Abingdon, 1989.

Zink-Sawyer, Beverly. "A Match Made in Heaven: The Intersection of Gender and Narrative Preaching." In *What's the Shape of Narrative Preaching?,* edited by Mike Graves and David J. Schlafer, 41–53. St. Louis, MO: Chalice, 2008.

TOO BUSY TO GO HEAR THIS FRED CRADDOCK GUY ...

A Remembrance of Fred

Nancy Coil Lear

MY FIRST ENCOUNTER WITH FRED CRADDOCK WAS, MORE ACCURATELY, A missed encounter. Not long after my husband and I moved to Kansas City, there was a buzz among the leaders of our congregation about "a wonderful preacher," "one of the best of our denomination," who would be preaching one evening at our church. My husband and I both worked full-time, and we had two small children, so we decided we were too busy to go hear this Fred Craddock guy. Fortunately, that was a mistake I never repeated.

By the time I had another chance to hear Fred preach a few years later, I knew of his reputation. I went expecting to see an imposing figure, and was surprised to see this short, ordinary-looking man in the pulpit. But then he started to speak. And then I knew why he was so revered among Disciples ministers. What he preached was, to me, the essence of Christianity. This was a man who knew what it meant to be a disciple of Jesus, and he spoke that truth simply and with humility. He never seemed in any way ordinary to me again, and I never missed another opportunity to hear him preach. His words have helped shape my theology and my life.

I have had the opportunity to hear many outstanding preachers, but in the presence of two of them I felt that I was truly in the presence of Jesus (not Jesus the Christ, but Jesus the man): one was Archbishop Desmond Tutu, and the other was Fred Craddock. Both men were short, not particularly striking in looks, not bombastic speakers. But each of them was, I believe, the embodiment of true Christianity.

"IT'S NOT A LIST; DON'T CALL IT A LIST . . ."

A Remembrance of Fred

Rick Stern

I WAS ABLE TO ENJOY CRADDOCK'S PREACHING ONLY A COUPLE OF TIMES AT the Academy of Homiletics gatherings. Never in a parish setting. Much later I found some examples on the Internet. But one homily in particular has become a constant companion, "When the Roll Is Called Down Here." Hugh Daley told me about this homily at my first Academy meeting in San Antonio, 1987, and later sent me a cassette. Much later yet I came across the transcript in Joe Webb's *Comedy and Preaching.* I play it for every class I teach, whether for priests or permanent deacon candidates. I use it as an example of inductive preaching. I use it as an example of inspired delivery. He seems to break every rule in the delivery Bible and does it to magnificent effect. I pretend to play it for the students' benefit. But it's really selfish. I love to play it again and again, each time finding something new. "It's not a list; don't call it a list" has become code for, "I had Stern for homiletics when I went to Saint Meinrad."

I figure I have listened to that sermon eighty or more times. And if you have a few minutes, I'll cue it up again. You just have to hear it.

"THIS SERMON ONLY WORKS *IF . . .*"

A Remembrance of Fred

Christopher Wilson

FRED HAD SOME OPENING COMMENTS OF WELCOME AS HE BEGAN TEACH-ing his homiletics class, "Preaching the Letters of Paul," at a summer class at Brite Divinity School. I relished the chance to take a class from him knowing his formal teaching was soon ending. I had heard Fred preach on multiple occasions. I had shared many private conversations with him. I had also discovered that he had preached in my home congregation the day of my baptism. I so wanted to take a preaching class from him.

He used this mantra in his opening hour of the first class by saying, "It's a good time for preaching in the church these days." He would share a few anecdotes and stories following his evocative phrase. I realized after absorbing these captivating stories that helped me travel in my mind and affirm his phrase about preaching that I should be taking notes. Fred had a way of teaching in which you felt you were sitting in his den by the fire and reflecting on life and love.

Fred spoke conversationally in his teaching style. You were warmed into the depth that lay beneath the surface of his words. Words, themselves, took on a richer meaning when you were in his presence. Every story was powerfully told, yet you knew the story had a deeper metaphorical significance. He was so selective in how he weaved together Scripture and life stories. As the class progressed the letters of Paul made the transition from biblical letters to personal mail that told of my very own ancestors.

The greatest challenge and opportunity in the class came toward the end of process, when each of us would preach to the class. This meant Fred would listen to my sermon and give me a grade for preaching. The sermon constituted a high percentage of the class grade. We pulled Scriptures out of a hat to determine our preaching text. I reached in and found myself intermingled with the church in Corinth and 2 Corinthians 9. I had preached on stewardship before, but I sought to do something different or unique for the class.

I wrestled with the text like Jacob did with God. I kept trying to live with and behind the text. I brooded over the style and presentation. Fred always said the order of your sermon material can be just as powerful as the message itself. I designed my sermon conclusion to let the text be read at the end. I would dress up as Paul and deliver the sermon from a first-person perspective. I entered the room in character and began my one-way dialogue as though the class participants were one of Paul's companions. I preached as though it was in conversation and struggled to offer Corinth a way to understand and embrace the power of giving because of Christ's gift to us. I sought to channel Paul from the cloud of witnesses as I summoned words of passion and discernment as Paul might have possibly done in his crafting a letter to one of the churches he helped start, that was now in a challenging place. I ended the sermon as if I had finally come to a conclusion about what I would write to Corinth. I opened the text and read what I (Paul) would finally write to the church. I ended the sermon and waited.

The evaluation process had two parts. First, the preacher would receive written and oral feedback from the class. I received this with lesser weight. Second, Fred would speak and the real weight would be the words flowing from Fred's mouth. I remember two distinct comments from Fred. First, he confessed he had never heard a first-person sermon before. I quickly thought this might give me an advantage with little to no comparison with other sermons. Second, he stated, "This sermon only works if you were a convincing Paul. If you were not Paul the sermon falls flat on its face."

I did not know my grade until after the class was complete. Fred left a letter for each student to pick up at the seminary. I got an A-. I was thrilled with the grade, but I was more thrilled to be challenged into the depths of how God's word is made known to those who listen to our words. I am forever grateful for Fred's gift to me that summer in his preaching class.

— 7 —

INVOCATION VOCATION

Preaching and Praying

Luke A. Powery

MY CHILDHOOD: FAMILY AND PRAYER

Growing up as a "PK" (and no this doesn't mean "party kid" or "problem kid"!), a preacher's kid, in the home of a Wesleyan Holiness minister, meant many things: no dancing, no movie theaters, no "secular" music, no playing outside, and no TV on Sundays. There were lots of "Nos," but there were also lots of "Yeses": yes to God, yes to each other, yes to making music together, yes to board games, yes to laughter, yes to family prayer. There is the worn-out saying, "A family that prays together stays together," and, of course, this is not true in every single case. Prayer can be used as a weapon of spiritual destruction, especially when prayers function as mini-sermons directed towards people rather than God, or as local news reports to update us on current events while making political stump speeches, or as private conversations between family members gone public over unresolved issues. However, in my family of birth, prayer was like a musical motif woven throughout our life together, summed up in a song we would sing frequently: "Don't forget the family prayer, Jesus Christ will meet you there, when you get around the altar, pray until the Lord comes near." It was more than music too. Prayer was an animating thread of family life. In fact, it was the lifeline, my lifeline. This does not mean that I understood every word or every sound that came out of everyone's mouths, yet prayer was a matter of life and death, literally, on 216 Street in Bronx, New York, in 1974.

One afternoon resting in my mother's arms with a high fever, I began to struggle to physically breathe and convulsed. One of my older brothers had just arrived home from school and saw what was happening. He picked up the phone and called my father while crying and said, "Luke is dead, Luke is dead." The ambulance came and took me and my mother to the hospital while my father met us there. At some point between our departure to the hospital and while there, a neighbor came upstairs in our duplex on 216 Street to see what the noise was all about. She heard a lot of movement above her on her ceiling. When she arrived upstairs, she discovered that the noise she heard was that of my four siblings—ages fourteen, twelve, eight, and four—pacing the floor, praying for me. The noise she heard was the pacing of praying feet. My life was touched by death *and* prayer as an infant. Both inform and transform my work and ministry. The pacing of praying siblings, the echo of my father pacing the house floor in the midnight hour in groaning prayer, and the pace of the dropping of my mother's silent tears in prayer, set the pace of my life.

Prayer also sets the pace for preaching in that it places us in the time of God, divine *kairos*.[1] Prayer changes our spiritual and homiletical pace to help us enter the rhythm of God. Just as breathing brings life to our bodies, praying breathes the life of the Spirit into preaching to align our words with the word. This pace of preaching is not about the tempo of one's sermon, but about the sacramental presence of God in, through, and around preaching and encompassing all of life.

I live and preach because as the gospel song says, "Somebody prayed for me, had me on their mind, they took the time and prayed for me . . ." I am the product of prayer just as the church's proclamation is a result of prayer (Acts 1–2). As such, life and preaching are pure gift. The gift of preaching is not bought but given. With all of its criticisms and abuses as a theological art form, with all that is wrong with Christian preaching practices, there are also some things that are right. One such thing is that preaching is still an invocation vocation, that is, the practice of prayer is still interwoven with the ministry of preaching such that if there is no invocation, there will not be the authentic preaching vocation. Without prayer, preaching loses its core theological identity and becomes a mere rhetorical exercise. Whether in private during sermon preparation or as part of public worship, preaching

---

1. There are two Greek words used in the New Testament for time. *Chronos* most frequently represents "clock time," the passing of minutes and hours. *Kairos* on the other hand most frequently represents "God time," those instants when time stands still and God enters the moments we live in life-transforming ways.

and prayer fit like a hand in a glove. This partnership should be nurtured as I still hear the pacing of little feet on a floor in the Bronx echoing down the acoustical corridors of family spiritual history and encouraging me in life and the preaching ministry. In light of this backdrop, this essay will affirm the relationship of prayer to preaching as what is right with preaching today—congregationally, theologically, and rhetorically.

THE CONGREGATION: PREACHING IN PRAYER

In affirming prayer's relationship to preaching, it cannot be ignored that most preaching occurs in the context of corporate worship, which is really a setting of common prayer as a faith community communicates with God through various liturgical signs and symbols. Prayers of confession, prayers of the people, prayers of thanksgiving, "concert" prayers when people pray aloud simultaneously, and altar prayers surround the event of preaching, which arises out of the larger event of the common liturgy. Preaching is one practice among a liturgical network of other practices engaged in by an entire community. Preaching is an act of worship within the context of corporate worship. Most frequently, it occurs in a community of prayer, a local congregation, not apart from it, signaling how its very texture is prayerful in nature as an ongoing *epiclesis* to God, an eternal invocation, a calling to God to draw near to the people. In this way, preaching is an *epicletic* vocation. Thus, the articulation and reception of the spiritual word of God happens in a larger setting of communal prayer received as a divine gift (Acts 1–2). As I have written elsewhere, "All is gift. All of life is a gift. All of homiletics is a gift."[2] Praying in common positions worshippers to receive what God has in store for God's people and preaching is one practice in this wider context.

This larger congregational setting of prayer suggests the importance of those who are not preachers themselves, that is, the laity. It is important to remember that most members of the church are not preachers yet are vital to the life of the church, including its preaching. Every church member's gifts are critical for the growth of any congregation and most of those gifts or callings do not include preaching. But within the context of preaching, the topic of this essay, it is crucial to assert that without hearers of the word, there could be no doers of the word. Without a congregation of eager listeners, the sermon would land nowhere and only tickle the ears of the preacher. Moreover, in light of the focus on prayer in this essay, one should remember that the preacher is a member of the faithful community and this community prays for the preacher and his or her preaching. This can happen before

2. Powery, "In Our Own Native Tongue," 83.

the sermon, during the sermon, or after the sermon, and it is a reminder that preaching requires speaking and listening. The hearers are key to the sermon event as well, in terms of what is received from any given sermon. This, too, requires prayer, not only for the listener but for the preacher, with the hope that the word event would not return void but work in the lives of all. In some traditions, a congregation might be asked to extend their hands in prayer toward the preacher before he or she rises to give a sermon. In other settings, some may even lay hands on ministers before they preach a sermon or pray for them throughout the week while preachers are preparing. Others, during a sermon, might call out, "Help him, Lord!" which could be a prayer for the preacher if the sermon does not seem to be going so well! Nonetheless, preachers are not left alone in this ministry of proclamation but are buoyed by the prayers of others who desire to offer spiritual support in this way. This kind of prayer support from the community should not be underestimated because it is a great form of encouragement; it demonstrates that we are all on this journey together and even though a preacher may share the word, preachers also need to be ministered by that word too. Praying for them is one way to ask for ministers to receive the ministry of the Spirit as well. Praying for preachers acknowledges that preachers are not perfect and need God's ongoing intervention. As a preacher myself, I can say that it is a blessing to have laity sincerely tell me from time to time, "I'm praying for you." This is a gift beyond words for the "burdensome joy" of preaching.[3]

In addition, being situated in a larger context of prayer suggests preachers can never command blessing but only ask for it, as God is not controlled by our words or deeds. Our praying does not guarantee homiletical success. The longevity or brevity of a prayer for a sermon does not ensure a good sermon, whatever that might mean. A good sermon stems from a good God who alone is truly good. Any good that comes from a sermon is due to the grace of God, yet we, as a people of God, pray to worship God and to offer ourselves as ultimately dependent on God, just as the sermon is. As part of prayer and worship, preaching is not only doxological in nature but a prayerful recognition that the audience is really God in the presence of others, all of whom with the preacher are "standin' in the need of prayer." In light of this, the context of congregational prayer is a reminder that preaching is generally not over against the people but *with* and *for* the people. Preachers are pray-ers like everyone else in the church. This is why I always teach that before you take a text to preach, take time to pray before you preach. With this understanding, corporate prayer may keep preachers

---

3. Massey, *The Burdensome Joy of Preaching.*

on the right homiletical track of extending grace to others, as any good that flows from frail sermons is due to God's grace. A congregational setting of common prayer implies a context functioning by grace. All, including the preacher, are in need, thus we all pray together in community.

One Sunday morning grace was extended to me even before I ever stepped foot into the pulpit. I had just finished saying a prayer with the Duke Chapel Choir before the morning service started, per the norm. But on this Sunday, the Chapel Choir joined musical forces with the organization Kidznotes, which provides free orchestral music instruction to underserved children as a means to changing life trajectories. The children from that group were with the Chapel Choir when I prayed. After the prayer, I was leaving the room when a little boy from Kidznotes, maybe ten years old, stopped me. He said something to me but I did not hear him because he spoke as soft as a whisper. I leaned in closer while turning my left ear in his direction to ensure that I did not miss what he had to say and asked him to repeat his words: "Say it again, young man." "Will you pray for my grandmother? She just died last week." This was not what I was expecting to hear from this little boy right before the service. Maybe small talk was in order about his favorite sports teams (so I thought), but this child, and perhaps God, wanted something bigger to happen. The little boy made such an innocent request. I laid my left hand on his shoulder and there amid the noise of musicians getting ready for a procession, I prayed for this boy and his family, and of course, his grandmother. After the "Amen" I gave him a hug and as I walked out of that room into the sanctuary, I had a deep sense that I had already "had church" and experienced the holy sanctum of God in that moment. Before any sermon was proclaimed, prayer preceded it and was actually surrounding it, because preaching occurs in a congregational context where prayer occurs in many forms, inside and outside of corporate worship, influencing the tenor of the preaching moment. That little boy reminds us all that authentic preaching arises from genuine heartfelt prayer within the community of faith. If we do not pray, we might as well not preach, because if we do not pray, we do not believe in God and it is dangerous when preachers become practical atheists, attempting to engage in ministry without God.

THE PRESENCE OF GOD: PRAYER BEFORE AND AFTER PREACHING

Not only is being situated in a larger congregational context of common prayer something that is right with preaching, but more specifically, when a prayer is voiced before and/or after the sermon, this signals the right theological message. This is sometimes called the "prayer for illumination" before the Scripture lessons are read, or is an actual brief prayer before the sermon or a short prayer directly after the sermon. When Howard Thurman preached, his usual pattern was to offer a "meditation-prayer" before the actual sermon.[4] It was a way to signal the presence of the Presence in the preaching moment. Sometimes, one might hear a preacher pray before the sermon: "May the words of my mouth and the meditations of my heart, be acceptable in your sight, O Lord, my Rock and my Redeemer" (Ps 19:14). James Weldon Johnson's *God's Trombones* captures a prayer in poetic form that he often heard before a sermon. He calls it, "Listen, Lord: A Prayer," in which an old-time black preacher prayed such words as,

> *O Lord, we come this morning*
> *Knee-bowed and body-bent*
> *Before Thy throne of grace.*
> *O Lord—this morning—*
> *Bow our hearts beneath our knees,*
> *And our knees in some lonesome valley.*
> *We come this morning—*
> *Like empty pitchers to a full fountain,*
> *With no merits of our own.*
> *O Lord—open up a window of heaven,*
> *And lean out far over the battlements of glory,*
> *And listen this morning.*[5]

Whether in looking back to homiletical history or studying contemporary practices of preaching, what is intriguing about the placement of prayer before the sermon is how it suggests that praying is the beginning of preaching, thus preaching is an act born out of prayer, revealing that the word we proclaim comes from somewhere and someone else. Tom Troeger goes even further when he writes:

> Preachers who do not pray will never awaken prayer in those to whom they preach. Homiletics does not start with hermeneutics or rhetoric, it starts with God and our relationship to God and the vast repertoire of human prayer. All the scholarly disciplines that converge in homiletics matter greatly, but they are not the beginning nor the end of preaching. The end of preaching is prayer. The beginning of preaching is prayer.[6]

4. Thurman, *Growing Edge*, ix.

5. Johnson, *God's Trombones*, 11.

6. Troeger, "House of Prayer in the Heart," 1248.

Even when one prays directly after a sermon, it suggests that preaching ends in prayer as well and that the future of the word is left in God's hands. To pray before and after a sermon reveals that prayer surrounds preaching, even if figuratively, as preaching begins and ends in prayer. This is not a suggestion that every preacher must do this literally every Sunday, but knowing this link between praying and preaching in many congregations says something more deeply about what is right with preaching theologically.

The location of prayer, before or after a sermon, points to a theological conviction that God is the beginning and ending, the alpha and omega of preaching, engulfing preaching with divine presence. Prayer as communication with God, an act of primary theology, suggests that preaching is a theological venture and not a mere rhetorical act. The placement of prayer before and after a sermon indicates that preaching begins and ends with God and is always a gift and a visual, oral/aural sign of dependence on God. Through prayer, preachers reveal their faith and trust in God as they preach. One preaches, ideally, from a place of faith in God's promises. Praying before or after a sermon or even at other times in congregational prayer is not just a plea for God to speak but a belief that God will speak. This does not mean that there are not struggles and we cannot pray, "Lord, I believe; help my unbelief" (Mark 9:24). It means, however, that despite any trials, tribulations, or turmoil, preachers are paying attention to and being present to God from the beginning, through, and at the ending of a sermon, and hopefully through the entire process of sermon preparation, recognizing that sermons will only be a blessing if God blesses them.

By preachers being attentive to God, as revealed through prayer, this can lead others to also pay attention to the One who is already "with us" (Matt 1:23). Whatever the location of praying in relation to preaching, it keeps the focus on God and can function as a linguistic liturgical memorial to God, remembering God, the One who re-members us through the speaking of the word made flesh. Prayer is a gesture to the word beyond our words and calls us to humbly remember we serve God and not the other way around; thus, preaching is not about us but about God, for God, and with God. I do not want to run any preachers out of business (I am one!) but I must concur with George Herbert's keen insight in his poem, "ChurchPorch:"[7]

> *Resort to sermons, but to prayers most:*
> *Praying's the end of preaching.*

---

7. Herbert, "Church Porch," 135.

Some may think prayer is "a royal waste of time," but nothing that has to do with God is wasted because nothing is wasted in God's economy.[8] Our sermons may sometimes smell like natural waste but nothing is out of the reach of God's redemption, not even a sermon. This is why, ideally, we continue to "resort . . . to prayers most." If we are honest, our sermons need lots of prayer.

THE SERMON: PRAYER IN PREACHING

To say that what is right with preaching is its intimate connection to prayer may seem odd to some because preachers are supposed to be "talkers, speechifiers, nonstop voices."[9] One can twist what John says, "In the beginning was the Word . . ." (John 1) and think it means our words should come first in preaching when it means that the Word of God is primary. One can be speechifying so much that we never hear the Word speak, that Word who even spoke the world into existence and gives us a word to proclaim. What prayer does, however, is suggest not just speaking but listening as a key aspect of the preaching vocation. It means not solely a ministry of voice, but also a ministry of the ear. It means silence. It means pause, figuratively and literally, and it is in this rhetorical space where what is also right with preaching becomes clear.

Not only is praying connected to preaching in the larger congregational setting of prayer and in prayer before and after sermons, but a look at the actual sermon and homiletical speech reveals where prayer can be found in our very speaking. This may not be the usual way of thinking about the preacher's actual preaching rhetoric, but even in it, there are "prayer pockets." The first word in preaching is silence because the word comes out of silence and the first task of a preacher is to listen, thus in many ways a preacher's first word is "hush." Although there may be a holy hush before the sermon or after the sermon to allow hearers to focus on what is to come or what has happened already, there is also a "hush" while we preach. There is the pause and I want to give praise to the pause in preaching.

In his book *Preaching*, Fred Craddock writes, "God does not talk all the time" because the Word proceeds out of silence.[10] You might be asking yourself then, "Why do some preachers seem to rattle off words like a typewriter all day long seemingly without a breath, leaving no space for other sounds or voices?" That can be a critique of some preachers but it is not true

---

8. See Dawn, *A Royal Waste of Time*.

9. Killinger, "Preaching and Silence," 127.

10. Craddock, *Preaching*, 53–54.

for all. There are those who comprehend the proverb, "A still tongue makes a wise head." One afternoon, when I was a new seminary professor, I was sitting in a faculty meeting and things became a little tense! I did not say a word. I was new and trying to discern the political landscape of the institution (yes, there are politics in seminaries and churches!). When the meeting was over, I had not said a word in the exchanges that occurred. When I rose from the table, one of my senior colleagues stood across the table from me, shook my hand, and said, "Wise man, wise man," as an affirmation of my silence during the linguistic struggle. At times, the best thing you can say, in a work or pastoral setting, is nothing. Making space for silence can be helpful in various life situations and even sermons. Was not the Word, the Christ, silent at some point "like a sheep before its shearers is silent" and did not open his mouth (Isa 53)?

Wisdom says, "there is a time to be silent" (Eccl 3:7) and depending on the scenario, silence can speak volumes. Thus, silence is not an empty void or an abyss. There can be meaning in silence as one comes to realize "that a minister's life does not consist in the abundance of words spoken."[11] Those in the Protestant tradition might have a hard time with this because Protestants are logocentric, word-oriented, and words do matter, but sometimes there are preachers who talk way too much without saying anything at all. This may be why one writer said, "Blessed is the man who, having nothing to say, abstains from giving us wordy evidence of the fact."[12] On the other hand, I can hear the naysayers reminding me of the speech given by Martin Luther King, Jr. about Vietnam in 1967 at New York City's Riverside Church, in which he proclaimed that there comes a time to "break the silence" and "that the calling to speak is often a vocation of agony, but we must speak."[13] What he declared is true but King also knew how to pray and have days of silence.[14] There was a time to speak but also a time to listen. This is not an either/or scenario, but a both/and situation in preaching. Speech and silence, silence and speech. Voices and ears are both critical tools in preaching.

More specifically, in an actual sermon, it is a good thing that a preacher's sermon does not consist only of an abundance of words. There are silences, pauses between our words, demonstrating that the Word is not solely words but includes silence. It has been said that "poise is in the pause"[15] but

11. Craddock, *Preaching*, 55.

12. Thomsett and Thomsett, eds., *A Speaker's Treasury of Quotations*, 108.

13. King, "A Time to Break Silence," 231.

14. See Baldwin, *Never to Leave Us Alone*.

15. I am grateful to Professor Charles Bartow, Carl and Helen Egner Professor of Speech Communication in Ministry Emeritus at Princeton Theological Seminary, for this teaching.

preaching also reveals that "the Presence is in the pause" too. Preaching includes words but also silences or pauses. Derek R. Nelson writes:

> Speaking and falling silent are related to each other not as opposites, but as partners . . . The act of speaking itself is simply sound punctuated by silence, sound rendered intelligible by silence. Speaking is phoneme, pause, phoneme, pause, phoneme. Speaking without silence is incomprehensible. It would be like a typewriter whose carriage did not move with each new letter, so that every letter was struck on the same place on the paper.[16]

Preaching includes the silence of pauses and these pauses can be viewed as whispers of prayer or "prayer pockets." Every breath, every pause, is an inhale of the life of God. Pause allows for a speaking that is without our speaking. It allows space for the Other's voice among our voices. Pause ensures that we do not fill up all of the acoustical air with our words, recognizing there is a Word around, in, through, between our words, longing to be heard. This is why we might pray,

> *Silence in us any voice but your own,*
> *that, hearing, we may obey your will*
> *through Jesus Christ our Lord. Amen.*

The pause leaves space for the voice of God. This is also why we might say along with the spiritual, "Hush, hush, somebody's calling my name . . . Sounds like Jesus, somebody's calling my name, Sounds like Jesus . . ." But if you never "hush," you may never hear the sound of God.

This hush homiletic facilitates prayer in the pause and creates space, or room, for the Spirit and allows preacher and congregation to encounter God in the pause as we breathe and listen to "the music not heard with ears."[17] The sermon is speaking and listening, words and silence. This spiritual-homiletical framing of the phenomenon of pause may help preachers realize that a sermon is more than our words, latest rhetorical flips, or Red Bull-driven high energy. The pause implies that we need God to speak, for if God does not speak, we, preachers, have nothing to say. The sagely homiletical wisdom of Evans Crawford is insightful on this topic:

> The pause in the sermon is much more than a break in delivery that is used by skillful speakers. I see it as a metaphor of spiritual formation, as an acknowledgement by preachers that they must not cram the air so full of their words that they obscure the vast

---

16. Nelson, "The Speaking that Silence Is," 333.
17. Johnson, "O Black and Unknown Bards," 73–74.

and silent mystery from which true speech arises. Sermon pause represents not only a rest from the sound of the preacher's voice, but an opening in the preacher's consciousness through which the musicality of the spirit breathes so that the musicality of the sermon resonates with the living truth.[18]

As the sermon pause makes room for divine breath, the breath we take in the pause is a prayer for the life of God in the moment and beyond. We pause when we preach to inhale the Spirit and exhale her life to others. The pause allows our speech to make sense but that is only the case because our words are punctuated by pauses, allowing space for the interpreting Spirit to speak. The pause, the prayer pocket, signifies room for the Other. The pause reminds us that we should allow another Speech in these sacred spaces and in those spaces we experience the sacramental presence of God. This homiletical "hush" reveals the sacrament of pause.

Listen to preachers like Howard Thurman, Fred Craddock, and Gardner Taylor preach and you can hear the patience of pause in their sermons, not rushing but taking in the breath, the Spirit, for the next homiletical move. Their pauses were not only prayers but revealed a patient trust for what was to come next in their sermons. Their overall tempo was slower compared to some contemporary preaching, which appears to have increased speed.[19] The sermon pause is the gift that may redeem our sermons as it makes space for God with, through, between, beneath, beyond, and for our words. I recognize, however, that many are uncomfortable with silence, even in preaching. The truth is people are wary of silence in general and this bleeds over into perceptions of preaching.

August 29, 1952 is a case in point. That day, David Tudor walked onto the stage of the Maverick Concert Hall, near Woodstock, New York, sat down at a piano, and, for four and a half minutes, made no sound. He performed "4'33"," a conceptual work by musician John Cage. It has been called the "silent piece," but its purpose is to make people listen. Cage did not believe there was such a thing as silence because one could hear other sounds during that piece—the wind, raindrops, people talking or walking out. Many did not really care for this musical experiment, including his own mother who thought he went too far. Performance expectations were not met on that day but it may also be the case that people just have a hard time centering down in silence because we may not like what we hear from God or even our own hearts when we pause, even in preaching.

18. Crawford, *The Hum*, 17.
19. Simmons and Thomas, eds., *Preaching with Sacred Fire*, 589.

Yet the pause, the silence, could be what we most need today in a society full of talking media heads. The sermon pause may be a corrective to a word-centered spirituality that believes that the amount of words reveals how deep one's spirituality really is. Maybe it is true for preaching, too, that less is more. Fewer words may be where the Word is—in the music of silence and "prayer pockets." To pause in preaching is to pray. Some may criticize this idea, but in the pause, in the holy hush, we can enter the sanctum of God and encounter the Presence in and of preaching.

THE FUTURE OF PREACHING: RESORTING TO PRAYERS MOST

What's right with preaching? Prayer is still connected to preaching, around it and in it. Preaching is in prayer, surrounded by prayer, and prayer is in preaching. Herbert's advice is still relevant for today: "Resort to sermons, but to prayers most." The future of preaching depends on praying because praying is dependency on God. What's right with preaching today, that is, praying, will ensure that preaching has a future. If we subtract prayer from the equation of preaching, we delete God, who is a vital variable, the *fons vitae*, because prayer implies the presence of God. There is no future for preaching if God has no future with us, in practice or theory. Furthermore, there is no future for preaching without the future God promises. Without prayer, preaching becomes atheological or atheistic in nature and is no longer a theological art but purely rhetorical speech, making it something other than preaching in the end.

But there is a future for and of preaching in light of the resurrected God, therefore, we continue to pray as part of what it means to preach. There will always be prayer present as long as the church is in existence because the church was born from prayer and is a "house of prayer for all nations" (Mark 11:17). In addition, prayer will always be present, even if implicit, when preachers pause to take a breath in a sermon because this breath is a "prayer pocket" for God. Moreover, prayer will always be present if preaching is still about transformation, signaling a larger vision than a human one, because humans alone cannot transform; only God can, making preaching a divine venture of redemption. Finally, prayer will always be present if preaching is still centered on the crucified Christ for every sermon is a little plea to "Come, Lord Jesus" (Rev 22:20).

"Resort . . . to prayers most" because without them, we may think preaching has nothing to do with God although the power of preaching comes from God. To forget God is to demolish the future of preaching.

But as long as prayer has a future, this implies that God is involved, giving preaching a future. It is not that prayer saves preaching because God does that, but prayer might save the preacher from thinking the sermon is all up to him or her. All of this may seem overly pietistic or too confessional, but throughout the Gospels prayer is the one thing the disciples asked Jesus to teach them. Even after the masterful Sermon on the Mount, the disciples never asked Jesus to help them preach better or inquire about his sermon preparation strategies. They did not ask him how to do an effective rhetorical flourish in a sermon, how to do a sermon introduction, how to exegete a text, or what was his theology of the word. They made one simple request that ought to be on the tongue of every preaching disciple in the pulpit: "Lord, teach us to pray" (Luke 11:1). "Teach us to pause. Teach us to hush, for our future proclamation depends on it because it depends on You." Our lives, our preaching, depend on God so let us pray: "Our Father, who art in heaven . . ."

BIBLIOGRAPHY

Baldwin, Lewis. *Never to Leave Us Alone: The Prayer Life of Martin Luther King, Jr.* Minneapolis: Fortress, 2010.

Craddock, Fred. *Preaching.* Nashville: Abingdon, 1985.

Crawford, Evans. *The Hum: Call and Response in African American Preaching.* Nashville: Abingdon, 1995.

Dawn, Marva J. *A Royal Waste of Time: The Splendor of Worshiping God and Being Church for the World.* Grand Rapids: Eerdmans, 1999.

Herbert, George. "The Church Porch." In *George Herbert: The Country Parson and the Temple,* edited by John N. Wall, Jr., 121–38. Mahwah, NJ: Paulist, 1981.

Johnson, James Weldon. *God's Trombones: Seven Negro Sermons in Verse.* London: Penguin, 2008.

_____. "O Black and Unknown Bards." In *The Book of American Negro Poetry,* edited by James Weldon Johnson, 73–74. New York: Harcourt Brace, 1922.

Killinger, John. "Preaching and Silence." In *A Reader on Preaching: Making Connections,* edited by David Day, Jeff Astley, and Leslie J. Francis, 127–33. Burlington, VT: Ashgate, 2005.

King, Martin Luther, Jr. "A Time to Break Silence." In *A Testament of Hope: The Essential Writings and Speeches of Martin Luther King, Jr.,* edited by James M. Washington, 231–44. New York: HarperCollins, 1986.

Massey, James Earl. *The Burdensome Joy of Preaching.* Nashville: Abingdon, 1998.

Nelson, Derek R. "The Speaking that Silence Is: Prayer as Openness to God." *Dialog: A Journal of Theology* 52:4 (December 12, 2013) 332–39.

Powery, Luke A. "In Our Own Native Tongue: Toward a Pentecostalization of Homiletical Theology." In *Homiletical Theology in Action: The Unfinished Theological Task of Preaching,* edited by David Schnasa Jacobsen, 72–84. Eugene, OR: Cascade, 2015.

Simmons, Martha, and Frank A. Thomas, eds. *Preaching with Sacred Fire: An Anthology of African American Sermons, 1750 to the Present.* New York: W. W. Norton, 2010.

Thomsett, Michael C., and Linda Rose Thomsett, eds. *A Speaker's Treasury of Quotations: Maxims, Witticisms and Quips for Speeches and Presentations.* Jefferson, NC: McFarland, 2015.

Thurman, Howard. *The Growing Edge.* New York: Harper, 1956. 4th reprint, Richmond, IN: Friends United, 1998.

Troeger, Thomas H. "'A House of Prayer in the Heart': How Homiletics Nurtures the Church's Spirituality." *Hervormde Teologiese Studies/Theological Studies* 62:4 (November 2006) 1239–49.

A PIVOTAL PERSON

A Remembrance of Fred

Dan Moseley

SOME PEOPLE ARE PIVOTAL IN OUR LIVES. THEY ARE PRESENT TO US AT JUST the right time with just what we need. Fred Craddock was one of those people for me.

When I was a sophomore in college I was in Dr. Craddock's class on spirituality in novels. The seminar helped us explore the sacred in the mundane. I presented a paper to the class for my final. I wrote it and then presented the essence of it orally. I then turned in the paper. When I got the paper back, I had two grades: an A+ for the presentation in class and a B for the written paper. The note from Dr. Craddock below the grades read, "The moral of this is, always speak, never write."

So I became a preacher. I heard a call to speak and I did. But, I also wrote. I worked hard on writing sermons and articles, on trying to communicate as well on the page as I did orally. Sometimes a word at the right time gives insight and challenges growth. I think I wanted his, "never write," to become a challenge that drove me to be a better writer. It was a truly pivotal point in my life.

After I graduated from seminary I began preaching. I was struggling. My early training in preaching taught me to give a speech structured this way: "tell them what you are going to tell the, tell them, and then tell them what you told them." (And occasionally end with a poem!) I struggled with the question, "Where do I get the right to tell others what is true?" And then I read the newly published book by Dr. Craddock, *As One Without Authority*, and it changed my life. I remember the first sermon where I guided people on a journey of discovery rather than trying to tell people what to do. I had much more fun and the listeners seemed to enjoy the journey of discovery much more than my telling them what I thought was true. It was a decisive moment that made preaching the delightful center of my ministry.

As I think about Fred Craddock, I grieve his loss. His presence in my life was sheer grace. He had the courage to share his gifts and they hit home in me when I needed them. Neither he nor I manufactured the relationship, nor knew what would happen when we met. But my need and his gift resulted in my life changing. I call that grace.

And Dr. Craddock had another gift: humility. He simply offered who he was, not forcing himself on others, not trying to control what others thought or did. He shared his insights and his wisdom with quiet passion and compassion. I never felt coerced. I was simply invited into his journey of discovery as he allowed me to run my fingers through the treasures of his mind. I call that grace.

So, Fred Craddock was, and continues to be, a pivotal person in my life. And no one can ever know how the grace that came through his person to me changed me. But, in this time of remembrance and gratitude I can only say "Thank you" to God for allowing my life to be touched by such a kind and graceful soul.

"AND THEN I SAW THE LAMB . . . SO I STAYED."

A Remembrance of Fred

Donald Chatfield

ONE DAY MANY YEARS AGO, A STUDENT IN MY PREACHING CLASS CAME TO my office in great excitement. "Do you know Fred Craddock?" he asked. I said I did not. "I heard him preach a great sermon," he said, and proceeded to walk me through Fred's sermon, which spoke poignantly about bringing "Doxology." This encounter was repeated a number of times over the next few years, with the enthusiasts able to walk me through sometimes the whole of a Craddock sermon, almost line by line. And then at last I heard Fred preach, at an Academy of Homiletics worship service.

The text he'd been given was Revelation 21:22, "I saw no temple in the city, for its temple is the Lord God the Almighty and the Lamb." Fred said something like this (and it wasn't too much longer): "I entered the holy city, and to my surprise, there was no temple there. No temple! I've spent most of my life in the temple. I've spent days fretting about the temple and hours praying for the temple. I've prepared people for service in the temple. How could I stay in a place with no temple? In despair, I turned to leave. And then I saw the Lamb . . . so I stayed."

I can't recall when that Academy meeting was, nor where we met. But as with my students, my soul can still recall that sermon. And in the long years since that day, when I'm fretting about what's coming for me, or the world, or our half-empty local temple, I often hear Fred say, "I saw the Lamb. So I stayed."

Thanks, Fred. Your words have stayed my soul.

— 8 —

RECENTERING PREACHING

A Taxonomy of Gospel

André Resner

INTRODUCTION

WHEN ONE THINKS ABOUT CHRISTIAN PREACHING, IT IS COMMON TO
think of it as a kind of interpretation of the Bible. Many, including Fred
Craddock, trace the tradition of interpreting biblical texts in preaching back
to the synagogue:

> Historians of preaching generally agree that of all the influences
> affecting the evolution of the Christian sermon, none has been
> more significant than that of the Jewish synagogue. Embracing
> the synagogue practice of publicly reading and interpreting sa-
> cred texts, the church quite early joined the Greek homily not
> only to Christian subject matter in general but to the interpreta-
> tion of scripture in particular. So strong and lasting has been
> this union of the homily and the biblical text that to this day
> preaching is commonly defined as the interpretation of Scrip-
> ture for the needs of the particular community being addressed
> by the sermon.[1]

1. Craddock, "The Sermon and the Uses of Scripture," 7.

Augustine, in what is generally considered to be history's first homiletical handbook, canonized the notion of preaching as biblical interpretation
by describing the preaching task as essentially consisting of two movements:
first the preacher attends to the interpretation of the Bible and, second, the
preacher attends to the articulation of what has been interpreted. Augustine
writes:

> There are two things on which all interpretation of Scripture
> depends: the mode of ascertaining the proper meaning, and the
> mode of making known the meaning when it is ascertained. We
> shall treat first of the mode of ascertaining, next of the mode of
> making known, the meaning; a great and arduous undertaking,
> and one that, if difficult to carry out, it is, I fear, presumptuous
> to enter upon.[2]

The rise of lectionaries in the early church, a practice also borrowed
from the Jewish synagogue, led to a crystallization of the practice of reading passages from various parts of the Bible in the regular Sunday worship
services.[3] The preacher would then choose one of those texts from the
Bible as the platform for the sermon. This led to a "text to sermon" mentality. Thomas G. Long describes this understanding of preaching's essential
process:

> Once upon a time any preacher who wished to take up the chal-
> lenge of responsible biblical preaching could at least be clear
> about the task . . . Producing biblical sermons . . . involved two
> clear and distinct movements. First, the preacher turned toward
> the ancient text, withdrawing its internal meanings. Then, the
> preacher swiveled one hundred and eighty degrees toward the
> congregation, attempting to state the implications of those
> meanings for the current situation. The order was crucial and
> the direction of the flow immutable: first the text, then the con-
> temporary situation. Though sometimes difficult to perform

---

2. Augustine, *On Christian Doctrine*, bk. I, ch. 1, https://faculty.georgetown.edu/
jod/augustine/ddc1.html, accessed 5/21/2020. Robertson's translation reads: "There are
two things necessary to the treatment of the Scriptures: a way of discovering those
things which are to be understood, and a way of teaching what we have learned. We
shall speak first of discovery and second of teaching. This is a great and arduous work,
and since it is difficult to sustain, I fear some temerity in undertaking it." See *St. Augustine On Christian Doctrine*. Augustine wrote the first three books of *On Christian
Doctrine* in 397 and the fourth book in 426.

3. Palazzo, *A History of Liturgical Books*, 91.

and demanding specialized skills, this two-step procedure was nonetheless elegantly simple in design.[4]

In reality, there was something else lurking behind the scenes when a preacher worked with a biblical text with a view to "preaching it," namely the prior theological commitments of the preacher. This is true no matter how much the interpreting preacher may profess to follow methodologically pure procedures in order to guarantee a truly biblical sermon untainted by the preacher's own prejudices.[5] The prior theological commitments of the interpreter exert powerful influences on just how it is that the Bible is used in preaching.

One way of addressing the particular theological commitments that Christian preachers (as interpreters) bring to the Bible is through the lens of one of preaching's key terms, namely *gospel*. I contend that "gospel," understood systematically by means of a tripartite taxonomy, can bring needed theological and methodological clarity to homiletical theory and preaching practice.

This essay celebrates the work of theologian Edward Farley, whose incisive exposure of a fatal flaw in the prevailing paradigm of preaching has led to a more theologically conscious approach to the relationship between the Bible and the sermon.[6] In what follows, I will lay out Farley's bold attempt to reconfigure preaching's paradigm, then I will propose an alternate perspective by means of a taxonomy of gospel.

FARLEY: PREACHING THE BIBLE AND PREACHING THE GOSPEL—1994

In three successive articles, Edward Farley called into question prevailing assumptions about the relationship of the Bible to preaching the gospel.[7]

---

4. Long, "The Use of Scripture in Contemporary Preaching," 341. As a prime example of this method see Best, *From Text to Sermon*.

5. Hans Georg Gadamer was clearer than anyone in exposing the fallacies of objectivity in interpretation and the inability of historical method to guarantee interpretive results free of interpreter influence. In fact, for Gadamer "prejudice" is a necessary and positive idea for hermeneutics, for reader prejudices make interpretation possible. The key is for the interpreter is growingly aware of his or her prejudices. Gadamer, *Truth and Method*, 239, warned about a common hermeneutical ignorance among historicists, and I would argue it applies to fundamentalists as well: "It is the tyranny of hidden prejudices that makes us deaf to what speaks to us in tradition."

6. Farley was not the only, or earliest, protestor in this regard. See for example Allen and Williamson, *A Credible and Timely Word*.

7. These three articles are gathered in Farley, *Practicing Gospel*.

In 1994 Farley exposed the elephant in the homiletical room to be a way of thinking about what preaching's processes are that had calcified in both theory and practice, yet that were logically and theologically incoherent. The prevailing, and uncritically taught and practiced, paradigm of preaching set up preachers for failure because its stated tasks were not just difficult, they were impossible. Because of this, the generally and frequently acknowledged crisis of preaching did not have to do with preaching's inherent difficulty, but with what had become a standard operating procedure that could not be accomplished.[8] What was the prevailing paradigm as Farley saw it? I will list it here, as he does, in eight points:

1. What is preached is the Bible or its message.

2. The Bible becomes available for preaching only as it is divided into sermon-sized sets of verses. "Preaching is not preaching unless it is 'on' a passage."[9]

3. The Bible is not naturally divided up as preaching requires it to be so someone must do so, like the Consultation on Common Texts, who decide on the three year cycle of sermon-sized sets of verses, known as the lectionary.

4. What is preached is the word of God that works some divinely charged action in the hearers.

5. "Since the Bible (the Word of God) is present to preaching only in the form of a passage on which one preaches, each passage must necessarily and in an a priori way contain" the Word of God.[10] "This is the *that-which-is-preached*, the what of preaching."[11]

6. "Preaching itself is an orally delivered message to a congregation in a liturgical setting. The congregation in its situation is the *that-to-which* of preaching."[12]

---

8. Cf. the contribution to the conversation about preaching's crisis: Graves, ed., *What's the Matter with Preaching Today?* Interestingly, Graves includes a chapter by Cleo LaRue, which turns the "preaching crisis" issue on its head. LaRue observes that preaching in predominately African American churches is vibrant and talk of a crisis is largely absent. Things have changed since 2004, especially with the rise of the prosperity gospel and its infiltration of the black church. See Franklin, *Crisis in the Village*, and McGee, *Brand New Theology*.

9. Farley, *Practicing Gospel*, 72.

10. Farley, *Practicing Gospel*, 73.

11. Farley, *Practicing Gospel*, 73.

12. Farley, *Practicing Gospel*, 73.

7. Preaching takes into account the situation of the hearers, including cultural issues and congregational problems. "This is the *that-in-the-light-of-which* of preaching.

8. In mainline churches and their seminaries, the sermon is first written "with its introduction, movement through major points, narratives, and metaphors. In the crafted sermon, the above three concerns come together in the form of a writing meant to be delivered orally."[13]

The paradigm thus has two tasks: connect the passage, or the preachable "X" of the passage, to the situation of the congregation by means of the prepared sermon. Some homileticians focus more on the problem of exegesis, others on the application, others on the rhetorical dynamics involved, but all are essentially operating with a "bridge" problem in mind: how does the sermon bridge the gulf between the preachable "X" of the passage and the situation of the hearers? Farley notes a shift in the early church's preaching, "a shift from the preaching of the gospel, to a preaching of the contents of the new two-Testament Scripture."[14] He contends that we cannot assume that just because we are preaching on a discrete set of verses from that two-Testament Scripture that we are necessarily preaching the gospel. This is not to denigrate the Bible by any means.[15] It is rather to make a clear differentiation between the Bible (and what it says and does, in the way it says and does it), and the gospel (and what it says and does, in the way that it says and does gospel). It is also to say "that the content of most biblical passages is not as such the gospel or good news."[16]

Farley assumes that his primary audience is the mainline church whose ministers have largely adopted historical and literary methods for

13. Farley, *Practicing Gospel*, 73.

14. Farley, *Practicing Gospel*, 74. In his first article, Farley is inconsistent in capitalizing the word gospel.

15. Some have attributed Farley's reason for wanting to abandon the bridge metaphor to his "low doctrine of Scripture." I think, rather, that Farley is concerned that the prevailing paradigm of preaching that requires that we slice and dice it into sermon-sized sets of verses does irreparable violence to the nature of Scripture as Scripture. Farley is on a rescue mission of both the Bible and the gospel. As Farley himself says, "Ironically, the effect of this atomism and leveling of Scripture into passages is to suppress the power and beauty of that literature. If the Bible is not, in fact, an aggregate of 'passages' or texts . . . then to construe it as such is to distort it. To see a letter of Paul, a Gospel, or a prophetic tract as an aggregate of discrete units is surely to miss the writing as an argument, a polemic, a set of imageries, a theological perspective, a narrative. The very thing that gives the writing its power is its unity, its total concrete vision, its total movement" (Farley, *Practicing Gospel*, 76). See Wilson, *Preaching and Homiletical Theory*, 50–51.

16. Farley, *Practicing Gospel*, 75.

studying the Bible. Those methods help situate the texts historically, literarily, socially, and theologically. Of great irony to Farley is the subsequent homiletical commitment of such ministers, who in spite of their awareness of the historical situatedness of texts, and the varieties of theological trajectories that those texts espouse, nevertheless assume that each set of verses they are handed necessarily contain the preachable "X" that preachers have been called and sent to preach. "The whole paradigm of necessarily true passages breaks on the rocks of historical consciousness and requires a fundamentalist assumption to make it work."[17]

Farley vividly exposes the competing agendas of the Bible and the gospel. The many agendas (theological, political, liturgical, historical, and literary) of the Bible are at least obscured, often truncated, or lost altogether when the Bible becomes reduced to sermon-sized sets of verses. Yet, preachers are still required to take each set and find a preachable "X" in that set, and each must then be made into a lesson for life. Since the agenda of smaller passages is rarely about offering life lessons, the preacher must imaginatively fabricate the preachable "X" and the life lesson. Typical exegetical procedures that attend to the text in context work against the preacher's agenda. The preacher must "abandon exegesis" per se in order to fulfill preaching's agenda. For Farley, the competing agendas of the biblical texts and preaching are hopelessly at odds. This is why the bridge paradigm is a failed construct: "There is nothing about arbitrarily selected passages of the Bible that in some necessary or a priori way contains that-which-is-proclaimed."[18] Farley's counterproposal begins with a description of gospel not tied to any specific content. In sum, he asserts that preaching gospel has a temporal content, an embodiment in time, and an underlying "structure" or "conceptual framework." For Farley that structure is this: "To proclaim means to bring to bear a certain past event on the present in such a way as to open up the future."[19] The past event that Farley has most in mind is "the event of Christ," by which I think he means the life, death, and resurrection of Jesus. But he finds the structure at work in Israel's own preaching by the prophets in the way they tapped the exodus event of the past to address their later, particular situations, in order to reopen Israel's future to judgment and mercy. What we learn by observing these particular instantiations of gospel is the way these former preachers of gospel temporalized the kerygma for their situations and how that temporalization nevertheless cohered to deep structural elements.

17. Farley, *Practicing Gospel*, 75.
18. Farley, *Practicing Gospel*, 77.
19. Farley, *Practicing Gospel*, 80.

Farley also notes the "deep symbols" that attend to preaching the gospel, symbols such as "justice, community, evil, law, grace, and many other things."[20] The "world of the gospel" for Farley is one where God acts salvifically in face of human sin. The gospel is not sin simplistically defined or salvation formulaically explained. But there is "a paradigm of redemption."[21] The paradigm for gospel is "the bringing of a past event to bear on the present so as to open up the future." That is Farley's deep structure of redemptive action inherent to the preaching of the gospel.[22]

In a surprise move near the end of his argument, Farley gives preachers their Bible back. After jerking it from their hands long enough for them to get very disoriented (and really nervous), Farley finally concludes that in order to become acquainted with the world of the gospel and the deep symbols that resonate with gospel, one must study the Bible and theology. "For we enter the world of the gospel by way of the world of the Bible and the world of the interpretation of the Christian faith. To understand gospel and the world of the gospel is to struggle critically with the truth and reality of these things. It is, in other words, a theological task."[23]

This is not mere double-talk. Farley has an important word to say in differentiating the gospel from the Bible and helping preachers see the incoherency in thinking that the Bible divided up as it is by the lectionary editors necessarily delivers to the preachers in each of those divided up texts the gospel that we are called to preach.

His real beef with the bridge paradigm is revealed in the penultimate paragraph of the article. There he states, "the bridge paradigm connects preaching to some fields of theological study but not to theology."[24] Farley is concerned that *theology* has not been adequately consulted in the preaching process. "Three fields are pertinent to [the bridge paradigm's] process: biblical studies, cultural (sociological, psychological) studies, and rhetorical studies . . . The threefold requirement of the bridge paradigm shows why

20. Farley, *Practicing Gospel*, 81.

21. Farley, *Practicing Gospel*, 81.

22. One wonders just at this point if this is not just another bridge paradigm. Farley's bridge is *from* a past event *to* a present situation, with the result that a future is opened up. The images evoke both *temporal* and *spatial* bridging of then to now and then out into the future. The gospel for Farley begins in the past with an event, not a text, but the goal is the same, the bringing to bear of that past event onto the present. To use his own language, in the Farley bridge paradigm, the preacher's task is to build a bridge from *that-which-is-preached* (the God redemptive-event of the past, so it might be better expressed *that-which-was-preached*) to the situation of the congregation.

23. Farley, *Practicing Gospel*, 81.

24. Farley, *Practicing Gospel*, 81.

theology itself, the critical and constructive struggle with truth questions as they pertain to the world of faith, has no place in preaching."[25]

In the end, much like James Barr argued concerning the way the authority of the Bible ought to be understood for the Christian life and thought, I think Farley would agree that using the Bible is analytic in preaching the Gospel.[26] One cannot do the one without the other. However, one can violate the Bible's nature by turning it into sliced and diced sermon fodder and miss the larger sweep of the Bible's message and embedded symbols, which evoke gospel undercurrents for the preacher.

FARLEY: TOWARD A NEW PARADIGM FOR PREACHING—1996

Two years later Farley offered his second constructive attempt toward a new paradigm for preaching. His starting point was the typical North American situation of preaching, the Christian faith community gathered for weekly worship. He understands this gathering to be part of the redemptive purpose for the church. Living in a world where human beings are not cared for and God's ways are neglected, the church gathers as "a community of redemption." And as such the church takes seriously the "concerns about oppressive institutions, corrupted relations, or individual hopes for transformation." It doesn't park those concerns or problems outside the sanctuary door in order to practice a kind of spiritualism in denial of reality. It brings the world it lives in to church and sits with expectation for a word that will concretely address the broken world with a redemptive word. "The worshiper's posture is thus one of listening for what disrupts the hold of evil and offers hope for change. The posture (aim) of those who lead worship is to do and say things pertinent to this listening and to this expectation."[27] The progression then is:

1. Fallen/corrupt world of the Christian (Hearer Situation in the World)

2. Gathering for Worship, Bringing of Hearer Concerns Before God (Hearer Situation in Worship, Expectation for Redemption)

3. Listening Posture for a Word that will Disrupt the Hold of Evil and Offer Hope for Change (Listener Expectation and Preacher Responsibility)

---

25. Farley, *Practicing Gospel*, 81–82.

26. See Barr, *The Scope and Authority of the Bible*, 52.

27. Farley, *Practicing Gospel*, 85. I would say that this is Farley's ideal worship participant. Experience with real listeners suggests that most may be more concerned with the Cubs or Cowboys than cosmic corruption.

Farley discerns a theological dynamic at the heart of preaching, that of the "dialectic of critique and hope."[28] "Critique" is the preacher's interpretive disruption of the corruption in this world. Thus far Farley has described the contextual dynamic of the preaching situation, but what precisely is it that the preacher says? What is the gospel that is proclaimed in this context? Again, no one specific set of content suffices for preaching's gospel. Rather, the specific content for the sermon is given unity by the dialectic of corruption and redemption. "Thus, the formal structure of preaching the world of the gospel is this dialectic of critique and hope."[29]

The reason that what we preach cannot simply be the interpretation of an old text is that the world of the gospel is always present tense. "The what of preaching is . . . the concrete situation of the present. The God of this preaching is not stuck in the past, simply to be remembered."[30] Preaching, understood as discerning the mysteries of God's present-moment-workings in our specific, concrete situations is a theological task, not the task of "applied exegesis." The "safe and efficient world of applying verses and passages" gives way to "the muddier, unsafe, and uncertain world of interpreting the mysteries of faith."[31] Since the world of the gospel is the milieu in which the church lives, preachers do not produce it or deliver it to the church. Rather, they "render it into forms of self-reflection, remembrance, new interpretations, spiritual discipline, and education."[32]

What role then does the Bible play for the preacher? Farley expresses a high view of the Bible here as he says that it functions as Scripture for the church. Such a designation indicates that the church "is 'subject to' and 'lives from' this set of writings."[33] For the world of the gospel to be identical to the world of the Bible, however, is the definition of fundamentalism. Scripture

---

28. More broadly, Farley's "dialectic of critique and hope" is similar to the theological dynamic of Law and Gospel. This is reminiscent of Lischer's "Divine Dialectic," which he argued was the theological movement inherent in preaching the gospel, regardless of the surface shape or design of a particular sermon. Whereas Farley only lists one dialectical dynamic, Lischer lists a dozen antitheses and develops even more in explaining how they function in preaching. See Lischer, *Theology of Preaching*, 46–66.

29. Farley, *Practicing Gospel*, 86.

30. Farley, *Practicing Gospel*, 87.

31. Farley, *Practicing Gospel*, 87.

32. Farley, *Practicing Gospel*, 87. It is clear at this point of his argument that Farley has eliminated his own bridge paradigm espoused in the 1994 *Theology Today* article, namely, "the bringing of a past event to bear on a present situation." His focus now is on the present tense situation of the faith community and the way that it "lives, moves and has its being" in God. The preacher's task is to point to the living God at work to oppose corruption and renew hope.

33. Farley, *Practicing Gospel*, 88.

is the written record of God's people's life before God in the world. As the "discursive embodiment of the world of the Gospel" it norms the present day community of faith in two ways.[34]

One way that the new Israel's character as redemptive community became concretely manifest was that it shattered all boundaries of ethnicity, thus becoming *radically inclusive*. The community that would continue into the present will continue to embody this same ethno-clastic ideal. At the same time, it would embody the dialectic of its core message, namely that of *exposing and critiquing* the corruption of the time and the bringing to bear on that exposure and critique a *redemptive and hopeful word* from the world of the gospel.

The redeemed and redeeming community would be about the activities of exposing evil and instantiating freedom, love, and justice. Scripture continues to enrich this community with the resonance of its archived themes of redemption and by identifying the dissonance where the community has failed to live up to Scripture's depictions of redemption.

FARLEY: SACRED RHETORIC: A PRACTICAL THEOLOGY OF PREACHING—2003

Farley's third contribution to constructing a new paradigm for preaching addresses two problems that emerged from his continued analysis: 1) the relationship of five "constraints" or "criteria" for the new paradigm, and, 2) the need for preaching to transcend popular religion and piety. Finally, Farley begins to develop advice for preaching's necessary linguistic envelope, something he calls (to resurrect an old and oft maligned phrase) "sacred rhetoric."

Farley defines popular religion and piety as "finitized" versions of the sacred that a faith community necessarily constructs. Humans must make finite the infinite in order to make communication about the divine possible. Idolatry occurs when the finitized version becomes thought of as having a one-to-one correspondence with the infinite. When this occurs the religious community becomes very dangerous since its discourse "about what God wants or thinks, and even how God 'is,' coincides with what human beings do, think, write and create."[35] Farley is clear that this "finitizing idolatry of popular religion" is inescapable and preaching participates in it. What needs to happen alongside this idolatrous reductionism is an ongoing prophetic critique of the community's verbal formulations of faith. Thus

34. Farley, *Practicing Gospel*, 88.

35. Farley, *Practicing Gospel*, 94.

faithful communities live in a tension between finitizing reductionism and prophetic exposure of such reductionisms which aim to articulate "a desta-bilizing language of mystery."[36] "Preaching takes place in a dense, ambigu-ous, ever-changing congregational situation, marked by clashing paradigms on the use of Scripture, the status of popular religion, and congregational needs."[37] Thus, there is no single problem, as the bridge paradigm assumes, namely the bringing of the truth of a sermon-sized set of verses from the Bible to bear on the present, but a complex of problems and tasks. Farley identifies five "voices or criteria" that call preachers to their duties. These are preaching's 1) content, 2) audience, 3) tradition/text, 4) truth, and 5) ultimate reference.

1) Preaching's Content/the Gospel/the what of Preaching

What the gospel is takes on specific content in specific situations but no spe-cific content contains the totality of the world of the gospel. Nevertheless, for Farley, the gospel's world always pertains to redemptive transformation of some kind. This is what we see in Jesus' preaching of the kingdom of God, in Paul's preaching of the cross, and in Martin Luther King, Jr.'s preaching of freedom. When the Bible is preached, in the linear text-to-sermon bridge paradigm, varied views from disparate ancient authors become the (wrong) message with a tendency to moralism.

2) Audience/Congregational Situation/the to-which of Preaching

"Gospel is never something merely general or abstract. It is the good news of redemptive transformation addressed to specific, embodied, everyday life situations of oppression, lack of freedom, and despair."[38] Preaching's rhe-torical situation is a multifaceted web that includes a local congregation and its issues, but that congregation is not an island unto itself. It is imbedded in denominational and ecumenical networks, as well as the social, cultural, national, and global webs. Cognizant of these often conflicting influences, preachers speak from and into these complexes of influence. Preaching ordinarily takes place in the context of a community of faith gathered for worship, a fact that asserts its own constraints and criteria.

36. Farley, *Practicing Gospel*, 95.
37. Farley, *Practicing Gospel*, 95.
38. Farley, *Practicing Gospel*, 97.

3) Tradition/Text/the through-which of Preaching

Understanding how Scripture functions in preaching gospel is at the heart of Farley's programmatic new paradigm. He seeks a recovery of Scripture and truly biblical preaching by jettisoning the old, bridge, paradigm's insistence on preaching a discrete set of verses from the Bible. This move seeks to free Scripture to disclose the world of the gospel that is embedded in its various genres and theological trajectories. Scripture is not the *what* of preaching; it is the *through-which*.

While clear in his deconstruction of the bridge paradigm's use of the Bible, he is not so clear in his reconstruction of the Bible's place in preaching. I want to know what, concretely, this use of Scripture in preaching would look like. What would be helpful at this phase of his argument would be a critical analysis of a sermon that shows a use of Scripture that Farley deems credible. The image of *through-which*, however, is suggestive of a window or lens.[39]

4) The Question of Truth/the truth-of-which of Preaching

This is Farley's apology for the place of theology in the preacher's preparation. Rather than simply applying passages from the Bible rhetorically, the preacher must discern the truth that the Bible depicts in all the various ways that it does so. Simply repeating the Bible's words and metaphors (one hears a polemic against the postliberal school) does not get at the truth of these images for who God is and who we are as God's people today. "The preacher must probe further and ask how these motifs actually express something important, true, and real and whether they are extraneous to the Gospel."[40]

5) The Ultimate Reference/Divine Mystery/the for-which of Preaching

For Farley, this constraint permeates all other constraints and criteria. For this constraint is what makes preaching preaching and not mere human discourse about how to live and think. Verbal motifs that Scripture uses and that preachers formulate for present day hearers seek to bear witness to the presence of God, a presence that ever alludes literalistic capture.

---

39. This is similar to Calvin's famous depiction of Scripture as spectacles that give our dull vision a correction as we seek to see and know God. See Calvin, *Institutes*, 70.

40. Farley, *Practicing Gospel*, 98.

> Further, every motif in the world of the Gospel is brushed with
> the divine mystery: redemption, creation, divine presence, rev-
> elation, human evil, justice, the ecclesial community. Because
> the very meaning of all these things is tied up with the mysteri-
> ous Presence of God, each one carries with it a horizon, a refer-
> ent to something not known, something not quite articulated,
> something still expected.[41]

In affixing "sacred" to "rhetoric" Farley repeats an oxymoron from the homiletical tradition.[42] But that oxymoron is descriptive of an inherent tension in preaching's nature. For Farley the phrase is appropriate for describing a kind of language that the preacher must use, or create, that permits "all five constraints to resound."[43] The divine mystery "suffuses preaching's language with an aura of transcendence."[44] As such, preaching's language is inherently dialectical since its task is to "give voice to what cannot be voiced and communicate what cannot be communicated—the mystery of God."[45] Literal language flattens the gospel into mere "finitizing idolatries of popular religion."[46] To preach means to use language set "atremble" by the divine mystery, metaphor that "shimmers" with that mystery, all the while plotted by a dialectical expression "that constantly undermines itself, that indicates its own inadequacy."[47] The preacher's task is to find "words that bespeak the divine mystery."[48] A dialectic of metaphor, qualification, and negation is a necessary component of all the preacher's interpretive work. The only way clear is for the preacher to use language artfully to evoke the holy in such a way that it becomes an experience of beauty. Farley uses Jonathon Edwards's definition of beauty: "primary beauty (loveliness) is the disposition of a loving and compassionate heart toward the welfare of whatever is in being."[49] For Farley this is a definition of the holy and the world of the gospel and implies that preaching itself be an exercise in the creation of such beauty.

---

41. Farley, *Practicing Gospel*, 99.

42. I call the term *sacred rhetoric* an oxymoron with tongue only slightly in cheek as a nod to the checkered history that rhetoric has had since the Sophists in ancient Greece. As Thomas Sloane has said, "Often called the world's second-oldest profession, the teaching of rhetoric has probably derived as little benefit from books as has the world's oldest profession." See Sloane, *Encyclopedia of Rhetoric*, ix.

43. Farley, *Practicing Gospel*, 100.

44. Farley, *Practicing Gospel*, 101.

45. Farley, *Practicing Gospel*, 101.

46. Farley, *Practicing Gospel*, 101.

47. Farley, *Practicing Gospel*, 101.

48. Farley, *Practicing Gospel*, 102.

49. Farley, *Practicing Gospel*, 104.

Anticipating possible distortion, he warns that beauty not be confused with self-indulgence or entertainment. But that would only happen if the five constraints were compromised by a preacher's narcissistic misuse of preaching's art.

REFLECTIONS ON FARLEY'S CONTRIBUTIONS AND A PROPOSAL FOR RECENTERING PREACHING

As I noted earlier, Farley was not the first voice of protest regarding the traditional paradigm of preaching which uncritically and often unreflectively operated in a "text to sermon" movement, assuming that the gospel (or preachable X of preaching, or the message of preaching) was essentially guaranteed to be delivered to the preacher by means of a passage from the Bible.[50] Fundamentalists operate this way, as a matter of theological conviction regarding the nature of the Bible (cleverly named "pericopal theology").[51] But non-Fundamentalists, most often employing the historical critical method as their primary exegetical tool, do the same thing interestingly.[52] Strange bedfellows indeed.

50. The strongest voices of protest, and the most constructive, theological alternatives have been offered by Allen and Williamson, *A Credible and Timely Word*; Allen, "Why Preach from Passages in the Bible?"; Buttrick, "The Use of the Bible in Preaching"; Buttrick, *A Captive Voice*; Wilson, *The Four Pages of the Sermon*; Wilson, *Preaching and Homiletical Theory*; and Wilson, *Setting Words on Fire*.

51. Kuruvilla, *Text to Praxis*. When the inaugural gathering of the homiletics section of the Society of Biblical Literature occurred in Boston in 2008, Abraham Kuruvilla and I presented papers back to back. He argued for pericopal theology as the theological and methodological backbone for preaching. I then laid out Farley's argument, which was essentially the opposite of Kuruvilla's, and offered my evaluation of it. I watched carefully as (largely) the same people listened to both papers. I was struck by the fact that no one in the room seemed to have noticed what had just transpired. Kuruvilla and I, who sat next to each other on the dais, just looked at each other after the session then walked out in silence. It seemed odd at the time, but now it seems like it was probably the only thing he and I could do. It's certainly the way that the discipline tends to proceed, those with theologically and methodologically incompatible positions passing like ships in the night.

52. Best, *From Text to Sermon*, and many others. It's been interesting over the past twenty-five years to engage in informal conversations with homileticians old and young, usually at the annual meeting of the Academy of Homiletics (the annual professional meeting of teachers of preaching from North America, with increasing attendance by scholars from around the world) about Farley's challenge. Some find it intriguing, but aren't sure it's worth the effort to address it. Some find it altogether specious. Some are just wed to what has been passed down through the tradition, as if it cannot, should not, or need not be questioned. It raises an interesting question about how tradition gets challenged and altered, how entrenched paradigms get overturned and better ones take their place. I know one seminary that asked as part of its interview process for

For those willing to consider the methodological and theological problems that occur when a preacher gives voice to a given set of verses from a different locale within the Bible every week, Farley is a more than interesting conversation partner. In what follows I will summarize Farley's key contributions to this issue, pinpoint what I see as the most urgent thing his work calls us to in the discipline of homiletics, and finally I will make a proposal for a tripartite taxonomy for gospel that aims to bring theological clarity and methodological functionality.

Illuminating Exposure of a Problem Spot in the Prevailing Paradigm

An exposure of a problem is a prophetic action. As Garrison Keillor put it, the prophet tells people the truth that they have been successfully avoiding.[53] Traditions tend to calcify over time and operate unquestioningly. It sometimes takes someone from the outside to see something that the insiders have become largely unable to see.[54] The tradition of taking a biblical text in the assembly gathered for worship and then interpreting it for those gathered is so taken-for-granted that it's hard for some people to even understand what all the fuss is about. This may explain why some insiders to the homiletical conversation who raised red flags earlier about the problematic relationship between the Bible and the gospel in preaching were not seriously heard. Farley's provocative, even inflammatory, language (e.g., "a failed paradigm, fostering an impossible task for the preacher") functioned as a megaphone on the matter.[55]

If homileticians have ears to hear, I believe that one of the chief contributions Farley makes is a kind of prophetic exposure. He forces us to address the issues he raises. We cannot, in my opinion, avoid the questions. And to this point, not many have made any attempt to do so, which makes his challenge a continuing matter of importance in the discipline of homiletics.[56]

---

prospective teachers of preaching: "What do you think of Farley's challenge?" The follow up question was: "Are you currently, or do you plan to, address his challenge?"

53. Keillor, "Prophet."

54. Abraham Heschel asserted that humankind's chief problem was thinking we know what we see when we look at a situation, thus God had to send the prophets to expose what was really there. That's why the prophets are called "seers." "What impairs our sight are habits of seeing as well as the mental concomitants of seeing. Our sight is suffused with knowing, instead of feeling painfully the lack of knowing what we see." Heschel, *The Prophets*, xiii.

55. Farley, *Practicing Gospel*, 72.

56. On the downside, and hurting his own case, Farley may have overstated his case,

Yet, his exposure of problems in homiletics and preaching demands that we push for greater clarity in homiletical theory and preaching practice. Here are some of his some of his important exposures:

1. The discipline of homiletics is not clear about what gospel means and how it functions in preaching theory or practice.

2. Within the discipline there are simplistic and sometimes fundamentally wrong understandings of what the Bible is and how it functions in preaching.

3. There is a lack of clarity at best, and a complete miss at worst, on what the purpose of preaching is.[57]

4. The Bible and the gospel often have competing agendas and to preach a passage from the Bible may obscure the gospel or even preach "another gospel."[58]

5. The missing ingredient in preaching's operational paradigm is theology and the way that theology mediates one's exegetical work for use in preaching.

A Call For Clarity on What is Meant by "Gospel"

One outcome from Farley's work is the call for clarity on the matter of "gospel." Arguably, this is not just preaching's most important term, but the heart of preaching's concerns from the very beginning of the Christian era. Indeed, this may well be the most important term in Christian theology. Not that there's a competition for most important term, but consider this. The gospel-birthed Christianity fueled the expansion and growth of the Christian faith and community, and sustained and nurtured it through the centuries. The gospel is what has challenged Christian community during periods of complacency, and when the church lost its way in the world. It continues to give faith communities hope, impetus, and the power to fulfill its mission. Paul, arguably history's first homiletical theologian, made a number of provocative and suggestive claims for preaching and the gospel.

---

which has caused him to be dismissed by some or not taken seriously enough by others.

57. One of the best books in this regard continues to be Childers, ed., *Purposes of Preaching*.

58. Piecemeal proof-texting can yield whatever gospel the preacher imagines. This is how alternative gospels get traction with seeming "biblical" warrant. The health and wealth gospel, now the prosperity gospel, is a case in point.

For me the most outlandish was that the gospel extends itself through time, largely, though not exclusively, by means of proclamation.

This is why Farley's concern about the prevailing paradigm of preaching in our time is legitimate: "As a way of thinking about preaching, the bridge paradigm is clearly a departure from primitive Christian preaching as we find it described on the pages of the New Testament."[59] This indictment is on point, especially when I observe the lack of clarity in the field of homiletics on the most important matter of "What is the gospel?"

It is definitely one of the dirty little secrets in homiletics and preaching that there is no consensus on what is meant precisely when one uses the word *gospel*. A brief perusal in any number of books and articles on preaching shows that the word *gospel* gets thrown around like we all know what we're talking about, and we're all on the same page. But examine more closely and you'll see that often gospel is used as a synonym for many other things like "word," "message," even "Bible," "biblical passage," or it is simply and literally translated from the Greek as "good news, or "good news about Jesus Christ."[60] Other times it refers neatly and exclusively to some specific content, most often the life, death, and resurrection of Jesus. This lack of precision is problematic.

In any scholarly discipline, the way key terms in that discipline are understood, how they function, the limits of what a scholar means and does not mean by a key word, is crucial to the discipline being a discipline. This has not been the case with regard to the key word, *gospel*, in the discipline of homiletics and it may explain in part how homiletics has historically, and is currently, still trying to justify its existence as a legitimate, scholarly discipline.[61]

To punctuate this point, it is more than notable that neither of the two most important reference works on the history, theology, and practice of preaching—the *Concise Encyclopedia of Preaching* (1995) and *The New Interpreter's Handbook of Preaching* (2008)—include an article on gospel.

59. Farley, *Practicing Gospel*, 72.

60. McClure, *Preaching Words*, 44–46, has offered a constructive definition of gospel, yet being just a little over a page in length he cannot address all of the complicated issues involved. Allen and Williamson, *A Credible and Timely Word*, 103, define gospel as "the good news of God's unconditional love for each and every created thing and the command of God that justice be done for each and every created thing." (In personal correspondence, Allen indicates that he would now substitute the word "persistent" for "unconditional.") This definition functions for them as a check on any witness of a biblical text that is being used in preaching.

61. Paul Scott Wilson has been one clear voice calling homileticians to account for doing their work in silos rather than in scholarly conversation with other pertinent voices in the field. See Wilson, *Preaching and Homiletical Theory*.

RECENTERING PREACHING BY WAY OF A
TRIPARTITE TAXONOMY OF GOSPEL

All this is to say that a clearer and more systematic way of thinking about gospel is in order. I am proposing here a tripartite taxonomy for gospel, three rubrics that categorize for homileticians and preachers alike the nature of gospel as:

1) *Previous Situational Witness*, i.e., concrete instances in the past of witness-bearing to the gospel. These are, to borrow Farley's term, finitized (fragile, time-bound, and situation-specific) versions of the gospel.

2) *Grammatical Substructure* to all faithful and fitting witness-bearing to the gospel. To speak of a grammatical substructure to the gospel is to describe a dynamic behind and within the particular witness that causes it to ring true to what we know gospel to be. The grammar of the gospel has elements of both form and substance.

3) *Working-Gospel.* This is a preacher's always-in-process core belief and central conviction about the center of the good news of God's redemptive work in the world. Every preacher's in-process, working-gospel serves a hermeneutical role in the reading of Scripture for preaching gospel.

A Proposal for a Tripartite Taxonomy of Gospel

Previous Situational Witness: Finitized Versions of the Gospel

Perhaps the most confusing aspect getting a grip on how to understand *gospel* is the variety of ways the term has been used, even within the Bible itself. Within the first fifteen verses of the Gospel According to Mark, the term *euangelion* (Greek for "gospel" or "good news") is used four different ways (if you include the title to the document, Mark 1:1). None of those connotations coheres with what Paul means by his use of the term, but even Paul is not monolithic in his usage. Luke's usage of the term is also interesting and diverse. John never uses the word in his Gospel or epistles.

One can become paralyzed when trying to make sense of the term when there are so many different connotations afloat. When Edward Farley said that the "Gospel is not a thing to be defined," he was grappling primarily with the tendency to define gospel in terms of its past expressions. Which of these is definitive, if any?

Farley meant that no single expression of the kerygma should be considered definitive. He insisted that gospel not be limited to any specific, static content. Rather, he urged preachers to examine the world of the gospel, a world to which Scripture bears witness. The world of the gospel, which includes things such as grace, justice, etc., is not to be confined to temporal expression.

Yet temporal expression of gospel, insofar as it extends out from the gospel world, is a necessary act of Christian existence and witness, including preaching. Farley calls these temporal expressions finitized versions of the sacred. They are time-bound, situation specific, and thus fragile and fallible. Though these finitized versions of the sacred are necessarily reductive and borderline idolizations of popular religion, they are necessary since the gospel is always a present tense expression of God's redemptive work in the world. Yet, once they are expressed, they become part of the church's previous situational witness.

In the taxonomy I am proposing, all prior moments of Christian witness are put under the rubric of *Gospel as Previous Situational Witness*. All have been attempts by witness-bearers to speak or enact gospel in particular places and times.

It can be argued that the "event of Christ," as it's often called, is the greatest finite formulation and witness to gospel because it points to the most momentous expression of God's redemptive work. Yet even if that is the case, it is still only one of the many concrete, time-bound, fragile, and situational witnesses to gospel. All others may point toward that event or back to that momentous event, but even so it does not forgo other instances of gospel that follow the a similar pattern of God's redemptive working in the world.

In addition, simply to repeat the actions of that event as they transpired in time does not express what those events meant and mean. "Christ has died, Christ has risen, Christ will come again" may repeat a tried and true liturgical witness, but what difference those confessional statements make for anyone and how they function as gospel declaration is far from self-evident.

One can also point to the pivotal, and arguably most significant witness to God's gospel in the First Testament, the exodus from Egypt. But one could also point to the moment that Moses is summoned to the burning bush and given his call. One could point to many similarly redemptive moments and name them as gospel, even smaller moments such as Jesus stopping for a man with a skin disease, touching him, and healing him (Mark

1:40–45). The Bible is full of such moments and each of them fit under this rubric of previous situational witness to the gospel, all of which are finitized versions of gospel.

The ongoing moments of Christian witness in the history of Christianity also fit under this rubric, including the sermons in the preaching tradition. Acknowledging this aspect of gospel's taxonomy answers the question as to why a study and exposition of a biblical text is not necessarily an instance of proclaiming the gospel. If the preacher stays solely within the confines of the previous witness, there is unlikely to be a present tense claim made on the contemporary hearers.[62]

Underlying Form and Substance: The Grammar of the Gospel

Farley identifies a dynamic inherent to the gospel, what I and others would call a deep structure or grammar, based on the nature of God's redemptive working in situations of compromise.[63] In any given language, there are constraints for what makes for proper sentence structure, and if these constraints or rules are violated, meaning is compromised. There is wide latitude for expression, of course, and deft wordsmiths and poets can riff in a variety of creative ways that defy grammatical logic, yet still work. Thus, in this second rubric I have not put a fixed restriction on any given, situational expression of the gospel. I do identify, however, both a form and substance that pertains to gospel preaching.

With regard to form, one way of understanding gospel syntax is to recognize a dialectic at its core. For Farley, that dialectic is corruption and redemption, critique and hope, or disruption of corruption and presentation of hope, though as Lischer and others have shown, the antitheses are almost endless.[64] What is signaled here is a "from . . . to . . ." dynamic. Though he does not use this language, one can see how the gospel's grammar has, as Wilson has emphasized, a bad news/good news cadence to it.[65]

With regard to substance, the gospel's deep grammar always has to do with God's redemptive transformation.[66] Redemptive transformation, the

---

62. To fill out the first rubric in the taxonomy I would consider the canons and criteria for assessing Christian witness. Space does not permit here, but Allen and Williamson, *A Credible and Timely Word*, ch. 5, and Wood, *Vision and Discernment*, provide helpful theological criteria for beginning the assessment process.

63. See Wilson, *Preaching and Homiletical Theory*, and Resner, *Living In-Between*.

64. Farley, *Practicing Gospel*, 85.

65. Wilson, *The Four Pages of the Sermon*.

66. This is true even of prophetic discourse that from all appearances may only appear as judgment or criticism. The good news of God's prophetic critique is that

heart of God's gospel activity, is necessary because of violations of God's good creation. Farley calls this aspect of the gospel, "preaching as a discourse of redemption."[67] The gospel is God's ongoing response to any reality that stands at variance to the vision of God's peaceful and peaceable kingdom.[68]

As I have described elsewhere, another way of describing the gospel's substructural grammatical dynamic is in its prophetic dynamic as the activity of gap-filling.

> Justice may be thought of as words and actions taken to close the gap between God's vision for healthy, loving, and harmonious community life and the reality of a broken, violent, and fearful world. Preaching social justice moves from the exposure and indictment of violations to the presentation of God's vision for healthy, whole, and peaceful life in community.[69]

This way of describing prophetic preaching does not prescribe any particular form or content, but it does describe the contours of the practice that pertain to authentic expressions of it. Note that inherent to this description is the dialectical element between God's vision and a compromised reality in the world, the bad news/good news cadence between vision and reality, the "from . . . to . . ." characteristic, all of which point to the redemptive pattern of God's gospel activity. Farley, too, notes how there is a substructual grammar to prophetic preaching as gospel witness:

> The world of the gospel does have certain recurring themes, even a certain structure . . . Gospel is—and this is its prophetic element—disruption, an exposure of corporate oppression and individual collusion, and, at the same time, an uncovering of redemptive possibilities. To say it is the good news of the [realm] of God is to say both of these things. And those who find themselves proclaiming these good tidings will surely be drawn to understanding the reality and power of the deep symbols in the world of the Gospel.[70]

God draws a line and unmasks our idolatries and violations to shalom and harmonious community life. One preacher likened this to a mother screaming at her little girl who is running headlong into the street and a moving vehicle. The child is frightened, but she also stops, and lives.

67. Farley *Practicing Gospel*, 84–85.

68. In describing his own grammatical construal of gospel, Wilson points to Michael Root's description of redemption's inherent movement: "a state of deprivation (sin, corruption) and a state of release from that deprivation (salvation, liberation)." See Wilson, *The Four Pages of the Sermon*, 24.

69. Resner, "Social Justice," 135.

70. Farley, *Practicing Gospel*, 81.

Preaching that participates in the world of the gospel of God has a fidelity to its underlying, deep structure, contours and can be assessed based on that fidelity. This realization heightens the need for preachers to be clear about the deep grammar at the heart of their own theologies of the gospel.

Working-Gospel: In-Process Synopsis and Hermeneutical Guide

The third rubric in the taxonomy of the gospel is "working-gospel."[71] Though usually not fully conscious of it, every preacher has what I call a "working-gospel." I will briefly describe three dimensions of working-gospel.

1) A working-gospel is a synoptic view and theological perspective on the heart and core of what Christianity is all about, what God's chief involvement with creation is, and how humankind is involved as well (theological anthropology). Elsewhere I have described the preacher's working-gospel as treating four questions: what is wrong, what is God is doing about it, what difference does it make, and how will it end?[72] One's "working gospel" is one's ongoing process of discerning the ways that God is at work in the world to accomplish what God wants done in human and divine relations. It is shaped by our multilayered experiences with life, with the Bible, with worship and the community of faith, ordinary life experiences, but perhaps especially with those experiences at the edges and limits of life moments, such as times of trauma and loss. "This is because our efforts to make meaning from our most important resources for meaning-making, like Scripture and worship, kick into gear at such times." I describe the notion of working-gospel at present this way: "The gospel is something that God does, that human beings cannot do for themselves, that concretely changes a situation from . . . to . . ." The "from . . . to . . ." dynamic is not specifically named

---

71. Tracy, *The Analogical Imagination*, 254. I coined the term "working-gospel" by analogy to Tracy's category "working canon," a term he believed to be more accurate than "canon within the canon" in describing how interpreters actually use the Bible in theological formulations. He argued that in reality theologians have a "working canon," an ever-flexing and evolving perspective of Scripture's influence on their thinking. The "working canon" idea allows for the criteria of fidelity as well as flexibility for diversity of expression. He says that one need not fear a "rubber ruler," i.e., the ability to say just anything about God and the kerygma. In the same way, with the idea of a "working-gospel" I do not think that preachers need fear a "Gumby gospel," something so flexible that it departs from the key instantiations of gospel from Israel's and the church's historical and testimonial record. According to Tracy, one's "working canon" is under constant negotiation based on one's continued reading of various parts of Scripture and the influence such readings have on the ongoing reshaping of one's theological convictions. The same holds for one's "working-gospel."

72. Resner, *Living In-Between*, 4–8.

because I do not know how my context or my various conversation partners for the sermon, including Scripture, will fill in the ellipses. Nevertheless, to be "grammatically correct," the sermon will participate at some level in the syntactical dynamic of "from . . . to . . ." Reflecting my personal perspective on working-gospel, I follow the lead of Paul's portrayal of the gospel in Romans 8 and 1 Corinthians especially, where he portrays an apocalyptically shaped gospel. Within the apocalyptic worldview, when God breaks into this world to work redemptive transformation, it is always somewhat incomplete while at the same time bearing witness to a hope in God's ultimate finalization and rectification of all things.[73]

2) Working-gospel serves a hermeneutical, i.e., interpretive, function in helping the preacher read Scripture with a view to discerning what God has done and is doing to address, undress, and redress situations where God's desired state of being has been violated.[74] Reading the Bible to preach the gospel has this presupposition: that gospel preachers are to continue to look for and assert God's vision for how things ought to be in a world where powers in opposition to God's will and way work to thwart that vision. The Bible helps us see that vision and refine our vision, and the continual rub of ourselves with the biblical vision for God's shalom, refines and reshapes what we understand to be the heart of things. Of course, there is no singular "vision" within the biblical record. Elsewhere I have highlighted the vision within the prophetic record of a community of shalom: "Preaching the gospel is the act of bearing witness to the actions of God, actions which work, primarily, for the purposes of right relationship. God's desire is that love, harmony, goodwill, reverence, justice, and compassion characterize all relations . . . It is not too much to say that all God's actions work toward the end of God's peaceful and peaceable [Dominion]."[75]

3) From a pedagogical standpoint, identifying the working-gospel of the preacher/interpreter provides a heuristic portal into their entire homiletical theology, how they read the world, Scripture, and what needs to be said, why, and how. Starting with a descriptive analysis of the preacher's

73. See Resner, *Preacher and Cross*, Kay, "The Word of the Cross," and Resner, *Living In-Between.*

74. J. Christiaan Beker's work on Paul is helpful for preachers here. For every "contingent situation" that was in violation of the gospel or the church's life as the body of Christ, Paul would bring some aspect of the "coherent core" of the gospel. Paul never wrote about the gospel in the abstract, but rather brought different aspects of the gospel to bear on specific needs and situations. The situation was what determined for Paul the aspect of the gospel that he would bring to bear. In homiletical terms, the bad news situation of the hearers would be the key for knowing what aspect of the Good News was more appropriate for that people at that time. See Beker, *Paul the Apostle.*

75. See Resner, "At Cross Purposes," 55.

working-gospel gets one beyond the "right" and "wrong" dilemma of evaluation of sermons. The teacher of preaching is not looking at the preacher from one's own vantage point and how one might treat a particular text or shape the sermon, but from the vantage point of the preacher. Teaching preaching requires an attentive and empathetic posture. The teacher asks above all else, what is this preacher trying to say and why? What drives this message for the preacher? The gospel has potential to be perceived in a wide variety of ways depending on a myriad of factors from one's personal history, ecclesial traditioning, gender, socio-economic status, ethnicity, etc. The most helpful thing the teacher of preaching can do in this regard is listen carefully to each preacher first to discern what's going on in their articulation of the gospel. This is why, in teaching introductory preaching courses, I always start with the sermons of my students. I hear what my students bring before I say anything about what I believe about preaching or preaching's gospel. Preaching pedagogy isn't really about my working gospel or how I think preaching ought to be done. It is about hearing what each student thinks it is and working from there.

Augustine is an interesting case study in how one's working gospel affects one's reading of the Bible and one's use of the Bible in preaching. As we observed earlier, Augustine described the study of scripture for preaching as essentially a bi-fold activity: one first interprets what the text says, then one articulates what one has interpreted. This seems to fit well with the traditional bridge paradigm, though it does leave some questions unanswered, such as, what if a particular text's meaning is obscure? How does one preach from a difficult text whose meaning is not clear? I choose Augustine as my case study here because his theological commitments, his working-gospel that informs how he interprets what is most appropriate in the Bible for the purposes of preaching make the major point of this essay.

In his laying out his guidelines for interpretation, Augustine lands on what for him is the center of Scripture's, and thus God's, concerns: love. Specifically love of God and of neighbor.[76] Once he's arrived at Scripture's center and focus, he pivots to make that "working-gospel" his hermeneutical guide in reading scripture for preaching.

> Whoever, therefore, thinks that he understands the divine scriptures or any part of them so that it does not build the double love of God and of our neighbor does not understand it at all. Whoever finds a lesson there useful to the building of charity, even though he has not said what the author may be shown to have intended in that place, has not been deceived, nor is he

---

76. Augustine, *On Christian Doctrine*, bk. I, chs. 25–35.

lying in any way . . . [A]s I began to explain, if he is deceived in
an interpretation which builds up charity, which is the end of
the commandments, he is deceived in the same way as a man
who leaves a road by mistake but passes through a field to the
same place toward which the road itself leads.[77]

We would typically label that eisegesis (an imposing onto the text a
meaning foreign to it) a high crime and misdemeanor in exegetical court.
Yet Augustine is guided hermeneutically and theologically by two places in
the Bible where he believes he has hit on the center and core of scripture's
message: 1) the great commandments to love God and neighbor, and, 2) 1
Corinthians 13, especially its conclusion, "And now faith, hope, and love
abide, these three; and the greatest of these is love." These, to Augustine,
following his working-gospel, are the most important guidelines for interpreting the Bible.

In this every student of the Divine Scriptures must exercise himself, having found nothing else in them except, first, that God
is to be loved for Himself, and his neighbor the sake of God;
second, that he is to love God with all his heart, with all his soul,
and with all his mind; and third, that he should love his neighbor as himself, that is, so that all love for our neighbor should,
like all for ourselves, be referred to God. Then it follows that
the student first will discover in the Scriptures that he has been
enmeshed in the love of this world, or of temporal things, a love
far remote from the kind of love of God and of our neighbor
which Scripture itself prescribes.[78]

In Book III Augustine shows us concretely how this hermeneutical
and theological orientation to interpreting Scripture through the lens of
love of God and love of neighbor plays out. Figurative language in Scripture
raises particular questions about meaning.[79] So in order to make sure that
figurative language is handled rightly one should think thusly: "Therefore in
the consideration of figurative expressions a rule such as this will serve, that
what is read should be subjected to diligent scrutiny until an interpretation

77. Augustine, *On Christian Doctrine*, bk. 1, ch. 36, para. 40–41.

78. Augustine, *On Christian Doctrine*, bk. II, ch. VII, para. 10.

79. I am convinced that the early church's use of allegory in preaching was a creative
effort in which the preacher's working-gospel hijacked any text it encountered, turning
the various features of the text into a vehicle for the preacher to proclaim what he (or
she) believed was most pertinent for that day and place. The theological competence
of allegorical preaching (regardless of its exegetical questionableness) is completely
dependent on the theological competence of the preacher and the sturdiness of his (or
her) working-gospel.

contributing to the reign of charity is produced.[80]" This will begin to work itself out in the actual interplay of texts where Augustine urges interpreters to the practice of explaining obscure texts by means of clearer texts. The clearer texts are those that express Augustine's working gospel of love. So when he encounters a line in Psalm 35:2, ultimately he needs Ephesians 6:16 as the key to unlock its mystery.

> In no better way may we understand what is said to God in "Take hold of arms and shield: and rise up to help me than by consulting that passage which reads, "O Lord, thou hast crowned us, as with a shield of thy good will." But we should not pursue this practice in such a way that everywhere we read of a shield raised for defense we should think of nothing except the good will of God; for it is also said that there is "the shield of faith, wherewith you may be able to extinguish all the fiery darts of the most wicked one." Nor again with reference to this kind of spiritual armor must we attribute faith to the shield alone, since in another place the breastplate is said to be faith: "having on," he says, "the breastplate of faith and charity."[81]

As contemporary interpreters, Augustine's treatment of the text here may make us cringe, but if you are a teacher of preaching, you have heard students, as well as seasoned preachers, do similar things with the Bible in preaching. Our impulse as pedagogues is to guide the student to a better use of Scripture so Psalm 35's integrity is maintained at the same time as that of Psalm 5 and Ephesians 6. But the teacher can learn something very important by listening carefully to what the student is doing, namely unveiling his or her working understanding of the gospel. Their hermeneutical gymnastics, bouncing here and there throughout the Bible, playing fast and loose with the text, is actually a theologically coherent action from the vantage point of their working gospel. That doesn't, of course, mean that anything goes in interpretation. Rather, it helps the teacher know what the core belief of the student is. Pedagogically the teacher can now work from where the student really is theologically, to better readings of the texts, to sharper, more critically aware formulations of their working gospel, and to more incisive and fitting instanciations (finitizations) of the gospel in their preaching.

80. Augustine, *On Christian Doctrine*, bk. III, ch. 15, para. 23.
81. Augustine, *On Christian Doctrine*, bk. III, ch. 26.

CONCLUSION

This essay began with an observation that an accident of history, the early church's adoption of the synagogue practice of reading Scripture in the assembly and then engaging in interpretation of that Scripture for those gathered, supplanted the early church's proclamation of the gospel, a Spirit-inspired and empowered proclamation that was not necessarily tied to an interpretation or exposition of a biblical text. Calling an entire discipline (homiletics) and ministerial practice (preaching) back to its roots and core, Edward Farley sought to reroute preaching by way of the gospel. Building off of his work, and addressing a lack of clarity about preaching's central term, gospel, I propose a recentering of preaching by way of a tripartite taxonomy of gospel that takes into account its three historic and theological dimensions: 1) the times of its historic deployment by preachers in various places, at various times, and in various ways: the church's *Previous Situational Witness*. These are instances of Christian witness, which are finitized versions of the gospel (i.e., time-bound, situation specific addresses) each with their own strengths and weaknesses. 2) Authentic Christian witness participates in a deep structure inherent to gospel proclamation, a *Grammatical Sub-Structure*, that has elements of both form (e.g., from . . . to . . .) and substance (e.g., redemptive transformation of situations of compromise and violation of God's good creation). 3) The last rubric in the taxonomy is the always-in-process *Working-Gospel* of the preacher. This is the preacher's synoptic understanding of the central matters pertaining to God and what God is doing to address our world in a redemptive and transformative manner. The preacher's working gospel functions hermeneutically when the preacher reads the Bible with a view to preaching the gospel. It discerns in reading the Bible and evaluating the context of preaching, what in the text should be preached as gospel.

To touch on the theme of this book, one of the things that is right about preaching today is the theological turn toward the gospel as the most appropriate orienting posture for preaching, for the interpretation of the Bible for preaching, and for assessing our socio-cultural contexts with a view to proclaiming God's gospel anew. To recenter homiletics and preaching on the gospel has profound implications for clarifying preachers' purposes and their use of the Bible, but no one should fear that such a turn constitutes a reduction of Scripture's authority. As John Barton asserted, "If we start at the centre with the gospel of Christ, we shall have no difficulty at all in discovering how indispensable the Bible is."[82]

---

82. Barton, *People of the Book?*, 89.

BIBLIOGRAPHY

Allen, Ronald J. "Why Preaching from Passages in the Bible?" In *Preaching as a Theological Task: World, Gospel, Scripture*, edited by Thomas G. Long and Edward Farley, 176–88. Louisville: Westminster John Knox, 1996.

Allen, Ronald J., and Clark Williamson. *A Credible and Timely Word: Process Theology and Preaching*. St. Louis, MO: Chalice, 1991.

Augustine. *On Christian Doctrine*. Translated, with an introduction by D. W. Robertston Jr. Indianapolis: Bobbs-Merrill, 1958.

———. *On Christian Doctrine*. https://faculty.georgetown.edu/jod/augustine/ddc1.html, accessed 5/21/2020.

Barr, James. *The Scope and Authority of the Bible*. Philadelphia: Fortress, 1980.

Barton, John. *People of the Book? The Authority of the Bible in Christianity*. Louisville: Westminster John Knox, 1988.

Beker, J. Christiaan. *Paul the Apostle: The Triumph of God in Life and Thought*. Philadelphia: Fortress, 1980.

Best, Ernest. *From Text to Sermon: Responsible Use of the New Testament in Preaching*. Louisville: John Knox, 1978.

Boers, Hendrikus. "Historical Criticism Versus Prophetic Proclamation." *Harvard Theological Review* 65 (1972) 393–414.

Buttrick, David. *A Captive Voice: The Liberation of Preaching*. Louisville: Westminster John Knox, 1994.

———. "The Use of the Bible in Preaching." *The New Interpreter's Bible*, vol. 1, edited by Leander E. Keck, 188–99. Nashville: Abingdon, 1994.

Calvin, John. *Institutes of the Christian Religion*, vol. 1. Edited by John T. McNeill. Translated by Ford Lewis Battles. Louisville: Westminster John Knox, 1960.

Childers, Jana, ed. *Purposes of Preaching*. St. Louis, MO: Chalice, 2004.

Craddock, Fred B. *Preaching*. Nashville: Abingdon, 1985.

———. "The Sermon and the Uses of Scripture." *Theology Today* 42 (1985) 7–14.

Farley, Edward. *Practicing Gospel: Unconventional Thoughts on the Practice of Ministry*. Louisville: Westminster John Knox, 2003.

———. *Theologia: The Fragmentation and Unity of Theological Education*. Philadelphia: Fortress, 1983.

Farris, Stephen. *Preaching that Matters: The Bible and Our Lives*. Louisville: Westminster John Knox, 1998.

Franklin, Robert M. *Crisis in the Village: Restoring Hope in African American Communities*. Minneapolis: Fortress, 2007.

Gadamer, Hans Georg. *Truth and Method*. New York: Seabury, 1975.

Graves, Mike, ed. *What's the Matter with Preaching Today?* Louisville: Westminster John Knox, 2004.

Herbert, George. "The Windows." In *George Herbert and Henry Vaughan*, edited by Louis L. Martz, 58. London: Oxford University Press, 1986.

Heschel, Abraham. *The Prophets*. Peabody, MA: Hendrickson, 2007.

Kay, James F. "The Word of the Cross at the Turn of the Ages." *Interpretation* 53 (1999) 44–56.

———. *Preaching and Theology*. St. Louis, MO: Chalice, 2007.

Keck, Leander. *The Bible in the Pulpit: The Renewal of Biblical Preaching*. Nashville,: Abingdon, 1978.

Keillor, Garrison. "Prophet." *Lake Wobegon, USA: Fertility.* Cassette: HighBridge Company, August 13, 2010. Also available at https://www.youtube.com/watch?v=8exNJkoBa8.

Kelsey, David. *The Uses of Scripture in Recent Theology.* Philadelphia: Fortress, 1975.

Kuruvilla, Abraham. *Text to Praxis: Hermeneutics and Homiletics in Dialogue.* London: T&T Clark, 2009.

Lischer, Richard. *A Theology of Preaching: The Dynamics of the Gospel.* Nashville: Abingdon, 1980.

Long, Thomas G. "The Use of Scripture in Contemporary Preaching." *Interpretation* 44 (1990) 341–52.

————. "The Use of Scripture in the Sermons of Barbara Brown Taylor." *Anglican Theological Review* 99 (2017) 291–97.

McClure, John S. *Preaching Words: 144 Key Terms in Homiletics.* Louisville: Westminster John Knox, 2007.

McGee, Paula. *Brand New Theology: The Walmartization of T. D. Jakes and the New Black Church.* Maryknoll, NY: Orbis, 2017.

Miller, Donald G. *The Way to Biblical Preaching: How to Communicate the Gospel in Depth.* Nashville: Abingdon, 1957.

Palazzo, Eric. *A History of Liturgical Books from the Beginning to the Thirteenth Century.* Collegeville, MN: Liturgical, 1988.

Resner, André. "At Cross Purposes: Gospel, Scripture, and Experience in Preaching." *Preaching Autobiography: Connecting the World of the Preaching and the World of the Text,* edited by Dave Bland and David Fleer, 47–74. Abilene, TX: ACU Press, 2001.

————. "Do You See This Woman? A Little Exercise in Homiletical Theology." In *Theologies of the Gospel in Context: The Crux of Homiletical Theology,* vol. 3, The Promise of Homiletical Theology, edited by David Schnasa Jacobsen, 15–41. Eugene, OR: Cascade, 2017.

————. *Just Preaching: Prophetic Voices for Economic Justice.* St. Louis, MO: Chalice, 2003.

————. *Living In-Between: Lament, Justice, and the Persistence of the Gospel.* Eugene, OR: Wipf and Stock, 2015.

————. "Logos." *The New Interpreter's Handbook of Preaching,* edited by Paul Scott Wilson, 353–54. Nashville: Abingdon, 2008.

————. *Preacher and Cross: Person and Message in Theology and Rhetoric.* Grand Rapids: Eerdmans, 1999.

————. "Preacher as God's Mystery Steward: Preaching Healing in an Apocalyptic Frame." In *Slow of Speech and Unclean Lips: Contemporary Images of Preaching Identity,* edited by Stephen Reid, 57–88. Eugene, OR: Wipf and Stock, 2010.

————. "Reading the Bible for Preaching the Gospel." Paper presented at the 2008 annual meeting of the Academy of Homiletics and at the 2008 Society of Biblical Literature Convention, both in Boston.

————. "Social Justice." In *The New Interpreter's Handbook of Preaching,* edited by Paul Scott Wilson, 135–37. Nashville: Abingdon, 2008.

Sloane, Thomas O., ed. *Encyclopedia of Rhetoric.* New York: Oxford University Press, 2001.

Thomas, Frank A. *They Like to Never Quit Praisin' God: The Role of Celebration in Preaching.* Revised and updated ed. Cleveland, OH: Pilgrim, 2013.

Tracy, David. *The Analogical Imagination: Christian Theology and the Culture of Pluralism*. New York: Crossroad, 1989.

Wilson, Paul Scott. *The Four Pages of the Sermon: A Guide to Biblical Preaching*. Revised and updated ed. Nashville: Abingdon, 2018.

_____. *Preaching and Homiletical Theory*. St. Louis, MO: Chalice, 2004.

_____. *Setting Words on Fire: Putting God at the Center of the Sermon*. Nashville: Abingdon, 2008.

Wilson, Paul Scott, gen. ed. *The New Interpreter's Handbook of Preaching*. Nashville: Abingdon, 2008.

Wolterstorff, Nicholas. "Justice and Worship: The Tragedy of Liturgy in Protestantism." In *Until Justice and Peace Embrace*, 146–61. Grand Rapids: Eerdmans, 1983.

_____. "Justice as a Condition of Authentic Worship." *Theology Today* 48:1 (1991) 6–21.

Wood, Charles. *Vision and Discernment: An Orientation in Theological Study*. Atlanta: Scholars, 1985.

MY LAST MINUTE LION'S CLUB SPEECH

Remembering Fred

Houston Bowers

IT WAS THE 1960 FALL SEMESTER AT PHILLIPS UNIVERSITY, AND I WAS A junior who had registered for a three-hour class in homiletics taught by Fred Craddock. While I had heard Professor Craddock preach in chapel on several occasions, what truly excited me was the fact that I was finally taking a class in the very thing I wanted to learn. I was going to learn to preach! I will always remember the first day the class met. Professor Craddock said, "I am assuming that each person in this class has felt a call to ministry and hopes one day to preach in front of a congregation. Therefore, I am teaching this class with that in mind."

Professor Craddock reviewed the syllabus and class requirements, which included preaching three sermons from a list of Scriptures, then verbally added a terrifying item, "I will call you the night before one of your class sermons and give you a surprise assignment in addition to the sermon." I was hard at work on my first sermon when Professor Craddock called me posing as the board chairman of the fictional church I was serving and told me he was the president of a Lion's Club whose speaker for the next day's noontime meeting was ill. "As my minister, I hope you can help me out," he said. He also made sure I was aware that my ten-minute presentation would be done for a club that had a lot of fun at meetings and disliked "stuffy preachers." Professor Craddock ended the conversation by thanking me for helping him "in a pinch." Since I was already having trouble with my first sermon in the class, I was, to say the least, stunned by the request. Throughout the semester, all my classmates received similar calls the night before they were scheduled to preach. All of us learned that PTA presentations, funeral meditations, and other requests to speak could be added to our list of ministerial duties when we served a church.

When, throughout my fifty years of ministry, I have been charged with the daunting task of unexpectedly searching for the right Scripture and words to meet the needs of people in congregations and communities, I remember the wisdom of Fred Craddock and how fortunate I was to be his student in two undergraduate homiletics classes.

"FRED CRADDOCK HAS NO PEER"

A Remembrance of Fred

Eugene L. Lowry

"Do you know Fred Craddock?"—a new student asked me, early on in my teaching of preaching. "No," I replied. "Who is he?" "Well, he teaches preaching at Phillips Seminary in Oklahoma. He just published a book that sounds a whole lot like how you talk about preaching." Immediately I looked him up. I have been looking up to him ever since.

We all are blessed beyond measure to have this world-renowned biblical scholar also be one who can then lead us with the text into a powerful sermonic design, enabling the word to become manifest in the world.

His depth of thought, his missional mind, and his communicational style all emerge by means of simple uncluttered sentences—empowered by the potency of sensory metaphors. His understanding of what he calls "triggering the mind" has enabled thousands of preachers to begin learning how to use the kind of language that serves "not to utter, but to evoke."

For example, the third sentence of one sermon begins: "The word is 'bitter.' Do you see a face? I see a face. I see the face of a farmer in western Oklahoma, riding a mortgaged tractor, burning gasoline purchased on credit, moving across rented land, rearranging the dust. Bitter." And the title of that sermon? "Praying Through Clenched Teeth." Oh, the juxtaposition!

And he makes a point of not concluding the sermon with the gospel's imperative claim. Too pushy. Rather, he returns with a *half*-reprise of the already named good news. Now, all feel like the closing sentence is about to be spoken. But no! No, he is walking back from the pulpit to take a seat. Oh my!

A number of years ago I underwent a bone biopsy on my hip. Upon my waking, the technician asked: "Who is Fred Craddock?" I inquired whether she might be a member of a Disciples congregation. "No, it is that, during the procedure, you kept repeating a name—saying 'Fred Craddock has no peer; Fred Craddock has no peer.'" To which I said: "There is only one reason I would have said that. Fred Craddock has no peer!"

ON FIXING A BROKEN SERMON

A Remembrance of Fred

Brian Nelson

EACH YEAR IN MY PASTORAL MINISTRY, I TOOK A STUDY LEAVE. IN 1980 I decided to take the course "Parabolic Preaching" that Fred was teaching in summer school at Candler School of Theology. I was the only post-seminary, practicing pastor in a class with Methodist seminarians.

Near the end of the course, Fred asked if any students would like to preach a sermon using what had been learned in class. One eager young student volunteered to preach a sermon in class. He preached on the story of Jesus and the Samaritan woman at the well. I held my breath as he finished. His sermon was terrible. I could not think what Fred could say.

Fred walked to the chalk board. "Let's see if we can work on it a little," he said as he began listing points in the young man's sermon. Then he began to rearrange them and change the emphasis of others. I watched awestruck as Fred shaped a powerful sermon using only the elements the young man had preached. Then, turning to the student, he asked: "What do you think?"

I know what I thought. It was a moment of powerful grace!

— 9 —

FINDING "SOUL" IN DELIVERY

Richard F. Ward

IN AN INTERVIEW WITH FRED CRADDOCK, DAY 1'S PETER WALLACE ASKED: "how should preachers improve their delivery?" That question takes us right to heart of the preaching moment—how preachers and their listeners are engaged with each other in the act of proclamation. How best to prepare for those moments? Craddock's answer began with a lament: "Too many candidates arrive at the first day of preaching class without ever having a speech course." He is evoking memories of an earlier era of theological education when younger candidates for ministry (usually men) were equipped with fresh experiences of undergraduate education as preparation for ministry. Training in public speaking in many cases was part of that liberal arts education and could be more easily assumed as adequate preparation for preaching.

Then things began to change. Older students with diverse backgrounds started coming to the seminary and for many of them undergraduate education was a distant memory. Preparatory training in public speaking could no longer be assumed. To cope with changes like these, homiletics began to busy itself with concerns with *how* a preacher should use one's voice or gesture with one's body so that the sermon could come to life. It cultivated its relationship with traditions of speech instruction to help with these matters. You can hear an echo of that relationship later in the interview when Craddock advises those who lack an adequate background in public speaking to "get a few sessions with a voice teacher, or someone who reads well publicly, who knows how to get you to lift the face and the voice."[1]

TEACHING SPEECH IN A THEOLOGICAL SCHOOL

I joined the faculty of Candler School of Theology precisely to be the person Craddock describes in the interview. I arrived with a fresh doctorate in the field of Performance Studies, awarded from the School of Speech at Northwestern University. My goal was to put into practice what I had learned about enlivening literary texts by means of oral interpretation and using voice and body to bring thought to life through speech. I was hired to teach speech communication to aspiring preachers at Candler School of Theology.

When Charles Bartow became the Carl and Helen Egner Professor of Speech at Princeton Seminary, he gave an apt description of what was expected of speech teachers in theological schools in his inaugural address: "We are here as servants of those we teach," he said, "which is to say that assessing and meeting students' personal speech communication needs is the focus of our attention."[2] For me, that meant assisting the preaching faculty in the development of a basic training program in speech communication within the seminary. "Basic" meant offering those courses and exercises that would help ministerial students learn to master a subject, organize it well, and have enough of a command of voice, body, and presence in the room to speak clearly and to good effect. The program in speech at Candler was designed to address the kind of stress one observer suggested was a common one:

> Something happens to the human animal when (he or she) moves from a sitting to a standing position. A person who possesses the God-given ability to talk, unique to the human animal, and is normally articulate, becomes something less than human when (she or he) finds (themselves) in front of an audience of more than two people, something happens to the link between mind and speech, and for some reason (one) believes (he or she) has to project something other than what (they) are.[3]

Mitties McDonald DeChamplain reminds us that "advising preachers on what to do in the pulpit is risky business," since in our pluralistic culture

---

1. Craddock, "Storytelling in Preaching."
2. Bartow, "In Service to the Servants of the Word," 274.
3. Keogh, "Forward," in Linver, *Speak Easy*, 13–14.

opinions quickly diverge on what is "good speech."[4] Can we even say anymore what "basic speech training" for preaching is? This could be an essay that echoes so many other voices that lament that adequate training in communication arts is among the things that have gotten lost in the changing, evolving world of theological education.

This is not going to be that kind of chapter, though. There has been enough lament over losses and not enough celebration of the rich diversity that the study of preaching now enjoys and the progress made in meeting the challenges of the communications culture we live in. I certainly won't suggest that training in public speaking is now irrelevant to the demands of the preaching ministry today because, as Fred Craddock says, "Nothing has replaced the power of the human voice. In a room full of ears and voices that might speak back is a vulnerability and a dynamic that is still unmatched."[5] I will urge caution, however, on a naïve, uncritical reliance on techniques and theories of communication when coaching preachers. When delivery of the sermon is the subject matter, preaching needs the discipline of theology. Preaching, like other ministerial practices, is not immune to the lure of a "professional model of ministry" that reduces ministerial practice to a series of ordered techniques that promise "success." Besides, many who are well trained in the theories and techniques of public speaking soon realize that preaching a sermon makes a different set of demands on them.

I recall a seminary student who had his doctorate in the speech arts and was coming from a career as a motivational speaker, who confessed to me after the first preaching class that he was terrified to preach his first sermon. He sensed that there was something more being asked of him than the application of what he had learned from his profession as a public speaker. Ruthanna B. Hooke makes a similar observation:

> I am always interested to note that the students who come to me with experience in other forms of public speaking usually find preaching just as frightening as those who have none. Former trial lawyers, salespeople, business men or women, and musicians will occasionally begin the preaching class claiming a greater confidence, but usually that self-assurance dissipates once they begin the practice of preaching.[6]

While speech training is a valuable asset, it doesn't tell us all we need to know about communicating a sermon, especially when it comes to the role that voices and bodies play in that communication.

4. DeChamplain, "What to Do While Preaching," 99.
5. Craddock, "Storytelling in Preaching."
6. Hooke, *Transforming Preaching,* 3.

FINDING VOICE: YOURS AND GOD'S

Speaking of "voice," there is a sense of urgency about preachers' beginning to find their "public" voices, that is, for learning how to give voice to the claims of God's gospel in the communities they serve. This means expanding our concerns beyond finding one's pulpit voice in favor of giving body and voice to those in communities whose voices are silenced and whose bodies are devalued. This calls for a balance of focus in Christian preaching between "how" we speak to "what" we say, a shift from method to message. If there is a shift away from "how" to "what," it may seem that traditions of speech instruction have little to contribute to that kind of effort since they focus primarily on the performance of individual preachers, not on how the gospel takes shape in the lives of the community addressed by sermons. The presence of God's gospel in the world at large is supported by a preacher's oratorical prowess but it is certainly not dependent on it. In fact, the dazzling display of a preacher's techniques might very well obscure the more urgent claims of Christian preaching on one's life and entire ministry. For the sake of those claims, the lens in our homiletical imaginations needs to open wider and new sources of inspiration need to be found.

Narrow thinking about the instrumentation of the message takes our homiletical imagination and ties it to the ground. One thing we are getting right about the way we teach preaching is that we have become aware that the methods we have used in teaching preaching are never theologically neutral. Tom Troeger writes: "The way a classroom is set up, how teachers use their authority, the feedback that is provided, the focus of evaluation, the selection of books, the diversity or lack of diversity in the student body—all of these have theological consequences."[7] What is the implication here? There is a push in theology away from exclusive attention on the preacher, as if effectiveness of a preacher is entirely dependent on that preacher's command of body and voice. Preachers, after all, are not to stand in front of the community to get attention as a soliloquist or master of verbal artistry. They are to lead a community to become present before God and the world through its engagement with its texts, its songs, its prayers, and yes, through a sermon.

FINDING VOICE AMONG GOD'S PEOPLE

A "ritual view of communication" supports this communal action by decentering the role of the preacher in favor of "the ceremony that draws persons

7. Troeger, "The Implicit Theologies," 94.

together in fellowship and commonality." Within ceremony other forms of speech and gesture are highlighted, such as prayer and chant.[8] Consequently, there is less of a tendency to isolate and parse out a student preacher's difficulties with the basics of public speaking from her overall formation as a minister within worshipping and learning communities. The role of those communities in the preacher's formation is expressed by Stephen Webb: "Voice does not come from deep within us but rather emerges in the give-and-take of listening and speaking to others."[9] Yes, preaching calls upon one's *whole self,* not just body and voice, but it also urges participation of a whole community in finding its collective voice and presence as a witness to the gospel. By performing the sermon, the preacher is becoming a part of the community's performance of God's Good News, not only in God's presence but in the world God has chosen to love.

To empower the community's performance of God's gospel, Richard Lischer has urged us to revive our concerns with the "credentials, character, competence, and holiness of the one who speaks."[10] One's work on a sermon arises as a fruit of one's devotion to one's personal development as a preacher and to one's community, but also to God. "To devote oneself to any task, person, community, or ideal is to give oneself wholly to that object of desire. In the case of religious devotion, the object of desire is God," says Barbara Brown Taylor. "Devotion to God and neighbor is the primary prerequisite for preaching the gospel."[11] The use of one's voice and body in preaching—like all the practices that go into the making and speaking of a sermon—must flow from one's devotion to the values of God's gospel as they are lived out in the world.

How does one teach this? I have found the discipline of oral interpretation to be helpful. I have identified biblical texts or written prayers that express that kind of devotion and have asked students to speak the words "as if" they are the student's own. The aim is to experience the text's affect and be able to share that experience using the language of the text. When the student's self is brought into the service of the persona of the text, student, text, and listener are transformed. "Devotion" is experienced and shared.

8. Carey, "A Cultural Approach," 16.

9. Webb, *The Divine Voice,* 59.

10. Lischer, "Before Technique," *178.*

11. Taylor, "Devotional/Life-Style," 227.

THE COMMUNICATION OF THE "RICH" AND "POOR"

The traditions of instruction and the models of communication that inform the preaching moment are laden with values that can train the preacher in the fullest dimensions of devotion. They aim at human freedom, empowerment and transformation, the freedom to express oneself openly and honestly and without fear or feelings of personal inadequacy. They also aim at respecting the "other" through the practice of active and attentive listening. In that tradition of instruction there is openness to change and a resistance to consensus about "the right way" to preach. The best way to approach issues related to sermon delivery are rooted in the assumption that "nearly all people have voices and bodies capable of expressing fully whatever is on their minds."[12] The point of instruction is often to help a preacher identify and then release those habits that prevent her from fully speaking what is on her heart for the sake of the gospel. Dig down far enough into those traditions and you will find that behind the rush towards "technique" or "mechanics" there is a slower search for "soul." In the 1940s, for example, H. E. Luccock urged his students to concern themselves with "the soul moving through the action of utterance, with the mood out of which moving preaching comes."[13]

Focusing on "soulful delivery" helps us faithfully respond to the temptation to succumb to what Pierre Babin has called "the Hollywood model" of communication or "communication of the rich."[14] By "rich" he means something broader than material wealth—it has more to do with tone, presence, and with attitudes like sufficiency, hardness of heart, or insensitivity. For example, if the "rich" were to offer a preaching workshop in effective communication, it would feature an easily marketable method whereby participants would be guaranteed "success" by becoming known through the mastery of those techniques and processes. Babin gives us permission to play with the idea of Jesus attending such a seminar! When Jesus spoke, he was not always clear. Sometimes he was quite incomprehensible, even to those that were closest to him. His disciples occasionally complain: "who can understand these things?" Nevertheless, Jesus remained a compelling communicator, unpredictable, primarily in his dealings with the poor in his midst. You might say that Jesus' devotion to God and to the poor shaped the way he communicated.

---

12. Bartow, "In Service to the Servants of the Word," 275.

13. Luccock, *In the Minister's Workshop*, 193–94.

14. Babin, *The New Era*, 100–109.

In the face of challenges and temptations offered by the "communication of the rich" (and perhaps because of them) our thinking about sermon delivery has deepened and matured. Creative methodologies are being employed and new guiding metaphors are emerging in research and practice. For example, to counter the image of "communication of the rich" there is "preaching in the poverty of spirit." To preach in poverty of spirit means to follow the example of the woman who enters the company of suspicious and skeptical men with the jar of costly nard and breaks it open in order to anoint Jesus (Mark 14:3–9). Similarly, we don't bring in the perfect form of the sermon into the ceremony and speak it with a fine-tuned voice so that it leaves the assembly untouched, safely tucked away in the folder under our arm. Since God allows God's self to be pierced and broken open in order to communicate love for us, we bring our sermons into the ceremony to be "broken open" by the chants and prayers that bear praise but also that carry the cries of human suffering. Preachers are caught in grace by means of a paradox, best expressed by Paul: "for whenever I am weak, then I am strong" (2 Cor 12:10b). It is a way of speaking where gentleness converges with conviction, humility with confident strength, and clarity of intention and purpose. Since Fred Craddock was such a careful student of language, of how people put things into words and what those words do to shape the imagination, I would like to reflect on a few words that pertain to the speaking of sermons in a "poverty of spirit." The words we put around the event of preaching are changing. They serve as stepping stones through a refreshed and renewed homiletical imagination.

RE/FORMING OUR TERMS

I will start with the word *delivery*. The word has a distinguished ancestry. As it is used today, "delivery" is the descendant of two words from classical rhetoric, *elocutio* (Latin, *eloqui*, elocutus=speak out) and *pronuntiatio* (proclaim, pronounce), meaning how one manages one's voice and body in the act of speaking. It describes "a speaker's distinctive way of bringing thought to expression"[15] or as John McClure puts it "the entire physical process of giving a sermon."[16] If we turn to the chapter marked "Sermon Delivery" in the preaching textbook or look to the bottom of the preaching evaluation form to find "delivery," we are likely to find some other words for assessing how well a preacher has used one's voice and body to "get a message across."

15. Bartow, "In Service to the Servants of the Word," 275.
16. McClure, *Preaching Words*, 20.

Scratch the surface of "delivery" and you will find a metaphor that is deeply embedded in our thinking about communication. It is a "transmissions" model that at first had theological implications, specifically the establishment and extension of God's kingdom on earth. But as it became more secularized, it has spun out an "impersonal language of input, feedback loops, and receiver-interactants."[17] Delivery has the hint of objectivity in it, that is, more of a concern with "efficiency" than with "holiness" or soul competency.

Issues like this soon come up when the call comes from the Regional or Conference minister, or the District Superintendent, asking if I might come and offer some assistance to some pastors who are struggling with their preaching. "Delivery" is a word they often use to discuss what the matter is. But often, when I listen closely to their concern, I hear that they are not talking so much about techniques of vocal production like articulation, inflection, or gesture. They are more inclined to use more evocative words like "connection," as in, "the sermons are just not connecting" or "the preacher seems to be detached from what is being said" or "the sermon isn't saying anything—it is too small." They usually start reaching for something more than moving a message across a space between speaker and listener.

One word that arises from their concern is *detachment*, a word that suggests some incongruity between the speaker and the message. Perhaps the preacher is saying something she or he does not really believe or perhaps vocal and physical behaviors are revealing an attitude that doesn't fit the message. Whatever the reason, the listener is getting mixed messages in the sermon delivery; the sermon is saying one thing but the preacher's body language or attitude in speaking is saying something else. How does one begin to address this sort of delivery?

RE/MEMBERING OUR TRADITIONS OF SPEAKING

Grateful that homiletics has not lost its memory in postmodern culture, I dig deep down for help in traditions of teaching preaching. I hear the voice of one of my former professors: "You are not the first to struggle with such things," he says as he takes down an old book with a faded cover, and opens it. There is a good bit of underlining in the old text and when I look to where his finger is pointing I find evidence of early discomfort with the term "delivery" as a description of what happens (and what does *not* happen) when the sermon is preached.

17. Lischer, "Before Technique," 178.

It's 1877 and none other than Phillips Brooks, the rector of Trinity Church in Boston. He was preparing to give a series of lectures on preaching at Yale. Eventually they will be published in the very volume that my professor is holding, *Lectures on Preaching,* but for the moment in my mind's eye, Brooks is casting about for images that will help him say what preaching is to his listeners. He gets an idea of what preaching is *not* when he imagines a delivery boy in transit on a bicycle across town—an early version of "text messaging." The delivery boy is the ancestor of those who deliver packages to our door in the afternoon. Brooks knows that the boy is carrying a message from someone to someone else. He does not know what is in it and so has no relationship to it, just the resolve to do what he has been given to do. This is a far cry from the classical notion that "delivery" means "bringing one's thought to expression." Some sort of connection between speaker and message is assumed there. Brooks remembers that the preacher must have an investment in the message and so he will go on to write: "The fundamental conception of the matter of all Christian preaching is that it is to be a message given to us for transmission, but yet a message which we cannot transmit until it has entered into our own experience, and we can give our own testimony of its spiritual power."[18] So it is connection or a bond between what a preacher has lived, what the preacher says, and the attitude of conviction in which it is spoken that Brooks (and his descendants in homiletical tradition) are reaching for! It is this sort of power that Brooks's biographer remembers about his preaching. After the manuscript was done, it "rested in the drawer; mere paper and ink, but instinct with fire, pathos, reason, humor, and passion. The sermon, however, was in Brooks himself, like a banked furnace waiting to break forth with heat."[19] You can see why Brooks thought "delivery" to be a weak way of describing what happens in the preaching moment!

Meanwhile, over at Princeton Theological Seminary, a tradition of instruction was beginning to develop that aimed at teaching the values Brooks's preaching demonstrated. It was looking for "the most successful way of making the . . . instrument reflect the mind's message while at the same time calling the least attention to itself."[20] This is what Brooks, for example, thought was a fundamental principle: "truth through personality is our description of real preaching. The truth must come really through the person, not merely over (one's) lips . . . [I]t must come through (one's)

---

18. Brooks, *Lectures on Preaching,* 14.

19. Lawrence, *Life of Phillips Brooks.*

20. Powers and Powers, *Fundamentals of Expression,* 13–14. As quoted in Bartow, "In Service to the Servants of the Word," 278.

character, affections, (the) whole intellectual and moral being . . . [I]t cannot be the mere training to do certain tricks."[21] "Tricks" might allow for "the exhibition of graceful bodies, or the exploitation of beautiful voices" but little else.[22]

"Truth through personality" is a dynamic in communication that resonates from deep in the wells of homiletical tradition. The use of the word *performance* aims to catch the energy of that dynamic when the subject of the discussion is the preaching event. It is true that "performance" has too often been used to describe the kind of trickery and artifice described above. We all have complained about "pulpit performers" who aim at effect and applause even as they distance themselves from their subject and their congregations. In recent discussions about preaching, however, we have not confined ourselves to these pejorative uses of performance. In fact, rehabilitating and then repurposing the term for use in homiletics is one thing we have gotten right! We speak now of the form of the sermon coming through the body and voice of the preacher when the sermon is spoken. What the classical use of the term *delivery* offered—"thought coming to expression"— is what performance describes with one modification. The sermon in performance is "thought becoming embodied."

A sermon is embodied by means of the selfhood of the preacher. Body, voice, and presence "body forth" a sermon that has been practiced well enough so that its language and structure are internalized and becomes a part of the preacher. We do not need to become a different person in order to preach a sermon like that or adopt vocal and physical behaviors that are alien to us. We might not know we have certain gifts for bodying a sermon forth until we make use of them or perhaps some gifts we do have might have been suppressed.

REPURPOSING VOICE AND BODY
FOR SERVICE TO THE WORD

In a continuing education workshop, or on that first day of the preaching class, a student brings in a lifetime of speaking habits, vocal patterns and rhythms that that need not be erased but refined, repurposed, and brought into the service of God's gospel. When we address such things in the preaching class, we do so as a part of "self-exegesis." "In such an exegesis," explains Stephen Farris, "the preacher examines the characteristics and tendencies

21. Brooks, *Lectures on Preaching*, 8–9.

22. Powers and Powers, *Fundamentals of Expression*. As quoted in Bartow, "In Service to the Servants of the Word," 278.

that impinge most directly on the preacher's task."[23] These aspects of preaching deserve our close attention because, as DeChamplain says, "A central fact of the preaching life is that the sight and sound of the preacher are themselves carriers of meaning."[24]

What carries meaning, then, is what speech consultant Sandy Linver calls one's "speaking image." This is how she defines what she means: "Our spoken image consists of much more than the words we say. It is how we say the words, the sound of our voice, the way we use our body as we speak."[25] This does not mean that a speaker crafts a phony speaking persona that he turns on in front of a congregation. Far from it. "You simply have to learn to project the person that you really are." Linver says. "The effective speaker is not necessarily polished and perfect. [The effective speaker] is energetic, involved, and willing to be a direct, open, human being. And the same principles apply whether [you] are talking to [your] closest friend or to an audience of five hundred."[26] Linver's concept of the "speaking image" allows us to talk about a value that preachers and their listeners appreciate when the sermon is spoken—congruity between how the preacher is experienced in ordinary conversation and how she is experienced in the sermon event.

Linver's "speaking image" reminds me of a place where contemporary communication theory and practice once again converges with homiletical wisdom. On the subject of the relationship between the person of the preacher and the sermon, Phillips Brooks says, "Every preacher should utter the truth in (the preacher's) own way and according to (one's) own nature." And he adds, "all successful preaching, I more and more believe, talks to individuals."[27]

What is a sign that a message has entered into a preacher's own experience and becomes embodied in the preacher's "speaking image?" Here is a prayer that helps us to find what we are reaching for. In the *Book of Common Prayer,* a prayer is said for "all bishops and other ministers, that they may, both by their life and doctrine, set forth thy true and lively Word."[28] The wedding of "liveliness" and "truth" in that prayer tells us something about the way that the "what" of the sermon is linked not only to the selfhood of the preacher (who) but also to the "how." If what I am saying is truthful and I believe it—even if it is a hard truth—then my body and voice will bring

23. Farris, "Exegesis of Self," 267.

24. DeChamplain, "What to Do While Preaching," 99–100.

25. Linver, *Speak Easy*, 18.

26. Linver, *Speak Easy*, 23.

27. Brooks, *Lectures on Preaching*, 23, 22.

28. *Book of Common Prayer*, 329.

a quality of liveliness that even perfection in technique cannot convey. As Jana Childers puts it,

> when questions about what is missing in contemporary preaching are put to laypeople, they yield an age-old and surprisingly consistent response: passion. Call it passion, life, authenticity, naturalness, conviction, sincerity or being animated. Call it fire, sparks, electricity, mojo, spiritual lava, or juice. It is what listeners want in a preacher. "We want our preacher to preach like (s/he) believes what (s/he's) saying!" says the pastoral search committee.[29]

What that committee is asking for is for fully embodied communication that leads them not only into the experience of the sermon but also to the community's own performance of the gospel. How do we get there with them?

We find ourselves at the point where this essay began, puzzling over Peter Wallace's question: how can the preacher improve "sermon delivery"? Of course, as Fred says, we can engage the services of a speech teacher, who is, as Charles Bartow says, "in service to the servants of the Word." At the same time, however, devotion to God's gospel pushes the preacher beyond a preoccupation with techniques and toward the development of character and "soul competence." More than "delivery of the message," the preacher aims at the community's performance of the gospel and offers the performance of the sermon as a love offering that is "broken open" in the presence of the holy. It is a difficult thing, particularly these days, to practice what Lucy Lind Hogan says of preaching, that it is a "way of thinking and of being before the Lord,"[30] much less to teach it!

Thankfully, we can glean spiritual direction from the conversations homiletics has had with communication studies. We have learned that it matters how we use our physical selves when we stand to bear witness to God's gospel in our preaching, and we have come to realize how important theology is to the instrumentation of our sermons as well as to what we say. This is certainly what we have been getting right about preaching today.

Prayer, practice, perform. We pray because we are not using the sermon to show off our prowess in public speaking or to apologize for our lack of knowledge about it. We pray because we recognize our dependency on God's Spirit to take what we offer in the form of the sermon and "break it open" for the benefit of God's people and the world it serves. We practice not to "put on a show" but because we want what we have composed in the sermon to become such a part of us that we can help our listeners revisit

---

29. Childers, *Performing the Word*, 18.
30. Hogan, *Graceful Speech*, 174.

their own experiences in light of the gospel and to lead them to enact its claims upon their lives and the lives of those they serve. And finally, perform, to allow the "truth to come through personalities" as lively, human speech. Such a performance will not sound like the "noisy gong" of artifice, but carry the ring of truth.

BIBLIOGRAPHY

Babin, Pierre, with Mercedes Ionnone. *The New Era in Religious Communication.* Minneapolis: Fortress, 1991.

Bartow, Charles L. "In Service to the Servants of the Word: Teaching Speech at Princeton Seminary." *The Princeton Seminary Bulletin* 13:3 (1992) 274–86.

Book of Common Prayer. New York: Seabury, 1979.

Brooks, Phillips. *Lectures on Preaching: Delivered Before the Divinity School of Yale College.* New York: E. P. Dutton and Company, 1878.

James W. Carey. "A Cultural Approach to Communication." *Communications* 2 (1975) 1–22.

Childers, Jana. *Performing the Word: Preaching as Theatre.* Nashville: Abingdon, 1998.

Craddock, Fred B. "Storytelling in Preaching." An interview with Peter Wallace on Day1.org. https://day1.org/video/5d9b820ef71918cdf20026b6/storytelling_in_sermons__dr_fred_craddock_on_day1.

DeChamplain, Mitties McDonald. "What to Do While Preaching." In *Best Advice for Preaching,* edited by John S. McClure, 99–115. Minneapolis: Fortress, 1998.

Farris, Stephen. "Exegesis of Self." In *The New Interpreter's Handbook of Preaching,* edited by Paul Scott Wilson. Nashville: Abingdon, 2008.

Hogan, Lucy Lind. *Graceful Speech: An Invitation to Preaching.* Louisville: Westminster John Knox, 2006.

Hooke, Ruthanna B. *Transforming Preaching.* New York: Church Publishing, 2010.

Keogh, Donald. "Foreword." In *Speak Easy: How to Talk your Way to the Top,* by Sandy Linver, 13–14. New York: Simon and Schuster, 1978.

Lawrence, William. *Life of Phillips Brooks.* New York: Harper and Bros., 1930.

Linver, Sandy. *Speak Easy: How to Talk your Way to the Top.* New York: Simon and Schuster, 1978.

Lischer, Richard. "Before Technique: Preaching and Personal Formation." *Dialog* 29:3 (June 1, 1990) 178–82.

Luccock, Halford. *In the Minister's Workshop.* Nashville: Abingdon-Cokesbury, 1944.

McClure, John S. *Preaching Words: 144 Key Terms in Homiletics.* Louisville: Westminster John Knox, 2007.

Powers, Leland, and Carol Hoyt Powers. *Fundamentals of Expression.* Boston: Leland Powers, 1916.

Taylor, Barbara Brown, "Devotional/Life-Style." In *The New Interpreter's Handbook of Preaching,* edited by Paul Scott Wilson, 227–29. Nashville: Abingdon, 2008.

Troeger, Thomas H. "The Implicit Theologies of How We Teach Preaching." *Papers of the 36th Annual Meeting.* The Academy of Homiletics (2001) 94–103.

Webb, Stephen H. *The Divine Voice: Christian Proclamation and the Theology of Sound.* Grand Rapids: Brazos, 2004.

I REMEMBER FRED CRADDOCK

Raymond Brady Williams

I REMEMBER FRED CRADDOCK AS AN OUTSTANDING TEACHER. HE TAUGHT at Johnson Bible College (now Johnson University) the four years I was a student (1953–57). Vivid memories—seated in his class on Romans, on the back row, as befits someone whose last name is Williams, three seats from the window to the left, a sunny day, Fred leading us in an exposition of Romans 3–4 on justification by faith. Mind and spirit soared as response in life's most significant theological moment. I remember thinking, "That's what my mother has been trying to teach me." When decades later an interviewer surprised me by asking what has been the most influential book, I responded immediately "the book of Romans" and remembered Fred standing behind the wooden desk in front of a cracked, dusty blackboard teaching at that transformative moment.

I remember Fred Craddock as a preacher and teacher of homiletics. Ironically, he taught our class on homiletics using the now-reviled Broadus textbook! More important was his example as a preacher. He had just completed seminary and regularly preached memorable sermons in the required evening chapel services, including a sermon over sixty years ago on James 1:17. The subject is still fresh: In God there is "no shadow of turning."

Fred also preached each Sunday for the Christian Church in Newport, Tennessee. He and Nettie drove up on Saturday, and he preached Sunday morning and evening. He reported that on one Saturday men of the church gathered for a workday, and he showed up in his work clothes. One of the elders took him aside and told him in effect, "Fred, your work and skills are far more important; let us do what we can do; you spend your precious time here as the minister of the gospel to our community."

Fred did not develop a theory about preaching and try it out. He preached—standing on a box or beside the pulpit, speaking calmly in his high-pitched voice—and the overwhelmingly positive responses surprised him, and his thinking about why his sermons were so effective eventually led to the transformation of the teaching of homiletics with salutary effect on preaching in America.

I remember Fred and Nettie Craddock as gentle friends. They were class sponsors for the Johnson Class of '57, and my classmates respected and loved them and continued a wonderful relationship for more than sixty years. On one Skip Day, when students left campus for a day in the mountains, our class faced a rugged Craddock exam the next day. It will surprise no one who knew Fred that the class was on Shakespeare and the textbook was *The Complete Works of Shakespeare*. We conspired, and when we got out of the cars at our destination, we quickly took our huge textbooks, gathered in a circle, and began "studying" for the exam. After a few minutes, Fred said, "Oh, all right!" We had a wonderful day with Fred and Nettie in the mountains, and Fred must have burned the midnight oil getting ready for class the next day.

I remember Fred Craddock as a valued counselor for our class. One day, walking beside him as he went home from class, he remarked casually to me, "You might want to continue on for a PhD after seminary and teach." It opened a door and career path I had not imagined. Think about it: my professor of homiletics recommended that it might be best to become a teacher! A good, wise, respected, and sensitive teacher influences lives in profound and unpredictable ways.

I remain enormously grateful for Fred's excellence as a teacher, preacher, gentle friend, and counselor, as do all my living college classmates.

"MY STORIES 'GET TUMBLED'"

Remembering Fred

Robert Garman

I REMEMBER COMPLAINING TO FRED THAT IN EACH OF HIS SERMONS HE had three or four wonderful stories driving home the point or points of his sermon but I, preaching to the same congregation forty to forty-five times each year, was hard put to find one good story per sermon.

Fred's comforting words were that his reputation as a preacher was occasioned by his having to travel widely preaching to supplement his income as a teacher. He was able to preach the same sermon in several places. He said, "You know those machines that can tumble roadside rocks into beautiful polished gems? My stories 'get tumbled' by being improved by each telling. Just do the best you can with what you have! Don't try to preach like me. Be you! Remember too that the exegesis of the congregation is as important as the exegesis of the biblical text."

Fred's greatness as a preacher came not from his having great answers but great questions—ones that troubled his hearers in just the appropriate way. He shared with each congregation his efforts as a biblical scholar to make sense of the questions and provide some insights so that his hearers could make sense of them also. Sometimes we get good answers too!

The memory of Fred Craddock is treasured by all who knew him!

— 10 —

HOMILETICS AS A BEHIND-THE-SCENES
PROMPTER OF PREACHING

Paul Scott Wilson

HOMILETICS IS A BEHIND-THE-SCENES PROMPTER OF PREACHING AND MAY be one of the less visible aspects of what is right about preaching today. Homiletics is the academic discipline that studies preaching and subjects that pertain to preaching, including its history, theology, theory, method, and practice. It devises processes to teach, evaluate, and mentor preaching. It celebrates fine preaching. It explores social concerns with a view to how they may best be raised in congregational settings. As in any theory/praxis pedagogy, homiletical theory strengthens the practice and the practice in turn tests and develops the theory. Homiletics is linked to the life and welfare of the church, it supports and nurtures preachers, and in this time of great and increasing change in the church, its importance may continue to grow.

BACKGROUND

To gain a sense of the significance of homiletics today we need some sense of the past—keeping alive the preaching past is one of the tasks of homiletics. Some time ago I came across a description of the Bachelor of Divinity (BD) course that was mandatory for ordination when my father attended the seminary in which I teach, prior to that degree becoming the Master of Divinity (MDiv). Preaching (including speech communication) was one of five year-long courses in each of the three years. Teaching preaching normally fell to someone in Bible or Theology, or to an experienced preacher. By the time I was a student in the late 1970s, the fragmentation of the theological curriculum begun in the 1950s was already complete: there were now four departments (Bible, Theology, History, and Pastoral Studies). While several electives were possible, only a single preaching course was required out of a total of thirty courses. By then the curriculum was trying to serve a broad and growing variety of responsibilities in vocational ministry.

Homiletics has been around since ancient times. Augustine's *On Christian Doctrine*, book IV, is often cited as the first homiletics book, though it would be appropriate to cite the whole volume since it, like homiletics, is largely concerned with how Scripture is interpreted. Countless manuals and books on preaching were written through the ages. However, it is relatively new as an academic discipline, as an area of study that is regularly taught at university level, that has considerable research and writing devoted to it, and that publishes material that conforms to academic standards. Evidence of this newness is seen not least in the founding in the last fifty years of three academies devoted to homiletic excellence, the Academy of Homiletics in 1965, and more recently the Evangelical Homiletical Society and the European-based Societas Homiletica. A common expectation today is that teachers of preaching will have a doctoral degree in homiletics, not just a related field.

Homiletics has become an important driver of preaching as we know it today. Some pastors and lay people imagine homiletics to have a role only in the seminary, where, in conjunction with other subjects, it helps to prepare students for the pulpit. In that capacity, it has a practical function, helping students to integrate and put to use much of what they have learned in their other courses.

The significance of homiletics extends beyond the seminary walls. The revolution known as the New Homiletic that has taken place especially in North America since the 1960s likely would not have taken place or achieved so much had it not been for the emergence of homiletics as an academic discipline. It holds its members to account for scholarly engagement of key biblical, theological, and social issues; it canvases the theological curriculum for new developments and encourages interdisciplinary discussion; and it helps uphold the centrality of the church and the gospel for the academy. It challenges preachers to identify preaching goals needed for a rapidly changing society. It offers assistance with ideas for weekly preaching through various commentary and other resources, many of them related to the interdenominational New Common Lectionary and the church year.

Its members lead continuing education events and offer other mentoring activities. As much as anything, homiletics seeks to offer encouragement of the word to preachers who seek creativity, strength, and guidance for their weekly demands. Homiletics meets these responsibilities with varying degrees of success, and much of its work is from behind the scenes, out of sight of the congregations it seeks to serve. Preaching would be much disadvantaged without it.

FIVE LIVELY TENSIONS THAT HELP PREACHERS

Homiletics, like other fields, is not homogenous. Some of its teachers are based in colleges or schools that are most interested in preaching as a vocational subject, while others are more concerned about research and publication in university-related seminaries where tenure and publication is an issue. Teaching degrees vary, anything from a basic degree for ordination in some schools to a DMin or more normally a PhD. Homileticians do not speak with one voice, even though on some aspects of the New Homiletic there is often a broad consensus. Rather, one can speak of certain tensions that mark important conversations within the discipline. Here we note five that have particular benefit for the pulpit:

1. The Tension of the New Homiletic and the Old

The New Homiletic is a term used by David Randolph in 1969 to describe a new approach to preaching (though the beginning of the New Homiletic is in the 1950s). For Randolph, preaching needed to be contextual, paying attention to listeners and their needs and the specific situations in which they found themselves. Rather than speak universal truths to general humanity, preaching should address the needs of specific people hearing the sermon in all of the particularity and distinctness of their individual and communal experience. Rather than proving an argument and convincing listeners primarily with information, sermons should elicit agreement through effective communication and by establishing relationships through words.[1]

Many of the features that came to be associated with the New Homiletic could be found in the changing culture at large, especially in mass media and later the Internet, with increased attention to story, metaphor, and image. Sermon form should be organic, fitted to each text and occasion,

---

1. Randolph, *The Renewal of Preaching*, 22–23.

having a life of its own, "an idea that grows," as H. Grady Davis advocated.[2]
Fred B. Craddock spoke of preaching that gradually unfolds the meaning
of the sermon, rather than discloses everything at the beginning and then
proceeds to prove it.[3] Preachers came to understand that preaching ought
not just relay important concepts, it can also provide an experience of the
biblical text and situations of people today. Sermons can employ narrative
principles. They can have plot or movement, generating a tension that is
eventually resolved. They can have episodes using various stories that work
to a common goal. They can present people to meet, characters doing things
to be visualized and heard, all the senses being addressed. The three kinds
of appeal advocated by ancient rhetoric were reclaimed: *logos* (logic), *pathos*
(emotion), and *ēthos* (ethics or character of the speaker). Further academic
support for many of these ideas came from other disciplines at the time, for
example Bible studies explored the role of parables in Jesus' preaching and
teaching, and theology appropriated narrative theory to give voice to the
experience of marginalized and oppressed peoples.

New implies old, and gradually the term "old" homiletic was attached
to the kind of preaching that Randolph and others reacted against, often
characterized as the three-points-and-a-poem deductive sermon designed
to prove a case. It was seen as relying too much upon reason, as though
communicating faith were a matter of giving hearers the right information
for their uncritical acceptance. It was seen as mechanical and rigid, lacking
beauty and aesthetic appeal. The old homiletic used stories but called them
"illustrations" and these were, in the eyes of the new homileticians, part of
the problem. They were often canned stories from books of sermon illustrations that often sounded corny or artificial and were designed to serve a
specific moral. If they ever were rooted in real life, all the wrinkles marking
real life had been ironed out. They lacked texture and contradiction. Most
often when used in sermons they were subservient to a propositional point
that had already been made and the illustration simply made it more visible,
but was not absolutely essential. The argument was central and could stand
without illustration.

The new homileticians claimed that authentic stories should reflect real
life and make their own points in their own ways. The story is its own point
and cannot be boiled down to a simple abstract idea without losing meaning. Rather, a story has many meanings, just as Jesus' parables may be read
in more than one way. Hearers bring their own meanings by having their
own stories evoked. What the preacher needs to do is what Jesus often did,

2. Davis, *Design for Preaching.*
3. Craddock, *As One Without Authority.*

he simply communicated the meaning he found in the story without reducing the story to only one understanding.

The story of the old and new homiletic is not the story of right versus wrong. No victory was fought on these homiletical plains. There is truth and overstatement on both sides and it is important that key insights from both camps be honored. Many people in the "old" camp felt they were unfairly characterized and put on the defensive, as though they were antique, trapped in the past, when even the notion of points was changing, not least in the adoption of PowerPoint after 1990. Those in that camp argued the success of established ways of preaching and could point to many booming churches to prove it. They pointed to the arguments some new homileticians made for open-ended sermons, where the listeners formed their own conclusions, as unhelpful or worse. They noted that single-story sermons are problematic, they leave the hearers either in the biblical time without connection to today, or in today, wondering about the relevance of the Bible. Most significant, they stressed that propositional preaching can make for good teaching. The new homiletic may teach, but inductive learning is indirect and, depending upon the material being taught, is not always best. Images can be good, but preaching that is too imagistic can have the effect of a sound and light show. Many people are unable to comprehend sermons that have poetic structure—the same criticism often leveled against abstract propositional sermons. Moreover, preaching that is mostly narrative may work best only with biblical texts that are mostly narrative.

Homiletics as a discipline covering many denominations did a good job overall in showcasing the strengths and weaknesses of both camps. Truths may be learned from both camps and there is an important tension to be maintained between appeal to experienced and ordered thought. In today's world, with so many interests competing with the church, the needs of listeners must be considered. People today do not generally like being talked at, they respond best to a conversational style. They want to be rhetorically engaged so as to identify with or be persuaded by what is said, and they seek meaningful guidance to live as disciples of Christ. If sermons are boring and develop a series of points on an uninteresting subject, or if they wander over hill and dale without a path or destination, people today are more likely not to listen, or no longer attend church. Both points and stories can be helpful and they can be woven into a structure that offers unfolding development, excitement, or plot.

2. The Tension between Divine and Human Agency

A second tension that homiletics keeps alive and vital for the pulpit is divine and human agency, or, said another way, between preaching the gospel and preaching morals and social justice. It is easy for preaching to get lost in one or the other. Most sermons focus on what is essential for every sermon, some kind of behavioral or attitudinal change brought by the word. Most sermons also are light on what is equally essential in order for the gospel to be the gospel, the gracious empowerment of God to provide what is required.

Throughout history until recent times, the primary purpose of preaching was to save souls. There have always been special occasion sermons, sermons to mark disasters or major civic events, coronations, and so forth. However, Sunday by Sunday, salvation of the individual soul was the chief goal of the church's preaching through the ages. On that topic alone one can locate the tension between human and divine agency. On the one hand Christ's followers must do something, they are to believe in Jesus Christ and follow God's commandments summed up in, "Love God . . . and your neighbor as yourself"[4] (Mark 12:30-31). On the other hand, salvation is by grace alone, it is by God's action, not based on human merit but on faith. Jesus says in John 15:5, "Those who abide in me and I in them bear much fruit, because apart from me you can do nothing." Paul says in Romans 11:6, "But if it is by grace, it is no longer on the basis of works, otherwise grace would no longer be grace."

While divine/human agency is an essential tension to maintain in preaching, it is often ignored. This may be in part due to an overly generalized understanding of what is the gospel. Much homiletical literature has tended to treat the gospel in vague terms, treating it as the overall message of the church. The New Homiletic brought an eventful notion of the word to preaching. The gospel thus offers not just understanding, but empowerment through the Holy Spirit. Preachers and listeners hear a message about God, but they also encounter the living God, as in the lively notion of the word in Isaiah 55:11, "So shall my word be that goes out from my mouth; it shall not return to me empty, but it shall accomplish that which I purpose, and succeed in the thing for which I sent it."

Loss of tension between divine and human agency can be an acute problem in our own age. Friedrich Schleiermacher (d. 1834) is generally recognized as the founder of hermeneutics, the study not just of what a text grammatically says but what it meant in its own time and what it means

---

4. Bible quotations unless otherwise indicated are from the NRSV.

today. In his 1819 lectures on the subject,[5] he argued that an author's context must be understood in order to understand a work's significance. Why was a work written and what was it trying to accomplish? Understanding is achieved by making a connection between the author's experience and the interpreter's, in a process that happens as a kind of back and forth exchange, spiral, or hermeneutical circle. He laid the foundation for contemporary hermeneutics, and he was also at the forefront of a movement to claim the importance of experience for theology.

Generally when preachers speak of human experience in preaching, the tendency is to speak of human agency. Cultural and social analysis leans in the direction of what is wrong, individual and corporate sin, and what humans need to do differently. Prior to the 1960s, when theology was focused mainly on key doctrines, theological topics were loci central to church beliefs, for instance human nature, the nature of God, Christology, soteriology, pneumatology, ecclesiology, word, and so forth. God was the assumed subject of theology and theology was broadly conceived as serving the pulpit through support, guidance, and correction.

Most of the key developments in theology in recent decades are based in the appropriation and implication of experiences of diverse peoples. Where the Enlightenment and modernity stressed sameness and uniformity, postmodernity has stressed diversity, pluralism, and difference. Perspective and context are now central. Systematic theology, that emphasized theological knowledge as a complete interconnected and rational system, has come under criticism for its own biases rooted in largely white, Eurocentric, male experience. One now speaks of constructive theology, that does not try to make everything fit into a grand logical system. The experiences of the marginalized and oppressed have become a new sun around which much theological thought orbits: liberation, feminist, black, womanist, Min-Jung, LGBTQIA, post-colonial, and more.

These theologies impact homiletics. Where human experience and social justice is in focus, human agency tends to take precedence. The old protest that the church is about saving souls and should stay out of politics has mostly yielded to an acknowledgement that nearly everything has political implications and politics cannot be avoided. Faith needs to issue in action and is not just a private or individual matter. Homileticians generally agree that the sermon is to result in some kind of change of behavior, transformation, or commitment in relation to others. Homiletics necessarily advocates strong moral, ethical, and social stances. Some homileticians would argue

5. Schleiermacher, "The Hermeneutics."

that this thrust is the gospel, it is all a part of God's saving action in making a new creation.

Nonetheless, there are those in homiletics who call for a more precise definition of the gospel, arguing that it has a content that relates to God's saving actions in Scripture and seen particularly in the life, death, resurrection, ascension, descent of the Spirit, and second coming of Jesus Christ. The gospel has form, it moves from crucifixion to resurrection, from sin to repentance, from despair to hope, from brokenness to new creation. The gospel has demand, repentance is required, and many people stop there with human action. Of even greater biblical importance is the empowerment of the Holy Spirit that comes as an action of unmerited grace on the part of God to enable humans to meet the demands. Some of us in homiletics would say that the sermon needs to be the gospel, it is not enough simply to preach a biblical text without getting to God's saving action. It is not enough just to instruct people what to do without offering them the help that a biblical text implies. There is an experiential dimension to the gospel, if the good news always sounds like bad news and is experienced as such by listeners, it may not be the gospel.

Unfortunately in the field of homiletics as in many pulpits, the emphasis seems to lie on one or the other, on ethics, social justice, and human agency or on gospel and God's agency. Both are needed. While there may be no broad consensus in homiletics on the need for both, or on how to achieve it in sermons, many scholars affirm that both are necessary. The presence of both provides a helpful tension that fosters faith and nurtures action.

3. The Tension of With and Without Authority

Our third tension concerns the changing role of the preacher and the changing role of the church in our current age. The civil rights and feminist movements together with opposition to the Vietnam War led the general public to question authority in new ways. Nearly every traditional institution, including the church, was critiqued by postmodern scholarship for bias and hidden assumptions, and along with it, the authority of the preacher was challenged, often with good cause. Authority is now often a contested term yet it is still important. Homiletics helps to maintain a tension between the preacher as one with authority and as one without authority.

The "with authority" part of our claim is clear in the Bible. Early in Mark, at the beginning of Jesus' ministry, he teaches in the synagogue "as one having authority, and not as the scribes" (Mark 1:22; Matt 7:29; Luke 4:32). Jesus commissions preaching at the end of Mark, instructing the disciples,

"Go into all the world and proclaim the good news to the whole creation" (Mark 16:15). In the great commissioning in Matthew, Jesus gives his authority to the disciples, "All authority in heaven and on earth has been given to me. Go therefore and make disciples of all nations, baptizing them in the name of the Father and of the Son and of the Holy Spirit, and teaching them everything that I have commanded you" (Matt 28:19-20). In Luke 10:16, Jesus says, "Whoever listens to you listens to me . . ." The church continues to bestow the authority for ministry of word, sacrament, and pastoral care through the laying on of hands in ordination.

At issue is the nature of that authority. Authority was once conceived in vertical fashion and the pastor, priest, or minister was granted it even outside the church as one of the most educated people in the community. The high pulpit that was seen as "ten feet above contradiction" was eventually seen as part of the "old boys network" style of ministry that used power in hidden ways sometimes for selfish gain, abuse, or suppression of other voices.

Fred B. Craddock was one of the first homileticians to offer an alternative in his 1971 book *As One Without Authority*. He understood inductive preaching to be less vertical and controlling, it invited participation of the listeners by appealing to their experience through metaphor, narrative, and the senses. Rational or propositional argument was not the only way to communicate effectively in the pulpit. His *Overhearing the Gospel* in 1978 continued to develop the theme: instead of the sermon being a lecture in which the speaker has all the knowledge, it should be like a conversation that is overheard that incorporates perspectives of the congregation, and to which individuals add their own understandings.

In this more horizontal model of preaching, the preacher stands with the people under the word, as their representative before God, rather than over the people with the word, more or less as God's chief prosecutor. This was a freeing notion for many preachers including women, in a time when more women were being ordained and were looking for less authoritarian models. Some critics seemed unable to get past the title of Craddock's initial book and argued that Craddock had given away the biblical authority to preach. Jackson W. Carroll responded to Craddock with his *As One With Authority: Reflective Leadership in Ministry*. He argued that leadership is necessary, even in the midst of changing ideas of ministry, cultural commodification of what the church offers, diminished importance of the preacher in society, and increased roles for laity. Ministers have authority and they need to exercise it in ways sensitive to the needs of the people and the mission of the church.

Our issue is best framed not as with authority or without, but as with authority *and* without. The preacher has authority given by Holy Spirit through the church, yet can act "as though not" (1 Cor 7:29) by guiding and enabling faithful discipleship in a ministry of service.

4. The Tension of Teaching and Proclamation

Proclamation is sometimes understood as a synonym for preaching. However, in homiletics proclamation is also often recognized as one dimension of preaching, alongside teaching. Gerhard O. Forde defined it as "present-tense, first-to-second person unconditional promise authorized by what occurs in Jesus Christ according to the scriptures."[6] Proclamation of this sort needs to be prepared for in the sermon by solid biblical teaching. In proclamation, the preacher dares to speak on behalf of God the words of the gospel, like "I love you. You are mine. I forgive you. I will give you what you need you. Peace I give to you. I will never let you go." Such words are attributed to God, not the person of the preacher. This is what Forde calls the "doing of the text to the people,"[7] or what I think of as "doing the gospel to the people."[8]

Some people in homiletics shun this kind of bold statement, rightly reciting a long list of terrible actions that have been done by the church through history under the claim it was the word of God. Some scholars would negate proclamation because it can be misused to support whatever claims a preacher wants to make. Such caution is appropriate.

Still, shedding authority is not so easy. Even donning liturgical garments, or entering the pulpit, or preaching the sermon in a section of the worship service entitled The Word of God, or praying before the sermon for the Spirit's guidance, or giving an ascription of glory to God following the sermon—any of these actions signal an event not simply human. In themselves they also signal in some way communication from God. However leery a preacher may be to proclaim God's words of love, congregants often listen to preaching in the hope and expectation of hearing God speak words that will sustain them and give them reason to live.

What people hear as proclamation is up to them in relation to the Holy Spirit. The Spirit can use even brick-like words to pluck the strings of the soul. In proclamation rooted in strong teaching from the biblical text, the preacher steps out of the way so that God's music can be heard. As John the

---

6. Forde, *Theology is for Proclamation*, 2.

7. Forde, *Theology is for Proclamation*, 155.

8. Wilson, *Setting Words on Fire*, 87.

Baptist said, pointing his finger to Jesus, "He must become greater; I must become less" (John 3:30 NIV). The preacher speaks the words of love and liberation that God covets for the people to hear on a particular Sunday. It is an offering of the good news in the present. It is an offering of the saving grace and empowerment of the Holy Spirit. It is an offering of the person of Christ to the people. As such it is sacramental.

5. Technology and the Spoken Word

A final tension that homiletics embraces is between technology and the spoken word. Many churches wrestle with whether to go with screens and audiovisual equipment, and many other churches have made that step. Is one better than the other? There are arguments on both sides and it may be too soon to make a broad determination. The church itself is evolving with technology, and perhaps only with time will we know what is best.

Still, technology is not new. Preaching from ancient times has been an oral/aural medium. Jesus says, "What I say to you in the dark, tell in the light; and what you hear whispered, proclaim from the rooftops" (Matt 10:27). Paul says, "So faith comes from what is heard, and what is heard comes through the word of Christ" (Rom 10:17). Even in the early church, preaching was not independent of technology. The first recorded instance of preaching in Nehemiah 8:8 speaks of the elders reading from the law: "So they read from the book, from the law of God, with interpretation. They gave the sense, so that the people understood the reading." In being dependent upon the written law, preaching was relying on the technology of writing. Paul compares individual witness to the same technology he uses to preach to the church in Corinth, "You yourselves are our letter, written on our hearts, to be known and read by all" (2 Cor 3:3). George Whitefield and John Wesley used a crude form of technology, natural land formations, to amplify and carry their voices in their outdoor preaching to tens of thousands of people. And of course our being indoors for worship with electric lights, heating, and microphones means that preaching is already deeply invested in technology. The issue today is not for or against technology, but what kinds of technology are best to employ.

Preachers throughout history have used object lessons to aid preaching. Alphonsus Ligouri (d. 1787) on his preaching missions sometimes would use a human skull for his sermons on death, or a large picture of someone who was damned in warning of the dangers of hell. Aimee Semple McPherson sometimes used a flannel board with cut-out figures to depict her preaching text. People tend to remember what is seen and heard better than what is only heard.

Use of visual devices like film today has present appeal, though caution is needed. In his 1967 book *The Medium is the Message*, Marshall McLuhan identified speaking as a cool medium and film as a hot one, that is, it involves listeners and addresses the senses in ways that speech cannot. Images, video clips, sound recordings, and live-streaming all can have their role in preaching, to mixed effect as preachers continue to learn how best to use technologies. When the technology works, the effect is often powerful, and when it does not, it can be a liability and distraction.

Homiletics is learning alongside the church as technology develops. Several theological implications are clear:

1. AUDIOVISUAL TECHNOLOGY IS NOT NEUTRAL.

Use of it affects the preached message in ways of which we are only beginning to be aware. We tend to think that preachers determine their message and add the audiovisual to it, much in the manner that illustrations or canned stories used to be commonly added to sermons. When preachers make minimal use of an image or two projected on a screen during a sermon, the affect of the images on the sermon is minimal. However, when preachers know they are going to use audiovisual aids on an upcoming Sunday, the need to find appropriate images can take priority over what is said. The preacher wrestles with what comes first, the images or the words? In other words, the technology starts to reach into the biblical text, possibly distorting it, determining what the sermon will say.

2. AUDIOVISUAL TECHNOLOGY MAY HELP PREACHERS TO COMMUNICATE, PORTRAYING SOME EVENTS MORE EFFECTIVELY THAN THE PREACHER ALONE COULD SAY IT.

These pictures can also add to the burden of preachers, for now there are in effect two areas demanding excellence, word and image, and they need to be carefully paired. However powerful a visual message, it usually cannot stand as the word without the spoken word. Alternatively, the spoken word can stand without the visual. Preachers can easily be seduced by the hunt for the visual when spadework with the text and our times is needed. Technology may not yet be sufficiently advanced to help preachers find appropriate images effectively, efficiently, and cheaply.

3. THE NATURE OF THE SERMON AS THE WORD OF GOD IS CHANGED BY USE OF MIXED MEDIA.

The New Homiletic speaks of making movies with words rather than conceiving of the sermon as writing an essay. Use of actual video clips adds a different dynamic. As McLuhan warned, there is an energy drop in the transition from a video clip to the preacher speaking (people may want to keep on watching the video). The function of the preacher and the center of the sermon may shift. The church still needs to determine the social and spiritual effects of audiovisual devices in the sermon. When a congregation meets through film people who are in need, situations of social need become more vital and personal than in the absence of visual aids. On the other hand the sermon as an encounter with God may be put at risk, as people are more conscious of interfacing with people and technology than with the divine.

4. THE CHURCH AND ACADEMY ALSO NEED TO DETERMINE HOW THE ROLE OF THE PREACHER IS AFFECTED BY USE OF MULTIMEDIA.

Does the preacher become more of a lecturer, director, or even entertainer? Is the ability effectively to teach a biblical text affected for the better or worse? Since proclamation arises generally only out of careful teaching and a relationship of trust with the people, is the sermon's capacity to support proclamation affected? Does the sermon now become an entertainment event, and if so, what does this say about the office of the preacher? Or, if in place of a preacher an entire sermon is broadcast live to other worship settings, is the connection between the preaching and pastoral offices lost? If so, what can be done to counter this? If a personal connection with the preached word is gone, will that affect the desire of the community to gather?

Obviously many important questions need answers that cannot yet be provided with confidence. The church is in radical transition, from what we know, but to what we do not know. What lies ahead? Might robots eventually preach better than humans? We get ahead of ourselves. Whatever the future, it belongs to God and we get there with God's help. For now it is enough that homiletics continues to support the preaching mission of the church and to identify the kinds of tensions that foment relevant discussion.

BIBLIOGRAPHY

Carroll, Jackson W. *As One With Authority: Reflective Leadership in Ministry.* Louisville: Westminster John Knox, 1991.

Craddock, Fred B. *As One Without Authority.* Nashville: Abingdon, 1979.

_____. *Overhearing the Gospel.* Nashville: Abingdon, 1978.

Davis, H. Grady. *Design for Preaching.* Philadelphia: Fortress, 1958.

Forde, Gerhard O. *Theology is for Proclamation.* Minneapolis: Fortress, 1990.

Randolph, David James. *The Renewal of Preaching: A New Homiletic based on the New Hermeneutic.* Philadelphia: Fortress, 1969.

Schleiermacher, Friedrich D. E. "The Hermeneutics: Outline of the 1819 Lectures," *New Literary History*, 10:1, Literary Hermeneutics (Autumn 1978) 1–16.

Wilson, Paul Scott. *Setting Words on Fire: Putting God at the Center of the Sermon.* Eugene, OR: Wipf & Stock, 2016.

"TELL THE GOOD CHRISTIAN FOLK THE TRUTH FROM YOUR SOUL AND YOU'LL BE ALL RIGHT"

A Remembrance of Fred

Ann Kircher

MY FIRST ENCOUNTER WITH THE GREAT "DISCIPLE STORYTELLER" WAS IN worship when Pastor Fred walked up into the pulpit (rather shorter in stature than I had expected of such a grand professor that I heard was a *giant* in his profession) and ripped open my understanding of how to preach the gospel. For a young minister experiencing the firestorm that ministry can often be, that sermon was as refreshing and sweet as a cool glass of sweet tea.

As a clergywoman in my twenties, I had the fortune to follow Professor Craddock around the country wherever he preached or gave a lecture. Professor and Pastor Fred was the best storyteller that I have ever heard and I miss hearing his straight talk and life-giving tales about Jesus. Fred was an inspiration to me as a young preacher and he always took time to engage in personal conversation on a personal level over a meal or during a coffee break between sessions.

Someday when I walk up into the pulpit for the last time, I hope to hear Fred's chuckle and his personal words of encouragement: "Ann, tell the good Christian folk the truth from your soul and then you'll be all right."

My last words to Fred were, "Thank you and God bless you."

I give thanks to God for the opportunity to know him and to have learned from a great preacher of the gospel truth on this journey of faith in Christ Jesus.

FRED B. CRADDOCK AND PREACHING
THE BREAD OF LIFE

A Remembrance of Fred

Frank A. Thomas

WHEN I WAS A PASTOR SEVERAL YEARS AGO IN CHICAGO, I DECIDED THAT I wanted to invite Fred B. Craddock to be our revival preacher. As a matter of fact, we called the event our "Festival of Preaching," to which we were proud to say that we invited the very best preachers from around the country. I sent the letter of invite and Dr. Craddock graciously consented to come. With all the particulars confirmed, I started to market and advertise. I put out Dr. Craddock's picture to the congregation and the community. And the response was swift and sure. Let me sum it up like this: "Pastor, I am sure that Dr. Craddock is a fine preacher, but everyone knows that black preachers are the best preachers and make the best revivalists." They said, "We want a stir-us-up, stomp-down black preacher to fire us up and revive our hearts." I persisted and held my position because I know good preaching when I hear it and Fred Craddock was a powerful preacher.

Swimming against the tide of public opinion, I ended up begging and pleading with the church to come the first night. I was worried that they would not come. Through all of my pastoral pleading, we were able to get the house full for that first night. Dr. Craddock came out and the first situation was the pulpit was too tall. I was embarrassed that I missed this detail of planning until he said, "Frank, I think your pulpit is made for adults." And he laughed and we laughed. Then he told a joke about his wearing Bermuda shorts, and it was on from there. They came back the next night and, like Luke 20:40 (NIV), "When he finished, no one dared ask him any questions."

Fred B. Craddock challenged barriers and broke down stereotypes with his humility, his depth, insight, understanding, scholarship, and ability to break open the bread of life, the living word of God, so that anyone who was hungry could come and eat. I learned that all people have a place at the table when the bread of life is being served.

ON HEARING FRED CRADDOCK

Remembering Fred

Bob Hill

BEFORE I EVER READ HIS BOOKS OR EVEN MET HIM, I *HEARD* FRED CRAD-dock. Not in a worship service or at a church convention or at a preacher's workshop. No, I heard him first on tapes. Cassette tapes. Some originated from the Thesis Theological Cassette series which were comfortably con-fined within the deep recesses of the divinity school library. Others came from friends who implored, "Listen to this!"

I had been stupidly arrogant and mischievously opportunistic with the loosey-goosey arrangements of the divinity school curriculum at the time and had "forgotten" to take any practical homiletics course during my three years of preparation for pastoral ministry. Thus, after graduation, when I found myself having to prepare weekly sermons for a small group of the faithful at a Disciples congregation in East Nashville, I was reading my eye-balls out and listening my ears off to catch up with what my classmates had already taken in.

So I met Fred Craddock on tapes. And how salvific those tapes were. Not merely because they were saturated with inspiring stories (from his childhood, his early pastorates, his academic compeers, and his encounters with students) and not simply because they were laced with extraordinary interpretations of Scripture. No, there was something else in those tapes, something that Howard Thurman might have called "the sound of the genuine."

There was in those tapes the sound of a personable preacher, a faithful follower of Christ's way, who listened with such intensity, such creativity, such authenticity to the call of the gospel and the lilt of God's presence in all of life, that one was compelled to begin listening in a similar fashion.

As my familiarity with Fred Craddock grew—through reading his books, through hearing him preach at Regional and General Assemblies of the Christian Church (Disciples of Christ), through countless discussions with professors and other preachers about the homiletical revolution he set in motion with his emphasis on inductive preaching, and through listening to yet still more tapes and CDs—so did my appreciation for the depth of his faith.

The initial oral introduction was transformed eventually into an epistolary connection. Once, while doing research for a sermon series on 1 Corinthians 13, I wrote to Fred to see if I was on the right track in my focus on the fascinating rhetoric and seemingly exemplary persuasiveness of Frederick Robertson, the nineteenth-century divine and a brand new source of inspiration for me at the time.

His response to my letter was what I would later come to understand as "vintage Craddock": *"You have stumbled upon the person whom I consider the greatest preacher in the English language."* Again I heard him and this time on a more profound level. *"Stumbled upon . . ."* With those humbling, chastening words, he was challenging me to go deeper and broader and with a more thorough scope of the possibilities of preaching and preaching well. His esteeming of Robertson as *"the greatest preacher in the English language"* disclosed that great preachers are always and ever students of the art and craft of proclamation and that great preachers themselves have homiletical heroes whom they believe are the "greatest."

In time Fred Craddock and I would become friends. I can't remember the exact "first time" he came to preach at Community Christian Church in Kansas City, Missouri. But I do remember that I kept asking him back, and he kept accepting the invitations. Several of the occasions were for what we called "Spirit Fests," since we were too progressive as a congregation (and the pastor too presumptuously elitist) ever to call a special three-day preaching series a "revival." In all of the occasions, it was a delight to be in the presence of someone who possessed such natural, disarming humility and such obvious loyalty to the gospel and the church universal. In all of those dear occasions, one could also hear his "high" ecclesiology, that is, his reverence for the church's perduring, though not unsullied, history of embodying the grace of God. While he likely would not have been comfortable with a description of himself as "a high-churchman," he obviously had a "high" view of church as a dependable vessel for the transmission of love, care, and empowerment.

I do remember one of the last times Fred Craddock spoke at Community, during a special service honoring Martin Luther King, Jr., "Requiem for a King." In that occasion, which included a presentation by Rev. Emanuel Cleaver II on "King the Prophet," Dr. Craddock inspired an enraptured congregation with his insights about "King, the Preacher" and what he heard in King's extraordinary sermons and public addresses. In his declension of King's essence as an "African American Baptist preacher," Craddock spoke powerfully about the African American rootage of King's oratory. He spoke winsomely, too, about King as a preacher above and beyond any other identity: *"Not every venue in which King spoke was an actual religious edifice, but after he spoke there it had become a sanctuary."* And he also unveiled his understanding of King's Baptist theology when he said that every address, speech, lecture, and sermon by King always contained *"an altar call."* In all of his civil rights efforts, Craddock went on to conclude, King issued *"an altar call . . . to save the soul of America."* In that conclusion Craddock revealed astute, razor-sharp scholarship and his keen listening ear regarding the famed organization that King founded, the Southern Christian Leadership Conference whose stated mission was *"To Save the Soul of America."*

In time I would no longer call him "Fred Craddock, "or "Dr. Craddock," or "Professor Craddock," but simply "Fred," just as countless others would. By the time this personal familiarity had been reached, Fred and I were talking a lot about prayer. Like untold legions of appreciative others, I came to pray after Fred's example, employing his daily recitative: *"Gracious God, we are grateful for a way of life and work that is more important than how we feel about it on any given day."*

It was in the arena of prayer practices and spiritual disciplines that I heard Fred anew, with a still deeper plumbing of the verities of the Christian path and the core essentials of authentic faith.

There was in Fred's demeanor and theological expressions a hesitancy to invoke the supernatural (what might even be called the "magical") power of God, even in service of someone else's benefit. Rather, Fred's encounters with God were moments of waiting, discovery, always leading to gratitude.

In an extended phone conversation, Fred spoke freely and forthrightly about his personal prayer disciplines. It was a rare and true blessing to hear Fred reveal his heart-anchored grasp of prayer and the disciplining of one's mind and soul: *"Sometimes my study moves into prayer—at the moment of discovery. Not that I petition God for a meaning of a text, but that as the text unfolds, there is a discovery and I offer a prayer, usually a prayer of gratitude for an insight . . . I don't make a lot of petitions for myself in my prayers, though perhaps I really should . . . I pray more as an intercessor for others; I have lists of people I pray for regularly . . . In my preparation for preaching I set aside Friday afternoon and Saturday for a time of entering into a mood, a meditation mood; I don't go to parties or to a lot of social events on those days; I'm trying to prepare myself and seeking God's guidance so that I will be an adequate instrument.* . . . *During the week I read in the morning, sometimes moving through a book* . . . *I've discovered that I ought to pursue what I naturally resist* . . . *An encounter with Albert Schweitzer altered my approach to scripture* . . . *Hermann Diem, professor of systematic theology, once asked me if I had read Kierkegaard, and I suppose that was a very significant, radical turning point for me* . . . *In the end, I suppose gratitude is the main substance of my prayers, yes, gratitude."*

"*In the end* . . . *gratitude."* That, I suppose, is—and always will be—the undeniable theological trace at the bottom of the cup, the core essential, the *sine qua non* of who Fred was and what he offered so generously, what I recall with affection and fondness whenever I remember him, what I cherish most in all that I learned from him and what I heard from him.

"Listen to this!" friends said, as they shoved a brand new cassette tape of Fred Craddock into my hands long ago. "Listen," God whispered in my heart, whenever I heard Fred preach, lecture, or talk over a cup of coffee. "Listen and give thanks," Fred said with his lips and his life. And so I have, and so I do now.

CONCLUSION

Mutation and Incarnation

André Resner

Mutation: *the changing of the structure of a gene, resulting in a variant form that may be transmitted to subsequent generations, caused by the alteration of single base units in DNA, or the deletion, insertion, or rearrangement of larger sections of genes or chromosomes.*[1]

IN 2020 THE CORONAVIRUS PANDEMIC INTRODUCED THE WORLD TO THE life cycle of a virus and the way that all viruses mutate, i.e., change in structure and in potency, either becoming stronger and more deadly, or weaker and less of a threat to health. The world has not been the same since, as individuals, families, communities, and whole countries have had to fundamentally alter the way they live and relate to one another. Not to adapt to a permanently changed and perpetually changing world is to cease to engage the threat at hand with a will to live.

I'm not sure there has been a greater—certainly not a more rapid—mutation of preaching practices and liturgical expression in the history of the church than has happened since March 2020. The very DNA of preaching,

---

1. https://www.google.com/search?ei=ymewXq2HKMOpytMPqZGd2A4&q=mutation&oq=mutation&gs_lcp=CgZwc3ktYWIQAzIECAAQQzIECAAQQzIECAAQQ-zIECAAQQzIECAAQQzICCAAyAyAggAMgIIADICCAAyAggAOgQIABBHOgUIABC-RAjoFCAAQgwE6BwgAEIMBEENQ6EZY_k9g51NoAHACeACAdoBiAHODJIBB-TAuNS4zmAEAoAEBqgEHZ3dzLXdpeg&sclient=psy-ab&ved=oahUKEwitlPDd85r-pAhXDlHIEHalIB-sQ4dUDCAw&uact=5.

226

worship, and the sacraments has had to undergo metamorphosis in order for the gospel, the word of God, and the liturgical and sacramental life of the people of God to be experienced and transmitted in this bizarre time.

Incarnational theology—the theology that examines the nature of God's own enfleshment among us—has consistently informed robust theologies of preaching and worship. The challenge now is, how does incarnational theology inform how we do preaching, worship, and the sacraments, in a post-Covid-19 world? How can the word become flesh if our flesh is always under suspicion of being infected with a deadly contaminant? How can the word become flesh if it must be transmitted virtually on Facebook, Instagram, or through a Zoom meeting? How can the bread and wine become the body and blood of Jesus if we cannot break it with our hands, drink it with our mouths, and hand it to each other in the scandalously messy interaction of one person being with another? How will the peace of Christ continue to pass from one reconciled sinner to another without hands in hands and cheeks alongside cheeks in loving embrace? Can the church survive social distancing?

It must be said that one of the things most right with preaching at this moment in history is that preaching and preachers have been mutating the delivery of the word, sacrament, worship, and other essential activities of the life of faith through a variety of creative media and means. I am writing these words on June 4, 2020, before we have discovered the needed vaccine for Covid-19, so there are still so many unknowns at the moment. Nevertheless, as I observe not only the way that ministers of the word are adapting to the ever changing landscape of health challenges, I am encouraged by the bravery and creativity of so many ministers and parishioners to venture forth in unprecedented ways out of a conviction that we must acclimate to whatever conditions we face.

That's true, too, for the way ministers are having to adapt the word spoken, written, and embodied to address the social unrest in the wake of the killings of Breonna Taylor, Ahmaud Arbery, and George Floyd. Covid-19 has been called the silent and invisible enemy that has attacked the world and killed so many, especially those who were already vulnerable. The same is true of the silent and invisible enemy of racism that is just part of the atmosphere of living in the (not) United States of America. Yet the invisible virus of racism makes itself graphically visible from time to time with startling clarity.

At the time I write this, the sitting president has had police in riot gear fire rubber bullets and tear gas into a peaceful protest so he could stroll down the street for a photo op with a Bible held aloft, and spout threats about using military force to bring about law and order by means of "domination." That tear gas cleared the church's clergy off the church porch so the president's entourage could hijack it. I know as you read this, that this is ancient news. Yet, my guess is that that moment will be a microcosm of a regime that threatened both civic and religious life like never before in American history. I don't know what the political conditions are at the moment you hold this book in your hands. But whatever they are, the task before those called to proclaim the gospel is still the same: to see what's going on, to evaluate what we see through the theological lenses of the gospel, to formulate a response, and to screw up the courage to speak it and embody it in the contexts to which we are called. Insofar as we continue to do this, we continue to answer our call to bear witness to God, God's gospel, and the kind of world that God wishes and wills to be in face of powers that oppose God's will and way.

In a book that has as one of its agendas to lift up what is right with preaching today, I cannot help but marvel at the ways that ministers and churches have used technology to overcome the barriers of the coronavirus pandemic and the necessary shelter-in-place restrictions. And although some people have "lost jobs" in ordinary practices of church life (Sunday school teachers, acolytes, etc.), other jobs have emerged that didn't exist before in order to meet the demands of the moment. I know ministers who have turned to their teenaged children, and other tech-savvy church members, to help them figure out how to best use technology to reach their parishioners for preaching, teaching, worship, and even pastoral care. And in face of the nationwide demonstrations of racial injustice we have seen old and new voices speak truth to power in prophetic ways not seen since the 1960s. And some of the bravest, most sincere, and authentic of those voices have come from young people who have braved the front lines of the protests. I would imagine that coming out of this time there will be a need for all churches and ministers to have matters of social justice on the front burner. I anticipate an increasing number of "Justice Committees" to arise within faith communities, a long needed component of any community that seeks to be about God's way in the world.

I am grateful to the authors of this volume who, each in their own way, are engaged in meaningful acts of justice and community building in their own lives and ministries. All of the other writers' work in this book were completed before the pandemic and before the protests erupted shortly after George Floyd was murdered. That's why they are silent on those matters. Yet, reading their work now, in the midst of the world-altering events of the novel coronavirus and the unfortunately not-so-novel racially charged killings, the authors here each give evidence of careful and passionate concern for the stewardship of the word in preaching. And that is a fitting tribute to the one to whom this volume is dedicated, Fred B. Craddock.

I've been teaching a course titled "Fred B. Craddock" at Hood Theological Seminary, a historically black seminary, for the past several years. When I initially offered it, I was not sure how it would fly, to be honest. Upwards of 80 percent of my students are African American. Long story short, it has been received very well. As Frank A. Thomas, my colleague in the PhD program in African American Preaching and Sacred Rhetoric at Christian Theological Seminary, has said to me: "Fred Craddock is my favorite preacher." One of my Hood students posted this yesterday (June 3, 2020) on his Facebook page: "Where did Byron De La Beckwith go after he shot Medgar Evers? Back to Bible Study; it was a Wednesday night!"—Dr. Fred Craddock.

Fred was not just a creative genius in flipping the pulpit from a deductive to an inductive logical flow; he had a heart that was attuned to the gospel's primary impulses of inclusion, justice, care for the most vulnerable, and confrontation and unmasking of the unjust, albeit by sly and indirect means. In one sermon, having read the story of Peter's denial of Jesus, Fred recalled one night during his graduate work at Vanderbilt where he found himself walking to a diner for a late night meal. He observed a man who was obviously not welcome inside the diner at the back door waiting patiently for the short-order cook to finally take an old, gray burger off the back of the grill, wrap it in a napkin, and hand it the man through the screen door. As Fred headed back to the library, he passed by an elderly black man eating his dinner on the curb of the highway where tractor trailers kicked up the salt and pepper for the man's burger from the road. As he walked past him, he heard a cock crow off in the distance. Fred is privy to the conversation between God and the angel who cheered as Pharaoh's chariots and men were destroyed in the sea when the waters closed up on them. The angel asked God, "Why are you not cheering too?" God replied, "They're my children too."

We never knew how Fred was going to get us when he preached, but we knew he would. And we wanted him to, because we trusted him to get us with what we most needed. And if there's anything in Fred's enduring legacy that we each of us can continue, I hope it's that. To care. To be passionate. To be creative. To be unpredictable. To be faithful to God and to the gospel and the continual need for it to be preached in a troubled and troubling world. Fred's still getting us, in his quiet, oblique way, and for that I think we all can be truly grateful.

The final words to this conclusion with be from Fred himself, who in a moment of reflective confession, shows us that our learning of the good graces of God is a never ending school of hard knocks and surprising revelations that potentially spawn transformations:

> Especially when I've come to a new insight, and suddenly my life is entirely different, if I'm not careful, I will attack people who are like I used to be. I made that mistake in the days of the civil rights movement in the South. I am from western Tennessee. I grew up in prejudice, strong, bitter, prejudice. It was part of my life. I recall once, I was maybe ten years old, my uncle Jim and I and Will, a friend of mine, were hauling loose hay to the farm. I was up on top of the stack. My uncle Jim was driving the team of horses. Will, my friend, who was an elderly black man, was sitting on the gate of the wagon. He was my friend; we played together. He was, I guess, eighty years old. He taught me things I never learned in school. He taught me, for instance how to tell if a watermelon is ripe by putting a broom straw on it. If it turns around, it's ripe. He taught me, for instance, why grape vines are scared and have to hang on to trees. He was a marvelous friend of mine. We were going to the barn, and he said something to me. I didn't hear him, but I knew he had said something. I just yelled back, "Sir?" My next conscious moment was looking up from under the front wheel of the wagon, my face half paralyzed from the blow that my uncle had struck, and his bitter face in mine saying, "Boy, if I ever hear you call a XXXXX 'Sir' again, I'll kill you, so help me, God." And that was the basic training for the minister of the gospel. Finally, by the good graces of God, I was able to move past that. I became mad at everybody who was prejudiced. Then one day my wife reminded me that I was more prejudiced against the prejudiced than the prejudiced were prejudiced."[2]

BIBLIOGRAPHY

Craddock, Fred B. *Craddock Stories*. Edited by Mike Graves and Richard F. Ward. St. Louis, MO: Chalice, 2001.

2. Craddock, *Craddock Stories*, 41–42.

ONE MORE CRADDOCK STORY

Mike Graves

I STUMBLED ONTO FRED CRADDOCK'S CLASSIC 1971 BOOK *As One Without Authority* while doing my doctoral work in preaching, a wonderful accident, since the book hadn't been assigned. It was like discovering Elvis Presley for the first time when all you had known before were old-fashioned crooners. Both of them shook up the world as we had known it, the one with his gyrations and the other by suggesting sermons need not give away the ending too soon. In the ABCs of homiletical history, there was Augustine, Barth, and Craddock. I introduced him that way one time. Over the years I became something of a regular at introducing him in Kansas City. He once joked that my next book should be called *Craddock Introductions*. Each time I tried to find something new to say, and to keep it short. When I put him alongside Augustine and Barth in terms of impact on homiletical theory, he naturally deferred. It seemed true to me.

When it came time to find a topic for my dissertation, Fred's model of inductive preaching was the obvious choice. We had visited in person once during my studies when he lectured at the seminary. When I wrote about doing a phone interview for my dissertation, he graciously agreed, which I not so graciously screwed up because of the time zone difference. I still have the audio of that conversation, Fred chiding me, before we talked preaching.

Not too many years later he was in Kansas City, speaking at a conference hosted by Church of the Brethren. I would have registered for the conference but I was going to be out of town for all but the first night. In my attempts to talk my way in, I told the man on the phone I had done my dissertation on Craddock and that I would be bringing some students. He said it would be fine. That same man introduced Fred, noting that one of Fred's doctoral students was also present. When he called my name, my eyes got big as saucers. I feared a public chiding this time. Instead, Fred graciously smiled and waved. I explained the misunderstanding afterwards and we both laughed. We would remember that incident many years later as well.

The highlight of my professional life, however, came when Fred agreed to have Richard Ward and I edit the collection called *Craddock Stories*. People have sometimes asked how that came about. It started when Richard and I were leading a workshop for preachers and Fred was in the hospital with a serious, life-threatening illness. Several of the pastors had heard and inquired, which led to everyone sharing their favorite Craddock story. Hardly any of us finished telling whatever story had occurred to us because someone would interrupt before it was over. "Oh, yeah, I love that one. But what about the one where . . ." That's when the idea hit. I wrote to him later, suggesting how it could be done. We agreed to talk about it the next time he was back in Kansas City. I still remember sitting at a red light on the way back to his hotel, when out of the blue he said, "Let's do that book of stories," although he had a hard time imagining people would be interested.

Believe it or not, there would be an even better moment as the book was coming to completion, my most cherished "Fred moment." I had listened to hundreds of sermon tapes, read every printed sermon I could get my hands on, and now we had the stories collected. The problem all along had been how they would be organized. On this particular visit to Cherry Log, Georgia, where Fred and Nettie had retired to, Richard and I sat on the back deck with him after dinner. Then came the oral examination, "So, Mike, how do you propose we arrange this collection?" I bounced several organizational ideas off of him that I knew wouldn't work even as I suggested them. He agreed. I did recall a collection of Robert Frost's poetry in which the first poem stood for the whole collection, with the remainder arranged at random. Before I could finish sharing that, I suddenly wondered if we might do something similar but with a twist. "What if the first and the last story stood for the whole thing?" He liked that idea, then added, "But which two stories?" He knew the answer already; that much was clear. I ventured, "The two that are about your dad." Test passed.

We stayed in touch over the years, and not just when he was in Kansas City with me to introduce him. I did one presentation with him at Candler School of Theology in 2010, and what a treat that was. He and Nettie invited me to dinner that evening. That was when we learned we shared the same wedding anniversary date, June 9. In what turned out to be the last few months of his life I shared how we were expecting our first grandchild, and they talked about their first great grandchild. During the Christmas holidays and then again around February of 2015, I visited with Nettie on the phone, only to learn Fred was in the hospital again. I said that maybe it was better I checked with her first anyway. I had this idea for a book, a sequel to the collection of essays I had edited some years back, *What's the Matter with Preaching Today?* Fred had contributed to that first collection, and now I was imagining a companion volume, *What's Right with Preaching Today?* I knew Fred would appreciate the positive emphasis, and that his health would not allow him to participate. His Parkinson's wreaked havoc in many frustrating ways, interfering even with his ability to read. I said to Nettie, "What if I flew out, had a conversation with him about what's right as he sees it, then wrote it up as a kind of introduction to the book?" She wasn't sure, but said when the time was right she would talk to him about it. She suggested I call back. I didn't get to talk to Fred again.

On the day he died, my wife surprised me with a dinner on the town, at which a dozen of our closest friends were there. My newest book, *The Story of Narrative Preaching*, had just been released, and my friends were there to celebrate. When I had gone to Candler on my last sabbatical to work on the manuscript for that book, I had driven up to Cherry Log to see Fred and go eat some BBQ at the Pink Pig. I told him how it was not only about narrative preaching, but was in the form of a narrative. He loved the idea. When I said I did too, but wondered if I should break that mold at the end and offer some concluding remarks as author, he chided once again. "No," he said. "No, the thing about stories is that they either work or they don't. Leave it at that."

Fred's stories, sermons, books, and lectures either worked or they didn't. We all know the answer to that one. Leave it at that.

ACKNOWLEDGMENTS

IF FRED CRADDOCK TAUGHT US ANYTHING ABOUT THE COMMUNICATIONAL event of preaching, it is that true communication is a team event between the preacher/speaker/writer and the congregation/hearers/readers. His inductive method at its core was about preachers understanding that the preaching moment was a collaborative moment of discovery. Preachers had to abandon an authoritative, top-down model of communication and instead serve in an invitational and hospitable role, welcoming the people in the pews into the process of discovery, and even being willing for the discoveries among the hearers to go beyond the planning of the preacher.

That team spirit is writ large into this present volume. As an editorial team of two, we extend profound gratitude to our colleagues within the Academy of Homiletics for their essays. They each responded to our requests for participation with enthusiasm and they have each been more than gracious as each draft underwent the necessary edits.

We also thank each of the contributors of remembrances. We put out a wide call for "Craddock stories in reverse," not stories that Fred told, but that were told by those impacted by his life and work. We received many more than we could possibly include in this volume. We apologize to those whose contribution did not make it into print, but are grateful to have been witnesses to your own appreciation of Fred's life and work.

(In Mike's own words:) As always, I'm grateful to my wife for her ongoing support of my work, whether in the academy or the church. Likewise, I give thanks to the colleagues with whom I labored at Saint Paul School of Theology, especially the faculty members who challenged my thinking at many places, always in order to make my work better. Lastly, I am grateful to the people of Country Club Christian Church who allow me to share my gifts of preaching and teaching with them.

(In André's own words:) I am grateful to President Lattimore, Dean Eppehimer, and the faculty at Hood Theological Seminary for granting me

236 *Acknowledgments*

a sabbatical leave in order to work on this book. I also thank Mark and Jane Ritchie for allowing me to do final edits of the manuscript at StillPoint. I do not know of a more conducive space for peace, quiet, and reflective renewal. Finally, I thank my children—Josh, Danny, Sarah, and Ana—for their continued love and support. You each make me so proud.

ESSAY CONTRIBUTORS

Ronald J. Allen is Professor of Preaching and Gospels and Letters Emeritus at Christian Theological Seminary. His most recent book is *I Will Tell You the Mystery: A Commentary on Preaching from the Book of Revelation*.

Mike Graves is Wm. K. McElvaney Emeritus Professor of Preaching and Worship, Saint Paul School of Theology and Scholar in Residence and Minister of Spiritual Formation at Country Club Christian Church in Kansas City, Missouri. His latest book is *Table Talk: Rethinking Communion and Community*.

Thomas G. Long is the Bandy Professor Emeritus at Candler School of Theology, Emory University. He is the author of *The Witness of Preaching*.

Barbara K. Lundblad is the Joe R. Engle Professor Emeritus of Preaching at Union Theological Seminary. She is the author of *Transforming the Stone: Preaching Through Resistance to Change*.

Alyce McKenzie is the Le Van Professor of Preaching and Worship the Altshuler Distinguished Teaching Professor and the Director of the Center for Preaching Excellence at Perkins School of Theology, Southern Methodist University. She recently published *Wise Up! Four Biblical Virtues for Navigating Life*.

Debra J. Mumford is the Frank H. Caldwell Professor of Homiletics at Louisville Presbyterian Theological Seminary. She is the author of *Exploring Prosperity Preaching: Biblical Health, Wealth, and Wisdom*.

Luke Powery is the Dean of the Duke University Chapel and Associate Professor of homiletics at Duke Divinity School. His most recent book is *Were You There? Lenten Reflections on the Spirituals*.

André Resner is Professor of Homiletics and Liturgics at Hood Theological Seminary and Professor of Preaching and Rhetoric in the PhD program in African American Preaching and Sacred Rhetoric at Christian Theological

Seminary. His latest book is *Living In-Between: Lament, Justice, and the Persistence of the Gospel.*

Richard Ward is the Fred B. Craddock Professor Emeritus of Preaching at Phillips Theological Seminary. He is the author of *Speaking of the Holy: The Art of Communication in Preaching.*

Dawn Ottoni-Wilhelm is the Brightbill Professor of Preaching and Worship at Bethany Theological Seminary. She is the author of *Preaching the Gospel of Mark: Proclaiming the Power of God.*

Paul Scott Wilson is Professor Emeritus of Homiletics at Emmanuel College of the University of Toronto. He is the author of *The Four Pages of the Sermon: A Guide to Biblical Preaching.*

Made in the USA
Las Vegas, NV
03 February 2022